German Panzers on the Offensive

The scene exemplifies dynamic command style in offensive maneuver war. The German column has not halted either to prepare tea or to wait for a commissar to countersign another order to continue an advance. The officer standing in the command car is likely a panzer division commander issuing "orders from the saddle" to the leader of a subordinate battle group at right in the cupola of the specialized command tank. The style is urgent with the actors to the front, the decision quick, the orders brief.

German Panzers on the Offensive

Russian Front • North Africa 1941-1942

R.H.S. Stolfi,

Professor Emeritus, U.S. Naval Postgraduate School

Schiffer Military History
Atglen, PA

Book Design by Ian Robertson.

Library of Congress Control Number: 2002115245

Printed in China.
ISBN: 0-7643-1770-9

We are interested in hearing from authors with book ideas on related topics.

Published by Schiffer Publishing Ltd.
4880 Lower Valley Road
Atglen, PA 19310
Phone: (610) 593-1777
FAX: (610) 593-2002
E-mail: Info@schifferbooks.com.
Visit our web site at: www.schifferbooks.com
Please write for a free catalog.
This book may be purchased from the publisher.
Please include $3.95 postage.
Try your bookstore first.

In Europe, Schiffer books are distributed by:
Bushwood Books
6 Marksbury Avenue
Kew Gardens
Surrey TW9 4JF
England
Phone: 44 (0) 20 8392-8585
FAX: 44 (0) 20 8392-9876
E-mail: Bushwd@aol.com.
Free postage in the UK. Europe: air mail at cost.
Try your bookstore first.

Contents

List of Figures

List of Maps

List of Illustrations

PART ONE:

Panzer Maneuver War on the Plains of the Western Soviet Union 1941

1

Introduction

The Germans launched the greatest coordinated set of military operations in human history on 22 June 1941. Beginning with the initial oral order of Adolf Hitler on 21 July 1940, to Field Marshal (five stars) Walter von Brauchitsch, Commander German Army, to begin to plan an attack against the Soviet Union, the Germans spent twelve months on preparation for the offensive. The chief of staff of the Army, Colonel General (four stars) Franz Halder, planned to destroy the main concentration of the Red Army in a period of approximately ten weeks while also seizing Moscow and then occupying Russia to the west bank of the Volga River. Revisionist historians claim that Hitler had no such intention but rather saw the advance into the Soviet Union as necessary to push back the wartime siege lines drawn around Germany to include Leningrad, the Ukraine, and the Crimea. Three weeks into the campaign, the blitz-oriented German Army stood almost 100 km east of Smolensk on the threshhold of victory over the Soviet Union but halted by the siege-oriented concerns of Hitler for the immediate seizure of the Ukraine. Deflected south and away from near certain victory in the war, German Army Group Center would reveal impressive mobility in the Kiev encirclement in September 1941, turn back to defeat the main concentration of the Red Army between Smolensk and Moscow in October, and then advance to the suburbs of Moscow late in November. From these vast operations, ground forces should be able to derive lessons for the conduct of mobile war.

In terms of distances covered in the face of resistance by a strong armored enemy, the 30 mobile divisions of the attacking German armies would achieve astounding results.[1] Colonel General Heinz Guderian, commanding Panzer Group 2, would move his ten mobile divisions approximately 1,970 km (1,202 mi) largely against strong resistance in the period June-November 1941. During this period, Panzer Group 2 would not move over a single bituminous or concrete paved highway but would operate exclusively on dirt and gravel roads. During two months of this period, Guderian would stand halted by Hitler's procrastination (August) and Russian autumn rains (October) that turned the unpaved roads into impassable swamps. During the remaining three months of actual movement, Guderian's panzer group participated in five major encirclements of Soviet forces that included necessary halts to set and defend lines around trapped Soviet armies. The mobile divisions actually advanced in several bounds each resulting in the encirclement of Soviet forces and involving movement of as much as 250 km by at least one division in a single day. Surely in these extraordinary movements, the analyst should be able to find useful lessons for the conduct of mobile operations by ground forces today.

Just what was the resistance offered to Panzer Group 2 in almost 2,000 km of advance through the Soviet Union? It might have been that the Soviets skillfully withdrew their forces leaving relatively few troops behind in the pockets formed by the Germans. In the recent 1991 Gulf War, allied forces through some combination of slow moving style and chance accounted for only approximately 110,000 Iraqi troops in killed and captured against a force estimated by allied intelligence at 550,000 and intended for encirclement in the ground attack. The same possibility exists that the Soviets through skill or luck eluded serious damage from German mobile forces advancing swiftly but possibly not effectually through the ample Russian countryside. Panzer Group 2, however, scores high marks for inflicting casualties and damage. In five major encirclements, it contributed as one wing of encircling forces executing double envelopments, and its effectiveness can be gauged by the results in terms of prisoners taken. Note the Soviet losses as summarized in the following listing:

Pocket	**Time to Effect Encirclement**	**Soviet Prisoners**
1. Bialystok	22-27 Jun 41	160,000
2. Minsk	22-27 Jun 41	164,000
3. Smolensk	3-16 Jul 41	315,000
4. Kiev	25 Aug – 14 Sep 41	665,000
5. Vyasma-Bryansk	30 Sep – 6 Oct 41	660,000
Total		1,964,000

The epic dimensions of the Soviet losses in prisoners show that the Germans and Panzer Group 2 conducted mobile warfare with special skill. The losses show that when the Germans intended to effect great envelopments they succeeded. German success is magnified by the difficulties of the Russian theater of operations. The Soviets fought in familiar terrain, largely among friendly populations, and in vast space in which to elude or threaten the Germans. The Germans faced the challenge of advancing great distances across a dense but extremely primitive road network over which they had to maneuver. Guderian, for example, in the first day of the drive south in September 1941 that would end in the encirclement of five Soviet armies east of Kiev, noted that he "drove along a terrible sandy track, a very bad road, and a number of … vehicles broke down." As early as noon on the first day of the advance he "had to signal for replacements of armored command vehicles, personnel lorries, and motorcycles … a grim omen for the future."[2] During this movement south into the Ukraine, Guderian's Panzer Group would advance 470 km with a logistical system that worked well enough to support success. German logistics truck columns ran supplies successfully from distant railheads that had been positioned just close enough to support such moves even though the Germans had to construct a new rail system to overcome the unique wide-gauge (extra width) Soviet system.

It must be evident that if Panzer Group 2 helped to force the surrender of almost two million Soviet soldiers out of five great pockets along a two thousand-kilometer route of advance, the reader is faced with an unparalleled example of mobility in war. The question arises though: just how well armed were the Soviets particularly in terms of tanks and artillery? Surprisingly, the German Army in its attack on the Soviet Union advanced against a Red Army that outnumbered it severely in tanks. Across the entire front, the Germans held 3,100 tanks according to reliable accounts.[3] Authorities quote figures for the number of tanks held by the Red Army that run from 17,000 to 22,000 vehicles. Western writers of general accounts of the war in the east tend to use the lower figure while Josef Stalin, the redoubtable first secretary of the communist party, used the figure of 22,000 tanks in a conversation with the visiting British foreign secretary in Moscow in December 1941. The author of this study estimates the number of Soviet tanks available to be inserted in combat at approximately 18,800—a staggering advantage in numbers for an army defending against a blitz-style attacker. Outnumbered almost 6 to 1 in numbers of tanks, the German Army cannot be said to have relied on overall numbers for success in mobile war.

It is possible though that the German Army had battle tanks that were superior enough to the Soviet tanks qualitatively that those qualities, along with artful concentration of force, counterbalanced the Soviet numerical advantage. The qualitative picture, indeed, is as surprising as the numerical one. Broadly summarized, the situation shows approximately half of the German tanks clearly dominating the vast majority of Soviet tanks in weapon system performance characteristics but in turn being dominated more decisively in tank-versus-tank combat by a small percentage but relatively large number of heavier Soviet tanks. In more detail the situation sorted itself out as follows:

Russo-German Tank Balance, June 1941

Russians		**Germans**	
T-26 A-C	c. 12,000	Pz.Kw. II	746
BT 2,5,7	c. 5,000	TNHP 38	812*
T-34 A,B	c. 1,200[6]	Pz.Kw. III	1,065
KV-1,2	c. 582[6]	Pz.Kw. IV	479
Total	c. 18,782	Total	3,102

*Number includes some older TNHS 35 Czech tanks.

The 1,544 German Pz.Kw. III and IV tanks dominated the mass of approximately 17,000 Soviet T-26 and BT tanks in terms of radio communication, optical sights and observation scopes, and spacious dimensions for upgrading with bigger guns and heavier armor. The German tank cannons were also capable of penetrating the armor of all of the Soviet T-26 and BT tanks out to extended ranges of about 1,100m. In a seldom made but important point, the Soviet 45mm tank cannon, which was found on most of these tanks, was capable of penetrating the armor of the German Pz.Kw. III and IV tanks in the Soviet Union in 1941. The 1,782 Soviet T-34 and KV tanks dominated in turn the German Pz.Kw. III and IV vehicles especially in terms of gun power and armor slope and thickness. In a crushing

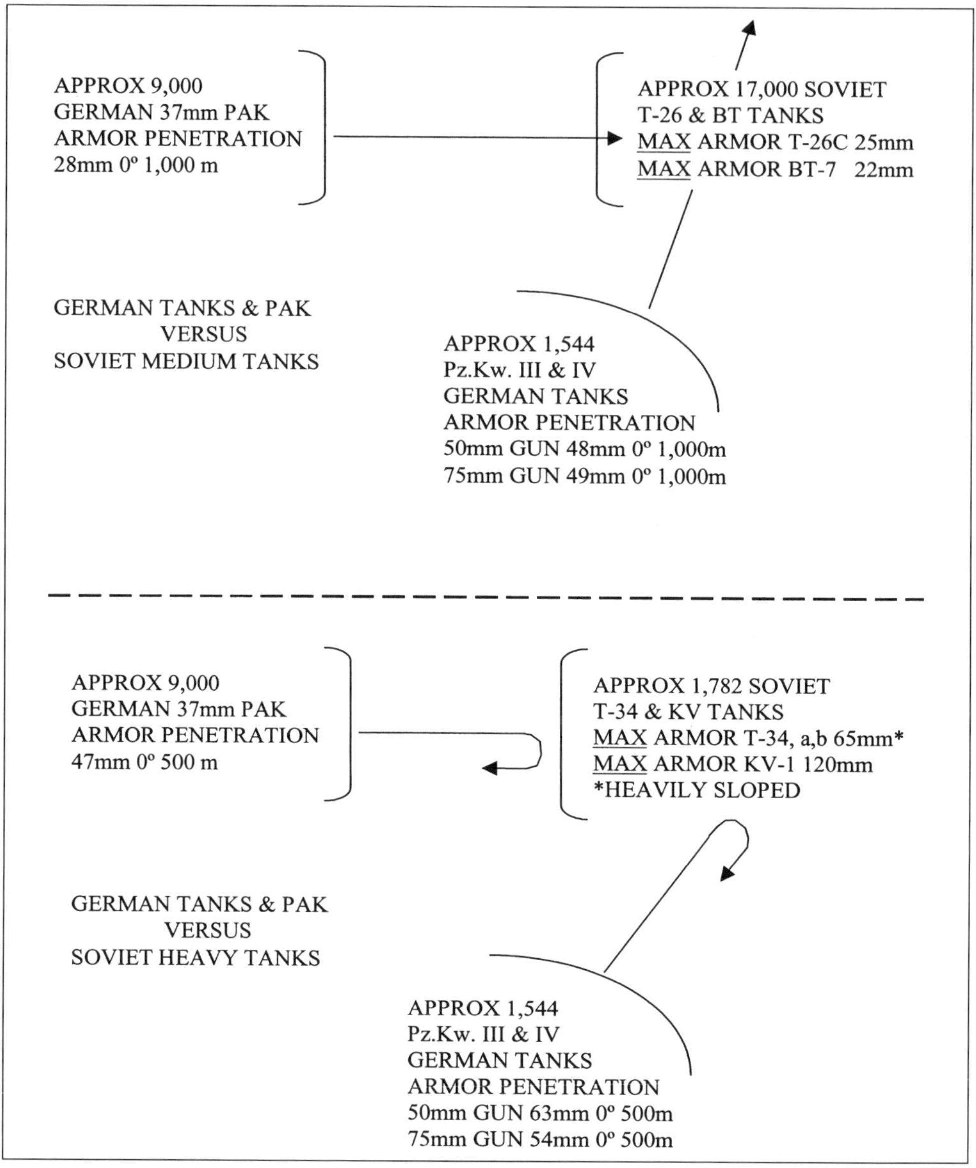

Figure 1: Projectile versus Armor Mismatches in the Russian Campaign (1941).

technical mismatch, the German tank cannon could not penetrate the front or side armor of the heavier Soviet tanks at any range while the Soviet tank cannon were able to penetrate German armor and destroy German tanks beyond 1,000m. The Germans survived this disastrous situation only because the Soviets scattered the heavier tanks across the entire front in penny packets and the Germans skillfully employed artillery, *Flak* (antiaircraft guns) and a few heavier antitank guns against them. Finally, the numerous German 37mm *Pak* (antitank guns) dominated the relatively thin armor of the Soviet T-26 and BT7 tanks but were unable to penetrate the armor of the Soviet T-34 and KV tanks, maintaining the sobriquet among German *Pak* crews as the "army's doorknockers."

Figure 1 shows the projectile versus armor mismatches among the German and Soviet tank and antitank weapons. All of the numerous German 37mm *Pak* and a smaller number of newer 50mm *Pak* were able to penetrate *all* of the armor on the 17,000 Soviet T-26 and BT tanks at ranges of 1,000m. None of the German tank cannons and *Pak* of June 1941 was able to penetrate the front and side armor of the hulls and turrets of the 1,782 Soviet T-34 and KV tanks at effective ranges of engagement, for example, over 500m. The German Army would inflict grievous damage on the Soviet tank force due to the technical mismatch illustrated in the figure and the tactical skill of the German soldier. The Army would survive the contrasting mismatch with the heavy Soviet T-34 and KV tanks through application of the same tactical skill.

In terms of numbers of men under arms, the Germans faced larger Soviet forces. The Germans concentrated approximately 3.0 million men for the opening attack and employed additional moderate sized allied forces from Rumania, Finland, Slovakia and Hungary. The Soviets in post-glasnost writings note the concentration of approximately 3.7 million men on the various Soviet western fronts by June 1941, and plans to mobilize more than 4.1 million additional personnel.[7] The Germans in their preparations for the attack, set up a pool of only 450,000 replacements, assuming that the campaign would be over by October 1941. The campaign in its all-important opening stages became, in effect, a race on the part of the Germans into Soviet mobilization space, i.e., the Moscow-Gorki space, to paralyze the arming and organizing of the additional 4.1 million Soviet troops. And if inferiority in numbers of tanks and men were not enough of a strategic burden, the Germans faced a larger Red Air Force. The Luftwaffe would deploy 2,230 aircraft for support of the attack including only 1,220 bombers, 660 fighters, and additional reconnaissance, transport, and liaison aircraft.[8] The Red Air Force would hold approximately 14,000 aircraft.[9] In a situation similar to the one between the opposing tank forces, the Soviets would have a very large body of outmoded aircraft and a smaller body of advanced fighter and ground attack aircraft just coming into production. Figure 2 summarizes the situations and shows the Soviet advantage in numbers.

	Armed Forces Personnel	
German:	**Ratio:**	**Soviet:**
3.00 million	3.70 million	
+ 0.45 million (Repl)*	1.00 : 2.27	+ 4.10 million (Mobl)**
3.45 million total		7.80 million total
	Main Battle Tanks	
German:	**Ratio:**	**Soviet:**
3,100	1.00 : 5.62	18,782
	Military Aircraft	
German:	**Ratio:**	**Soviet:**
2,230	1.00 : 6.28	14,000

* Repl or First Replacement Pool (German)
** Mobl or Initial Mobilization (Soviet)

Figure 2: Numerical versus Armor Mismatches in the Russian Campaign (1941).

Across the entire front in this battle between two Great Powers, the German Army scored unparalleled success in maneuver warfare. With only 30 motorized rifle and panzer divisions providing the strategic mobility, the Germans would achieve the following results:

In the North: Three motorized rifle and 3 panzer divisions would move almost 800 km to the outskirts of Leningrad between June-Sep '41.

In the Center: Seven motorized rifle and 9 panzer divisions would move 1,500 km in various drives culminating in the battle around Vyasma in early Oct '41.

In the South: Three motorized rifle and 5 panzer divisions would move 1,600 km in drives ending in an encirclement of Soviet forces against the Sea of Azov in Oct '41.

Across the entire front, the German mobile force in conjunction with the great mass of foot-marching infantry divisions achieved the results listed below. The listing contains numbers that the author has verified through original records as being accurate. In addition to the losses shown; the German Air Force (Luftwaffe) destroyed large numbers of Soviet aircraft in the first few days of the campaign. Although virtually all of the Luftwaffe records of World War II were destroyed under uncertain circumstances in the last weeks of the war, surviving records of reports made to the high command of the German Armed Forces (*OKW*) show that in the first six days of the fighting that the Luftwaffe destroyed 3,882 Soviet aircraft including 2,918 on the ground and 964 in the air. According to the Luftwaffe officer responsible for the target folders for every German air attack target north of the Pripyat Marshes on the first day of the war, these officially reported figures were shown through additional photographic analysis and physical examination of captured airfields to have been low by approximately 12 percent. [10] The Luftwaffe, therefore, destroyed approximately 4,348 Soviet aircraft in the first six days of the campaign.

The German Armed Forces paced by the 30 mobile divisions initially on the eastern front achieved advances of 800 – 1,600 km and inflicted the following casualties and damage to the Soviet Armed Forces:

Losses	**Seven Pockets**	**General Fighting**	**Totals**
Prisoners	2,256,000	756,000	3,012,000
Tanks	9,336	4,860	14,196
Guns (37mm or larger)	16,119	9,050	25,169

The German inflicted these casualties and damage in the period 22 June - 14 October 41, a period of little more than 3.5 months, and created most of the carnage in the fighting in seven encirclements effected by the mobile divisions. The numbers do not include Soviet personnel killed or badly wounded and evacuated for treatment estimated to last for more than 30 days, numbers that can be estimated to total an additional approximately 1.5 million personnel. How did the Germans achieve such results with a handful of mobile divisions in a country without paved roads and with a different rail gauge? The answer is an easy one to make at a general level of consideration. The Germans fought this mobile war in the opening stages of the Russian Campaign with unparalleled skill. For ground forces today there must be guides to greater combat effectiveness especially against a strong armored enemy in the German style of command, the organization and size of staffs, and the tempo of operations revealed by the fighting on the eastern front in 1941.

2

Centerpiece of the Advance into the Soviet Union, Army Group Center, Panzer Group 3: The Style and Achievements of the 7th and 20th Panzer Divisions

The Germans inserted the 7th Panzer Division (*7.Pz.D.*) into the fighting in the east as part of Panzer Group 3. Colonel General (four stars) Hermann Hoth commanded the group and possessed boldness hard to parallel in World War II. In March 1941, for example, faced with putting together his scheme of maneuver within the advance of Army Group Center toward Moscow, Hoth would advise the ascetic but fiery commander of the Army Group, Field Marshal (five stars) Fedor von Bock, that the initial encirclement of Soviet forces should close just east of Smolensk, an awe inspiring 700 km from the border.[11] It is not clear just how Hoth envisioned the setting of lines of encirclement around the Soviet forces in so big a pocket. The pocket could be estimated as being 350 km long, 120 km wide and holding perhaps 1.1 million Soviet troops. Bock notes in his wartime diary, however, that he was in essential agreement with Hoth but that the high command of the Army insisted on a more conservative encirclement closing approximately 350 km into the Soviet Union just east of Minsk. With such leadership above them in the chain of command, German division commanders could be expected to have advanced with a style exemplifying maneuver warfare. The fundamental qualities that characterize the style should also be independent of time and place, allowing analysts to apply the style and associated organization as appropriate to U.S. ground force operations today.

The *7.Pz.D* put together a series of advances more dramatic and effective than those of any other division in World War II. The division would attack out of East Prussia at 0305, 22 June 41, and seize the road junction 17 km northeast of Minsk, the capital of Byelorussia at 2200 on 25 June. For most intents and purposes, *7.Pz.D.* set the northern arm of the encirclement of the vast Soviet forces defending the road to Moscow in a war with Germany. The next morning, the division would advance 25 km farther east to seize the rail station at Smolevici and sever the main road and rail connections between Minsk and Moscow. The division would execute this coup in the face of imposing resistance and vast distance.

The Germans would first face the tough and tactically aggressive Soviets in a violent tank battle at Alytus (Olita) 80 km into Soviet-occupied Lithuania. The division's 25th Panzer Regiment quickly seized intact two bridges there over the Neman River in an impressive coup de main at 1245, but the Soviets recovered and launched strong tank attacks from the northeast against the German bridgehead. In the ensuing combat from 1430-2000 on 22 June 41, the panzer regiment would destroy 70 Soviet medium and heavy tanks for the loss of a handful of German tanks most of which were repairable and soon back in action.[12] The tank battle at Olita was bitter with the Russians showing their peculiar tenacity in defense, reckless courage in the attack, and unnerving capacity to take punishment. The Soviets however managed to halt *7.Pz.D.* for only the 5.5 hours of the tank battle and the Germans were ready to move again by around midnight on 22 June.

The *7.Pz.D.*, however, did not move again until 0900 the next morning held up by devastating fuel shortages caused by an overloaded road system outweighed by the innumerable army and Luftwaffe columns pressing into Lithuania and Byelorussia. In spite of the strategic, indeed, war winning necessity for *7.Pz.D.* to move on Minsk, division headquarters was unable to free its fuel columns from the masses of horse drawn infantry and Luftwaffe units and their logistics columns. Delayed by fuel shortages, the division headed for the great old city of Vilna 100 km from Olita with the leading 7th Motorcycle Battalion driving into and seizing the lightly defended city by 0840 on 24 June 41. As concerns German command style, the division commander rode with 25th Panzer Regiment beginning at 1900 the previous day, advancing personally immediately behind the motorcycle battalion and not returning to the division command post until 1300 on 24 June 41. At about midnight, after an earlier oral alert, the division received a short written order from 39th Panzer Corps directing it by 0600 the next morning, 25 June 41, to begin to advance from Vilna into the area north of Minsk.

The scene was now set for a sequence of events during the remainder of the day that gives unique insight into the German Style in maneuver war. The division commander, *Generalmajor* (one star) Hans Freiherr von Funck, set up a *Kampfgruppe* (battle group)[13] based on his 6th Motorized Rifle Regiment (*S.R.6*) to lead the advance. At 0600, notwithstanding the corps order, the enormous importance of continuing the advance, and the dedicated efforts of the division leadership, *S.R.6* (reinforced) had not received fuel for the move. The regimental commander therefore ordered the transfer of all fuel available to 2d Battalion, *S.R.6*, and set it on the road to Minsk as an advanced detachment with enough gasoline to move about 40 km of the 185 road kilometers to the area just northeast of the capital of Byelorussia, directing it to advance until it ran out of fuel![14] Just as the battalion began its move at 0900, the Germans discovered a Soviet fuel dump with satisfactory octane gasoline, fueled the entire *Kampfgruppe* and began the advance toward Minsk by approximately 1000.

During this determined rush of 25 June 41, the regimental commander of *S.R.6* positioned himself immediately behind his point company (*Spitzen-Kompanie*). On one occasion he was joined by the division commander who personally redirected the advance of the point company toward the north and east of Minsk after it had just turned south by mistake at a confusing road junction. During this rapid move, the German columns received fire from Russian troops in villages and towns along the route of advance. The columns in no case halted to deploy and beat down this resistance. The Germans continued the march through the fire using a technique of deploying motorized infantry to engage the enemy until the rear of the column passed and then having those motorized infantry and their vehicles rejoin the moving column. This extraordinary style of advance paid big dividends. By 2200, 25 June 41, German units stood on the road junction just northeast of Minsk and the next day cut the main road and rail lines connecting Minsk with Moscow.

Maps 1 and 2 show the extraordinary advance of 25 June 41 and three further equally dramatic rushes of the division in the opening stages of the campaign. The *7.Pz.D.* would remain fixed northeast of Minsk around Smolevici (shown on both maps) blocking the retreat of huge Soviet forces eastward that would give up 324,000 prisoners out of pickets formed east of Bialystok and west of Minsk. As shown on Map 2, *7.Pz.D.* would switch to the mobile role again from 3-15 July 41. It would advance from northeast of Minsk to the city of Jarcevo northeast of Smolensk on the latter day cutting the main rail and road connections between Smolensk and Moscow and lie 300 km (183 mi) from Moscow only 24 days into the campaign. As in the case of the drive to Minsk, *7.Pz.D.* would set the northern wing of the lines of encirclement around a pocket in the area around Smolensk that would yield an additional 310,000 Soviet prisoners. The Germans stood poised on the brink of victory over the Soviet Union at the end of July 1941.

Adolf Hitler, however, remained deeply concerned over the immediate seizure of the resources of the Ukraine, and instead of ordering the continuation of the drive to Moscow, froze the German forces around Smolensk, procrastinated about further goals, and finally diverted a large part of Army Group Center southward to seize the Ukraine in conjunction with Army Group South. The *7.Pz.D.* accordingly stood fixed in field fortifications and rest areas near Jarcevo for an epic 78 days from 15 June 41 through 2 October 41. Presented with this extravagant amount of time to survive a fatal blow at Moscow and the mobilization space around it, the Soviets massed freshly raised forces between Smolensk and Moscow and constructed vast field fortifications to prevent the fall of the capital. As the Germans retracted from their victory in the Ukraine and reorganized for the drive to Moscow, there seemed little hope of a swift drive through nine fully alert Soviet field armies massed for the defense of Moscow. As *7.Pz.D.* attacked from positions along the Wop River north of Jarcevo and the high road to Moscow, it is difficult to estimate what its troops thought about the chances of success. In yet another notable performance, however, the division broke through the Soviet defenses and 107 hours later on 6 October 41, cut the great road from Smolensk to Moscow at the city of Vyasma thus setting again the northern arm of a great encirclement around strategic level Soviet forces. The same day, 10th Panzer Division (*10.Pz.D.*) linked up from the south with *7.Pz.D.* closing a pocket in which 55 Soviet divisions would be destroyed and out of which the Germans would take approximately 463,000 prisoners along with 200,000 more from two additional encirclements farther south around Bryansk. The division would cover 110 km in the four days of an advance characterized by the same sense of urgency and continuous movement that characterized the advances to Minsk and Smolensk.

Heavy autumn rain set in about 10 October 41, and, although the Germans managed to eliminate the 80 divisions (!) they had trapped in three pockets, they stood immobilized on the unpaved, muddied roads of Russia for the remainder of October and into November 41. As the ground began to freeze toward the middle of November 41, the German high command ordered another advance toward Moscow to begin on 14 November 41. The high command ordered this attack with trepidation over the wear and tear on the armies resulting from Hitler's eccentric side excursion into the Ukraine, and with frustration over the opportunity to have won the war earlier in August 41. After two days of preliminary movement, *7.Pz.D.* launched a successful attack across the Lama River at 0630 on 16 November 41 as shown on Map 2 a scant 100 km from Chimki, the big northwestern suburb of Moscow. The objective of *7.Pz.D.*, however, was not Moscow but a crossing over the Moscow-Volga canal in the vicinity of Jachroma north of the capital in order to effect an encirclement similar to the ones earlier to Minsk, Smolensk, and Vyasma. Advancing against Soviet forces having been given a month's respite by the autumn rain to recover and in the face of the coldest winter in the climatological history of Europe (namely, from A.D. 1715 to 1941),[15] *7.Pz.D.* placed assault troops in the southwest corner of Jachroma at about midnight on 27 November 41. At 0600 the next morning an assault team under command of 1st Lt Reineck seized intact the 80m-long steel bridge across the Moscow-Volga canal—the startling final achievement in offensive movement of *7.Pz.D.* in the great battles of 1941.

The advances accomplished by *7.Pz.D.* in the periods 22 June—15 July 41 and 2 October—28 November 41 were so impressive that they demand inquiry into both the fundamental principles that seem to have been operating and the organization and techniques of the Germans in advancing in the face of a strong motorized and armored enemy. Just what was the "command style" of the German officers leading *7.Pz.D.*, the division organization that reflects that style, and what are the possibilities for extracting the ruling principles of operation of a foreign army and applying the superior elements to U.S. ground forces in a different time and a different place? The author of this piece in examining thousands of pages of the records of *7.Pz.D.* has arrived at several conclusions about what made the division tick. The following paragraphs present those conclusions and are followed by description of the achievements of other German panzer divisions in 1941 to verify the style.

The author concludes that *7.Pz.D.* operated with a command style significantly different from that of the U.S. Army and Marine Corps today. This conclusion is not surprising because the division was part of the German Army as it had developed especially since the time of the Prussian innovators of 1806. It is also not surprising because the division was an armored formation with deep strategic targets in a continental theater of war. The fact that the division was German demands recognition of the situation that the style developed as part of the general picture of German civilization and culture in the nineteenth and early twentieth centuries. That the division was a fully motorized armored unit demands recognition of its superior battlefield mobility and capability to engage an opposing armored enemy but its limited strategic mobility in terms of sea and air transportation. Neither of these impressive conditions—German development nor tank-centered organization—should prevent extracting the ruling principles and specific organizational structures for application to ground forces today.

The *7.Pz.D.* operated with a command style that accepted the fundamental factors of uncertainty and chance in war. The style rejected formula (*Schema*) and procedure (*Vorgang*) and demanded action and the exploitation of opportunity on the battlefield. The style embraced the idea that every combat situation is different and demands action on the part of the leader rather than application of rule. In the division, orders tended to be oral, brief, and general. In contradistinction to U.S. ground forces orders which tend to get bound up in how to accomplish a mission, German orders concentrated on the mission, or what was to be accomplished. Not surprisingly, in the advances of the opening battles in the east, the Germans emphasized movement and the formation of ad hoc *Kampfgruppen* (battle groups) more than the centralized organization of fire support and the establishment of phase lines for attacks. If there is some special, fundamental quality that characterizes maneuver war, it is probably the one suggested by the words "fleeting opportunity" within a realm of uncertainty and chance. In an early diary entry of World War II, the chief of staff of the German Army, General of Artillery Franz Halder, remarked laconically "the troops forever clamor for artillery; opportunities are being missed.[16] Marines may wince here, after all, what opportunities existed for maneuver on an Iwo Jima, a Pelelieu, or a Tarawa in World War II; but in a mobile war in Southwest Asia or the Middle East, maneuver would predominate and opportunities would beckon during the maneuver battle.

The *7.Pz.D.* illustrates German maneuver warfare at its peak in terms of advances accomplished, casualties inflicted, and encirclements effected. The factors that characterize and explain the success of the division may point the way to a more effective style of combat and organization for today's ground forces. But what about the achievements and style of other German mobile divisions in the first great advances into the Soviet Union? Just what were those achievements and are they associated with factors similar to those identified for *7.Pz.D.*? The following section on *20.Pz.D* and the three following chapters on the combat of other panzer divisions should give a complete enough picture of German maneuver war to suggest application to the present day style and organization of U.S. ground forces.

The German high command placed *20.Pz.D.* with *7.Pz.D.* in 39th Panzer Corps along with two additional motorized rifle divisions for the attack on the Soviet Union. On 22 June 1941, the division commander positioned himself at 0230 in the command post of the artillery regiment of the division to observe the opening actions of the attack set for 0305. The division commander, *Generalleutnant* (two stars) Horst Stumpff, decided to break through the Soviet border positions with his 59th Motorized Rifle Regiment and clear out the Soviet defensive positions and obstacles with its motorized infantry. Stumpff ordered the 21st Panzer Regiment with the attached 20th Motorcycle Battalion over the border at 0700 with instructions to overtake the advancing motorized infantry and cross the Neman River 80 km distant near Olita (Alytus on Map 1) in present day Lithuania later in the day. The division commander moved with the tanks of the panzer regiment, and the division war diary noted that at 1450 he was accompanying the farthest forward tanks of the panzer regiment in the drive to seize the bridges at Olita.[17] As the 21st Panzer Regiment arrived at Olita at approximately 1700, it discovered that the neighboring *7.Pz.D.* had already seized several bridges there intact. Corps headquarters ordered *20.Pz.D.* to move into the bridgehead now over 80 km into enemy territory and defend the northern sector with 21st Panzer Regiment initially under tactical control of *7.Pz.D.*, Stumpff and the first general staff officer of the division (the Ia) moved into the bridgehead at 1900 arriving in the middle of heavy fighting. The chaos, strain, and movement of maneuver war is illustrated by the situation at 2300 in which one of the two motorized rifle regiments of the division stood 50 km west of the Neman River and the panzer regiment. The panzers which now lay over the river, had completed 300 km of continuous movement including a night march of 220 km into position for their attack and an advance of 80 km into Lithuania.

The tempo of the attack and command style is illustrated by several events the next day, 23 June 41. At 0420, *20.Pz.D.* received a corps order to continue the advance alongside of *7.Pz.D.* to Vilna 100 km distant. The division distributed orders to units of the division from 0515 to 0700 for continuation of the advance ordering 21st Panzer Regiment to move out at 0900. The fuel truck columns of the division supply battalion continued to have difficulties in getting through with gasoline and the movement was delayed approximately two hours. As the division began to advance again, the division commander accompanied the "farthest forward march group" and the division Ia coordinated the necessary movement of the division largely on his own initiative in a command post from which the division commander was absent for approximately 24 hours (!). The last entry of the war diary, for example, notes about midnight on 23 June that "the division staff attempted to gain a connection to the front with the division commander."[18] The next morning at 0535, the Ia, well forward with the division staff received an order to meet the corps commander in the middle of a road 2 km south of Waka and 25 km southwest of Vilna. There he received oral orders to "lock up" but not advance into Vilna from the west and southwest with the division. Shortly afterward, alerted by the Ia by radio concerning the latest orders, Stumpff returned to the division command port.

During the rest of 25 June 41 and the next two days, *20.Pz.D.* advanced alongside of *7.Pz.D.* into the area immediately north and northwest of Minsk. On 27 June 41, the division lay in defensive positions near Minsk with the mission to block the escape of Soviet forces now trapped far to the west. The division had moved not quite so fast or so far to the east as *7.Pz.D.*, but its positioning around Minsk by 26 June 41 was impressive and the two divisions together were strong enough to block any attempt of the Soviets to save the forces inside the pockets. By 27 June 41, for example, the hard marching German foot and horse-drawn infantry had already completed a great encirclement of Soviet forces to the east at Bialystok. Large Soviet forces succeeded in eluding this encirclement and continued to flood eastward where they would be encircled in a second pocket near Minsk formed by the more deeply penetrating German mobile divisions like *20.Pz.D.*

Earlier, on 25 June 41, the day of the great surge to Minsk, the corps commander had shown a special kind of energy and leadership from the front that characterized the tempo of that extraordinary day. He issued orders at 0020, for example, for advanced detachments of *20.Pz.D.* to move through darkness toward Minsk and for the mass of the division to be ready to move by 1200. At 1100 the corps commander, *General der Panzertruppe* (three stars) Rudolf Schmidt, appeared at the command post and "expressed astonishment" that the mass of the division had not already moved off in the advance notwithstanding the 1200 time in the earlier order. Two hours later, his chief of staff appeared in the division command post and reiterated the urgency of completing the encirclement. Finally, at approximately 2000, the corps commander now moving with the advanced detachment of the 92nd Reconnaissance Detachment of *20.Pz.D.* and in the lead of the division was surprised by Soviet troops and cut off temporarily. The corps commander personally lost his command vehicle, and his staff suffered casualties in killed and wounded. At 0130 on 26.6.41, i.e., in the middle of the night, a *Kampfgruppe* rescued the corps commander and linked up with the "point" of the 92nd Reconnaissance Detachment that he had been accompanying. This action illustrates the German command style in maneuver war of leading from the front—a corps commander physically with the advanced element of one of his panzer divisions. The danger to the commander must be obvious and the necessity for a self confident chief of staff to keep the general flow of maneuver coordinated is impressive. What is most impressive though is the commander leading a key element of his force toward a distant decisive objective.

The *20.Pz.D.* spent the period 26 June—2 July 41 in defensive operations that blocked the escape of vast Soviet forces lying to the west. One map examined by the author shows that on 28 June 41 elements of 12 Soviet divisions were already pressing toward the lines established by *7.Pz.D.* and *20.Pz.D.* now joined by the *19.Pz.D.* and 14th Motorized Infantry Division and lying to the west northwest of the city.[19] By 1 July 41, however, the Soviets had disintegrated west of Minsk, and on the following day, *20.Pz.D.* began the next great mobile drive—to seize the so-called Smolensk land bridge to Moscow and encircle the Soviet forces to the west of it. Ordered by corps to begin the drive toward Smolensk at 0600 on 2 July 41, Stumpff organized an advanced detachment near Minsk to begin to advance to meet the deadline and on the same day seize a crossing over the Berezina River at Berezino a distance of 170 km across extremely bad, unpaved roads. The division commander rode with the advanced detachment while the mass of the division set out later in the morning toward the same objective. The division staff moved out at 1130 after turning over its sector to *12.Pz.D.* and continued forward attempting to link up with Stumpff. The division and the staff encountered difficult roads and the war diary noted that the Ia and division staff were unable on the evening of 2 July 41 to reach the division commander. Stumpff and the advanced detachment, however, crossed the Berezina at Berezino over a half-destroyed bridge at 2100, and German command style in maneuver war appears again with the commander in the lead seizing a distant objective. Stumpff did not orchestrate or manage the 170 km march of the division toward the Berezina, he led an advanced, heavily armed but mobile battle group in the seizure of a bridge over it.

The *20.Pz.D.* continued its advance to encircle Smolensk from the north, crossing the Dvina River at Ulla at 1600 on 7 July 41 and seizing the western part of the large city of Vitebsk by late afternoon of 9 July 41, 60 km farther east. The move from Ulla to Witebsk illustrates the flexible style and continuous movement on the part of the Germans and the apparent chaos of the situation. At 0100 on 8 July 41, division headquarters issued a brief written order for the advance out of the Ulla bridgehead later in the morning. At 0900, the pioneers declared the "war bridge" over the Dvina ready for use and at 0902 Advanced Detachment Bismarck, which included one tank, motorcycle, and artillery battalion each and supporting units, began to move across the Dvina. At 0950, the Chief of Staff, 39th Panzer Corps, assigned by telephone call the city of Gorodek as the objective for *20.Pz.D.* The division commander personally moved out with the strong advanced detachment commanded by Colonel von Bismarck. The division staff, organized in a march column under the Ia, and two additional strong march groups each with a battalion of artillery attached followed Bismarck. The division would move throughout the hours of darkness on the evening of 8-9 July 41 not stopping until the heavy fighting in Vitebsk that developed on the afternoon of 9 July 41. The style of advance was characterized by corps headquarters ordering the Ia of the division by telephone at 2050 on 8 July 41 to turn away from the advance directly east through Gorodek to a new direction directly south to Vitebsk. The Ia issued the new orders by brief radio message and informed the division commander who rode with the advanced detachment. Good natured frustration on the part of the advanced detachment and a special will to action on the part of Bismarck is shown in the following message sent to division at 0015 on 9 July 41: "Entire Advanced Detachment 15 km in front of Vitebsk. I will take Vitebsk. Approval please."[20]

After fighting its way through Vitebsk on 9 and 10 July 41, *20.Pz.D.* advanced directly east taking Surash on the south bank of the Dvina at 0515 on 12 July. The division moved with typical 24-hour a day tempo and arrived at Veliz (Welish) at 0700 on 13 July organized into three large *Kampfgruppen* operating widely separated. By evening of 14 July most of the division had passed through Veliz heading directly eat. At 2300 that evening, the division staff set up the division command post in a forest 8 km east of the town. All of the movements of the division from the time of the disengagement at Minsk two weeks earlier culminated at 0130 with the corps order passed on by radio message: "March objective: Petschanitschino (near west bank Vop River). Mission: Cover the Smolensk pocket from the east. Boundary on *7.Pz.D.*" By the evening of 15 June 41, as *7.Pz.D.* cut the main road and rail connections between Smolensk and Moscow, *20.Pz.D.* went into covering positions farther north near the Vop River.

During the time of this great encircling maneuver, *20.Pz.D.* moved almost continuously during the entire period in advances against the Soviets and the daily and sometimes more frequent reorganizations demanded by the German style of maneuver war in ad hoc battle groups. The division moved approximately 500 km over unpaved Russian roads (calculated in several straight-line segments; actual distance somewhat greater) reaching the close vicinity of the Vop River a straight-line distance of 370 km farther into the Soviet Union from Minsk. The division advanced decentralized in battle groups including the attachment of most of the organic and corps-assigned artillery to the *Kampfgruppen*. At any single moment in time, the combat and combat service support elements of the division would be found in movement and scattered over approximately 70 km of Russian roads. The division commander stationed himself consistently with the leading *Kampfgruppen* maintaining contact with the division saff and headquarters by radio. Division headquarters lay essentially with the Ia (operations officer) of the division and was dominated by operationally oriented considerations of movement, fire support, and logistics. The division commander and Ia arranged and controlled the supporting fires of the division through the headquarters of the Artillery Regiment or, as appropriate, an artillery headquarters assigned to the division. The division commander effected logistics support through his Ib (quartermaster, or logistics officer) who headed a logistics group called the quartermaster detachment, which functioned as the logistics headquarters of the division. With fire support controlled from an artillery headquarters and logistics from a headquarters commonly co-located with the division supply battalion, the division command post was uniquely light and mobile and dedicated to action and movement rather than the potential constraints of fire support schedules and logistical functions. In all of the things noted above, *20.Pz.D.* operated in a style similar to that of *7.Pz.D.*

Combat in *20.Pz.D.* was dominated by chance encounter and often wild intermixing of German and Soviet forces. The combat also showed the Germans imaginatively using unlikely weapons with effective results. The 74th Light Antiaircraft Detachment (*leichte Flakabteilung*, or *l. Flak 74*) supported various elements of the division in the crossing of the Dvina River at Ulla on 7 June 41 with the following interesting results. The action report noted that in spite of Stuka attack and the fires of various heavy weapons, enemy machine gun positions continued to fire from the opposite bank in the western sector of the attack. The 2nd Battery, *l.Flak 74*, intervened in the ground battle and silenced the enemy machine guns with 20mm automatic cannon fire. Through some surprising combination of physical damage and psychological effects, the German automatic cannon subdued the machine guns and also an enemy "observation position" and a Soviet artillery piece firing direct fire at the attacking Germans.[21] Chaos and chance encounter are illustrated by the experience of a corps unit, attached to the division—3rd Battalion, 51st Smoke Mortar Regiment. The 7th Battery of this mortar battalion was moving through the northern suburbs of Minsk at roughly noon on 29 June 41 when from a side street at an angle, six truckloads of Russian infantry suddenly drove into "the middle" of the battery. A wild and deadly street battle developed in which the German mortar crews killed 70 Russian troops and took 30 prisoners. The Russians in turn using hand grenades "blew up" two German munitions trucks and inflicted heavy casualties of 9 killed and 15 wounded on the Germans in this chance engagement.

Photo 1. The 7th Panzer Division probably in the first days of October, 1941, during the drive to Vyasma. Chaotic situation in a battle group. Note the Panzer III command tank in right foreground moving past a battle group 105 mm howitzer deployed just off the road in emergency direct fire (note leveled barrel) at likely Soviet tanks out of photo to left. Classical chance "meeting engagement" between German mobile force and defending Soviets (Bundesarchiv Bestand).

Photo 2. A 20th Panzer Division TNHP-38(t) battle tank in foreground with dismounted division motorized infantry. The division is advancing in early October 1941 south of the Smolensk-Moscow autobahn as part of the southern arm of the great mobile encirclement planned to close at Vyasma. After the neighboring 10th Panzer Division closed the trap on 6 October 41 from the south around 55 Soviet Divisions [!], 20th Panzer Division would form part of the intercepting line to prevent their escape. (Bundesarchiv Bestand).

3

Centerpiece of the Advance into the Soviet Union, Army Group Center, Panzer Group 2: The Style and Achievements of the 10th Panzer Division (10.Pz.D.)

At X-hour on B-Day, 0315, 22 June 41, *10.Pz.D.* lay in an accommodations area near Deblin in Poland approximately 135 km from where it would eventually cross the border into the Soviet Union. Unlike the case of most of the panzer divisions in the attack, the Germans would delay the entry of *10.Pz.D* into the war partly because of the overloading of the road system on the narrow front for the attack and partly as a mobile reserve to exploit opportunity or head off danger in the opening days of the campaign on the more northerly axis of advance. As the other divisions advanced deeply into Byelorussia, the headquarters of Panzer Group 2, committed *10.Pz.D.* across the border at 0700 on 27 June 41 as part of 46th Panzer Corps. Corps headquarters ordered the division to get to Slonim at the east end of the Bialystok pocket to prevent strong Russian forces from breaking out. As the division began to arrive in the area of Slonim in various march columns on 28 June 41, the Germans were under extreme pressure from masses of Russian troops attempting to escape eastward. Headquarters, Panzer Group 2, and 46th Panzer Corps committed the arriving parts of the division to various hard-pressed sectors leaving the division commander by 1900 with "not any troops at his disposal." This remarkable situation continued until late afternoon on 30 June 41, when the corps commander, General of Panzer Troops (three stars) Heinrich von Vietinghoff *gennant* Scheel, realized that *10.Pz.D.* had disappeared as a maneuver element and began to put it back together. On 1 July, the division commander, Lieutenant General (two stars) Ferdinand Schaal, regained control over most of the division and led it through Smilovici southeast of Minsk on that day. The division would go on to cross the Berezina River on 2 July 41 and move up against a strong Soviet bridgehead at Mogilev on the west bank of the Dnepr River on 5 July. The division went on to fight in the big battles south and east of Smolensk where it would remain frozen in August and September 41 by Hitler's aberrant decision to deflect forces of Army Group Center into the Ukraine to ensure its immediate seizure.

The great achievement of *10.Pz.D.* would come in autumn 1941 in the German offensive, code name, Typhoon, toward Moscow that finally began on 2 October 41. It has become well known in the literature that *7.Pz.D.* quickly arrived in the northern outskirts of Vyasma, 145 km east of Smolensk, setting the northern encircling arm around a pocket of Russian Forces that would yield approximately 463,000 prisoners southeast of that city. It is less well known that *10.Pz.D.* arrived in the southern outskirts of the city at virtually the same time and had covered more than twice the distance of its redoubtable northern running mate. The following paragraphs present the achievement and comment on the command style of the Germans and the confusion attending mobile war stemming from conditions of extreme uncertainty and chance.

The *10.Pz.D.* as well as the other German forces massed for the attack faced a nightmare situation of attacking against Soviet forces that in most areas had been preparing defenses for more than two months. On the main front west and southwest of Vyasma where the division was stationed, the Soviets had massed huge forces comprising more than 55 divisions based on the two additional months of mobilization. The Soviets would block the obvious direct routes to Moscow and the Germans would be forced to attack in the Smolensk-Vyasma area along those routes toward the capital and rail center of the Soviet Union. Unlike the case of the great Bialystok salient jutting into German-occupied Poland earlier in the campaign, the Germans would be attacking against a Soviet front that ran almost in a straight line north and south of the heights of Jarcevo 50 km northeast of Smolensk. The Germans would somehow have to penetrate prepared defenses and then quickly change the style of operations to advance quickly enough, far enough, and in the right direction behind the defending Soviet forces to cut them off from the rest of the Soviet Union and destroy them.

In preparing for the attack, the division commander and his staff concentrated roughly half their effort on the details of the breakthrough and the other half on the direction and tempo of the drive through and beyond the area of the breakthrough.[22] For the breakthrough, the corps commander reinforced *10.Pz.D.* with Artillery Headquarters 128 (*Arko* 128) to plan and execute fire support in the attack sector and direct and coordinate the organic artillery of the division's 90th Artillery Regiment and the corps and army artillery attached to the panzer division for the special demands of the breakthrough. The Germans located *Arko* 128, which served as the fire support control center for the division, away from the division command post. The division command post, as a result, remained light, mobile, and maneuver-oriented without the pressure of the fire support control apparatus and associated technical processes and procedures. For the breakthrough, the corps commander reinforced *10.Pz.D.* with Headquarters, Artillery Regiment 618, four additional artillery battalions, one special artillery observation battery, one smoke mortar battalion, and, of course, *Arko* 128 to control these assets and the fires of the division's 90th Artillery Regiment. The corps commander attached Infantry Regiment 479 to effect the actual breakthrough by infantry assault against the Soviet field fortifications and also assigned several corps and army pioneer formations to bridge the numerous water courses, to improve the difficult unpaved roads over the projected route of advance, and to negotiate several wide and lengthy antitank ditches discovered by aerial reconnaissance.

The *10.Pz.D.* attacked at 0530 on 2 October 41, with the elegantly general mission "to breakthrough the enemy Desna River positions and thrust deeply beyond" - - a German maneuver war mission at its best. The boundaries established by corps show the division advancing northeast parallel to and south of the main road from Roslavl through Juchnov to Moscow (see Map 2). In keeping with German operational flexibility and realism, it is evident that corps and army headquarters would only assign specific objectives along the way based on the actual progress of the battle. The artillery preparation lasted a compact 35 minutes fired against known targets thereafter changing to fire on call by artillery forward observers with the advancing German units. In keeping with German command style, the corps commander showed up at the division command post at 0620 to begin to observe personally the progress of the attack. The division commander reported that the attack was developing according to plan although later in the day challenges would develop in the building of the bridges across the Desna and several smaller water courses just beyond it and the use of several fords across the rivers. The corps commander accompanied this time for his chief of staff, visited the division command post again at 0805 and personally called for additional Stuka support. Then, at 0810, he ordered the rail bridge across the Desna that had been seized lightly damaged by the division to be made trafficable, a reconnaissance to be made for a location to ford the river, and the quickest possible advance by the tanks.

At 0910, the division commander ordered the reinforced panzer brigade of the division, consisting of 7th Panzer Regiment and several other combat elements, to advance across a passable ford discovered near a prefabricated war bridge that would not be ready until about 1200. As the first battalion of tanks crossed the ford and began to move through difficult terrain beyond, it became evident that the passage was going too slowly, and the division commander ordered the second battalion to shift to the rail bridge to cross. By 1620, the panzer brigade using a combination of the rail bridge and pioneer war bridges, had negotiated the Desna and several small streams just beyond. At this time it had been reinforced by 2d Battalion, Motorized Infantry Regiment 69 and an attached artillery battalion and had been turned into a strong *Kampfgruppe*. Accompanied by the division commander and staff, the tank-heavy *Kampfgruppe* began the mobile advance.

By early evening at 1930 on 2 October 41, the panzer brigade *Kampfgruppe* had moved well in the face of moderate Soviet resistance and extreme difficulties with the primitive roads and swampy off-road soil conditions. The division commander, observing "extraordinarily light" night conditions because of an almost full moon, ordered the *Kampfgruppe* to continue to advance during the entire night. He also directed the tank-heavy force to thrust in the division sector specifically for the city of Mosalsk approximately 75 km distant and in a location behind the defending Soviet armies that opened vast possibilities for encirclement. He also ordered his two motorized infantry regiments to advance along a separate axis but now with mission also to take Mosalsk (see Map 2).

On 3 October 41, the division continued to struggle with difficult road and cross country conditions and some tough resistance from strong Soviet units that had been deployed in depth. At 0700, the division commander moving forward behind the panzer brigade *Kampfgruppe* was fired on in his small group of command, communications, and escort vehicles by Soviet antitank guns from north of the road. Later at 0900 along the same road that seemed to have been reasonably secured, two radio trucks of the communications battalion were destroyed by "direct hits" from Soviet antitank guns, i.e., direct fire weapons evidently shooting from ranges of no more than about 800m. The understandingly annoyed commander of the accompanying division radio company picked up every man at his disposal in the area, three German self propelled antitank guns passing by on the road, and elements of 3rd Company, Panzer Pioneer Battalion 39, and attacked the Soviet force. As the attack developed, a light 105mm howitzer battery of 1st Battalion, 90th Artillery Regiment that was moving forward along the road on another assignment, spontaneously deployed into firing positions to support the attack. Finally, the radio company commander managed by radio through division headquarters to get Stuka air support that he directed into the target area by artillery smoke rounds and white light clusters fired by signal pistols. By 1140, 1st Battalion, Motorized Infantry Regiment 69, and the rest of the 1st Battalion, 90th Artillery Regiment, added their efforts to destroy an entire Soviet infantry regiment that had lain quietly in its positions and been bypassed by the preceding rapidly moving panzer brigade *Kampfgruppe*.[23] The action illustrates the chaos and chance of maneuver war and the impressive initiative of local German commanders in handling such encounters, e.g., a radio company commander (!).

Slowed by this engagement, continued difficult road conditions, and fuel shortages particularly for the advanced panzer battalions, the division headquarters at 0410 on 3 October 41, reorganized the division into two big *Kampfgruppen*. The maneuver elements of the right (southern) battle group consisted of 90th Panzer Reconnaissance Detachment, 10th Motorcycle Battalion and 89th Motorized Rifle Regiment. The maneuver elements of the left (northern) battle group included 7th Panzer Regiment and one light reconnaissance troop. The groups had all of the division artillery attached and moving in column with them. Artillery support, therefore, would be provided only by the artillery attached to each battle group commander but would be extraordinarily responsive with the artillery moving in column with the maneuver units. The commander and headquarters of 90th Artillery Regiment moved with the right battle and had the radio communications to mass the division fires. Central control of fires in the mobile advance was unlikely though because the two battle groups would advance too far apart and face tactical chance encounters too different and widely separated to permit centralized control of artillery support. The division commander ordered the two battle groups with their attached artillery to move through the night of 3 October 41 along routes that would converge on Mosalsk from two different directions toward the end of the advance.

Early the next afternoon of 4 October 41, as the division continued a slow but almost continuous move toward Mosalsk over the difficult routes, the corps commander appeared at the location of the division commander and staff along a road at the edge of a small town on the route of advance. The corps commander directed the division commander orally to turn north at Mosalsk and reach the big Roslavl-Juchnov-Moscow road. The division commander agreed requesting permission, though, to move one of the *Kampfgruppen* of the division as directly as possible to Juchnov to set up a bridgehead there across the Ugra River to fight off attacks on the flank of the division as it turned north to seize Vyasma. After this meeting, *10.Pz.D.* seemed to break into the deep rear area of the Soviets with the Germans overrunning enemy horse-drawn and motorized columns and with the Soviets giving up without resistance. For the first time in the campaign, *10.Pz.D.* directed prisoners rearward without escorts. In the lead of the northern tank-heavy battle group, the division commander entered Mosalsk at 1630, 4 October 41. Personally observing the clean breakthrough now achieved by the left battle group, he ordered a continuation of the advance again through the night this time to reach the Roslavl-Juchnov-Moscow road 25 km southwest of Juchnov (see all these cities and roads on Map 2).

As the tank-heavy battle group moved north at approximately 1730 on 4 October 41, with the division commander advancing in the column with the Ia, Ib, and both the operational staff assistants of the Ia, 12 Russian trucks suddenly drove into the column immediately in front of the division commander's vehicle. The *10.Pz.D.* war diary notes that all of the staff officers engaged in the ensuing fire fight and that 30 Russian prisoners were taken. The diary says nothing more about the division commander but it is difficult to escape a conclusion that he fired shots in this point blank, chance encounter. About two hours later at 1955, the division commander moved onto the road junction 25 km southwest of Juchnov far behind huge Soviet forces now in mortal danger farther to the west. At 2032 corps headquarters ordered *10.Pz.D.* to advance eastward toward Juchnov and seize both the city and the bridge over the Ugra River. In a telling commentary on effective maneuver war, the division commander had already on his own cognizance ordered part of the northern battle group to continue to advance and to take the town during the evening. In yet another display of initiative, the southern battle group that the war diary candidly notes the division staff had lost track, reported by radio at 0150 on 5 October 41 that its advanced element stood only 3 km by side road southeast of Juchnov. This battle group on the initiative of its commander had continued to march through the night toward an objective vital to the encirclement of the Soviet forces lying to the west. At about midnight in the middle of this fluid situation in which the two division battle groups lay spread out in movement at night over approximately 90 km of unpaved Russian roads bordered generally by impassable ground, the division commander, in yet another example of tempo and initiative in maneuver war had the inspired temerity to ask corps headquarters "whether the thrust to Vyasma remained, or whether a thrust to Gzhatsk (now the city of Gagarin) would not be better."[24] Gzhatsk lies about 110 km by road from Juchnov and 65 km to the northeast of Vyasma and represents opportunistic thinking on the part of the division commander at approximately two echelons of command above him. At 0300, corps headquarters replied laconically: "under cover of Juchnov and, advancing west of the Ugra, *10.Pz.D.* takes Vyasma."

The tempo of this drive continued at a pace that exemplifies maneuver war. At 0500, 5 October 41, the division commander ordered the left, tank-heavy battle group to advance into the area 12 km northeast of Vyasma beginning at 0530. Fuel continued to be in short supply; the division was only three days into its advance but 175 km by road from its original attack positions in front of the Desna River. The battle group commander did not have enough fuel for both of his tank battalions so he ordered one battalion to be "tanked up" to lead the battle group north toward Vyasma. He directed the other panzer battalion to wait for the struggling fuel columns, fill up, and then overtake the advancing battle group. As it turned out, a few of the compact, 600-gallon capacity German fuel trucks were not far behind, and by 0615, the remaining panzer battalion had been fueled and linked up with the rear of the battle group. The commander of the group estimated that he had enough fuel at that time to advance 60 km. The other battle group of the division, which held most of the motorized infantry, had the mission to hold on to Juchnov, develop a bridgehead over the Ugra, and cover the right rear of the division in its advance toward Vyasma. When the trailing S.S. Division "Das Reich" reached Juchov, the battle group would move out to reinforce the drive of the division northward.

As the division moved north on the road from Juchnov to Vyasma, it met even more difficult road conditions and also came under Soviet air attack through low level bombing and strafing. Near Slobodka, the leading panzer battalion that had been "tanked up" in the morning but with tanks only half full ran out of gasoline. At 1230 as the disaster halted the whole battle group, the division operations detachment, moving far forward arrived on the scene. To maintain the tempo of the advance, the division commander ordered the motorized infantry of the battle group to continue the march past the immobilized tanks and lead the advance against what he estimated as weak enemy resistance not absolutely requiring tanks in the lead. As a special lesson in tempo in maneuver war, the division war diary notes that the remaining panzer battalion at the rear of the battle group advancing now with almost full fuel tanks would not have to move forward through the long column and take over the lead hence "with that action no time would be lost" (!). At 1700, the leading motorized infantry unit, 2d Battalion, Motorized Rifle Regiment 69, radioed division that it had only enough fuel for about 25 km. Forty-five minutes later, the division staff overheard a message passed by the motorized infantry battalion to the commander of the battle group that it had reached the Ugra River northwest of Slobodka now only 40 km from Vyasma. As the sun fell, the division faced great opportunity but also darkness, lack of fuel, only a ford and no bridge across the river, and indications that the enemy was reinforcing.

At 2200 on 5 October 41, the panzer brigade commander, who led the battle group, radioed that the strength he had was too weak to hold the modest bridgehead across the ford in the Ugra River. Division calculated that it could provide no reinforcements before daylight and ordered the battle group to evacuate its bridgehead. In a formidable display of initiative after whining about his weakness in the bridgehead, the battle group commander proceeded to ignore the division order to evacuate the bridgehead and led a night tank attack at 0130, 6 October 41, that gained important high ground north of the bridgehead and obviously secured the crossing. At 0320, accordingly, division headquarters ordered the battle group not to evacuate the bridge head but rather to break out of it northward toward Vyasma. During evening darkness, numerous Russian columns ran into German units of the battle group on both sides of the Ugra River adding to the necessity for strong nerves on the part of the German commanders to maintain control over events.

By break of day, 6 Octrober 41, the division had been able to bring forward enough fuel to keep the battle group advancing for another 80 km, but as the group began to advance en masse at about 0700, it ran into a series of small bridges over the numerous brooks in the area that held up movement. Riding with the leading elements of the battle group, the division commander personally observed the situation and ordered all pioneers forward to bridge the gaps. In some cases the small streams were only 3 to 6 feet wide but presented bottoms and banks so soft that no wheeled vehicles could cross the tantalizingly short distances. The pioneers were not able until 1430 in the afternoon to put together the necessary bridges, and the new battle groups formed by the division earlier in the day were not able to push off until approximately 1600, 6 October 41. The two new *Kampfgruppen* formed out of the previous single strong group each had one panzer battalion, one motorized infantry battalion, and further attached artillery, *Flak* (antiaircraft guns), and pioneers. Then, unreasonably but in accord with the urgent tempo of its extreme style of maneuver war, the division ordered the left *Kampfgruppe* (Lieutenant Colonel Hauenschild) to seize Vyasma from the south and the right *Kampfgruppe* (Lieutenant Colonel Sternkopf) to block the great road to Moscow about 10 km northeast of the city and enter the city from that direction. The division commander envisioned, thereby, a night attack by tanks and various supporting units developing early morning on 7 October 41 and involving tired troops, delicate fuel situation, and advance over unknown terrain. The division commander ordered *Kampfgruppen* Hauenschild to seize the airport on the southern outskirts of Vyasma before midnight and *Kampfgruppe* Sternkopf to block the rail line east out of the city by the same time.

The corps commander, leading from the front, met at 1430, 6 October 41, with *Generalmajor* Stumpff near the division command post close to the Ugra River. In a sterling example of maneuver war, he was able to adjust immediately to the breakthrough of the division and ordered the advancing right column of his *2.Pz.D.* to move onto the route of the *10.Pz.D.*, clear its badly harassed supply route and reinforce its more successful advance. The division commander at 1530 moved forward to accompany the leading element of *Kampfgruppen* Hauenschild into the southern outskirts of Vyasma. In another noteworthy example of German tempo and command style, the division commander with the leading panzer battalion of the division noted that as the *Kampfgruppen* cleared the area of small streams there was virtually no contact with the enemy. Based on this personal "chance" observation, the division commander ordered the panzer battalion to move forward immediately without any other supporting forces and seize the airfield near Vyasma about 6 km northeast of the city. The division commander made this decision just as the panzer battalion seized intact a long wooden bridge at the town of Bessova and moved across it. To secure the bridge, the division commander personally stationed himself next to it along with the drivers and messengers of the vehicles accompanying him, the panzer battalion reconnaissance platoon and two light armored vehicles that he had suborned earlier in the day from 90th Reconnaissance Battalion.

The 2d Battalion, Panzer Regiment 7, now broke out into the clear and at 1915, 6 October 41, radioed division headquarters that it had seized the Vyasma airfield. In this position alone it blocked a significant part of east-west movement through Vyasma. About two hours later, the battle group reported that 2d Battalion, Motorized Rifle Regiment 69, had linked up with the panzer battalion at the airfield and that the reinforced formation had also blocked one of the two great rail lines leading east, i.e., towards Moscow and Kalulga out of Vyasma. A few hours later, the division would link up with elements of *7.Pz.D.* advancing from the north and block the escape route of 55 Soviet divisions now lying to the west of the two German panzer divisions.

Photo 3. Prisoners at pistol point. Operating north of 10th Panzer Division, German tank crew and infantry of 7th Panzer Division take prisoner the two Soviet tank crewmen first and third from right. This photo was taken on 27 June 41 near Minsk. Later in the year in deep four-day mobile drives, the two divisions would link up from the south and north at Vyasma to effect one of the largest encirclements of World War II (Bundesarchiv Bestand).

4

The Ukraine, Army Group South, Panzer Group 1: The Style and Achievements of the 13th Panzer Division (13.Pz.D.)

The German commander of Army Group South made the decision to break through the Soviet border defenses with his foot marching infantry divisions. As a result, *13.Pz.D.*, under the command of *Generalleutnant* Friedrich-Wilhelm von Rothkirch und Panten, crossed the Bug River near Hrubieszow (now Novovolynsk) at 1750 on 23 June 41 into Soviet territory on the second day of the campaign. As the division moved into the Soviet Union it immediately ran into difficult traffic conditions on roads jammed with the combat troops and horse-drawn supply trains of the infantry divisions on the unpaved roads of the Ukraine. Farther north in Army Group Center, the commander of Panzer Group 2 had insisted to his commander that he be allowed to launch the attack with the motorized infantry of his panzer and motorized infantry divisions to avoid the delays in struggling through the foot-marching infantry. The *13.Pz.D.*, nevertheless, moved its combat elements rapidly through the infantry meeting its greatest problems with its trailing supply trains particularly the fuel columns. Headquarters, 3rd Panzer Corps, in characteristic style, set the following elegantly succinct mission for the division: "Force a crossing of the Styr both sides of Luck, thrust in direction Shitomir (Zhitomir)."[25]

Where *13.Pz.D.* entered the Soviet Union, the city of Luck stood 90 km away. The division's 4th Panzer Regiment with various attachments led the advance in a formation designated March Group A that held both of the panzer battalions of the regiment. Halted briefly during the early morning hours of darkness on 24 June 41, the march group moved out again at 0500 and early in the afternoon ran into the combat elements of the German 299th Infantry Division (*299.I.D*) near Lokaci (see May 3). At approximately 1400, 1st Panzer Battalion, 4th Panzer Regiment, passed through one of the infantry regiments of *299.I.D* east of Lakaci now approximately 50 km into the Ukraine and into combat with strong Soviet forces. In the battle that followed during the afternoon, the panzer battalion "shot up" 23 Soviet medium tanks and in one part of the action overran a concentration of three Soviet artillery batteries destroying or capturing approximately 18 guns including several 152mm cannons. It should be noted that in the deep advances of offensive maneuver war, the German tanks in the battle groups commonly "overran" Soviet artillery positions but rarely suffered significant losses in the process probably through some combination of surprise and parallel boldness associated with the tempo of the advance. As darkness came, headquarters, 4th Panzer Regiment ordered the battalion into a "*Panzerigel*" or tank hedgehog perimeter-style defensive position reinforced by motorized infantry. The reinforced panzer battalion, therefore, spent the evening of 24 June 41 in a tight perimeter with no physical contact with any other German unit or unit of its own battle group. The 1st Panzer Battalion was a strong formation that started the day with 65 tanks ready for action and had only four tanks seriously damaged by Soviet gunfire in the day's fighting. In such a situation, it could effectively defend itself with modest infantry support.

The division continued its advance the next morning of 25 June 41 and the battle group built around the panzer regiment reached the city of Luck at 1800. Corps headquarters, concerned about the tempo of the advance, ordered that fighting continue through the night to assure the crossing of the Styr River in the vicinity of Luck. Thrusting just south of the great, wide, but unpaved road from the Polish border into Luck, the 2nd Panzer Battalion of 4th Panzer Regiment in March Group A reached the south entrance to Luck at 1630. Tanks of the point (*die Spitze*) fought their way into the city knocking out of action seven Soviet tanks in fighting through the streets leading to the big, wooden road bridge over the Styr River. The Soviets had set the bridge on fire, and as it burned four German tanks of the point crossed over to the east bank of the river. Then, as the fifth tank stood about to cross the bridge, explosive charges set on it exploded sending most of the bridge into the river at approximately 1830.[26] Moving closely behind the tanks, 3rd Company, 1st Battalion, 66th Motorized Rifle Regiment, was ordered first to clear the main street leading to the bridge and then cross the river to relieve the isolated tanks which had almost immediately come under attack. The German tanks had moved so boldly through the city that Soviet infantry still remained on the street down which they had passed to the bridge. The motorized rifle company quickly cleared the main street, and, reinforced by the rest of the battalion, using rubber boats, and supported by the fire of light and heavy machine guns (no mention is made in the record of either mortar or artillery support), crossed the river. Fighting continued sporadically, sometimes heavily during the hours of darkness and the four tanks on the east bank (two Panzer III with 50mm guns and two Panzer IV with 75mm guns) destroyed 14 medium Soviet tanks in the course of the battle.

During the next morning of 26 June 41, Rothkirch reorganized the division into three battle groups for the drive toward Rovno. Because of difficulties encountered by *16.Pz.D.*, the left neighbor of the division, corps headquarters ordered *13.Pz.D.* to advance south of the great road from Luck to Rovno on an assigned front of approximately 30 km (!) at the beginning of the advance. The division commander could advance through only two bridgeheads over the Styr, the one at Luck and another 30 km farther south at Tarcowica (half the distance to Demidovka shown on Map 3). Rothkirch, accordingly sent the 13th Motorized Rifle Brigade with most of the elements of the two motorized rifle regiments of the division and the entire 13th Antitank (*Pak*) Battalion as the right *Kampfgruppe* through Tarcowica northwest of Dubno. He organized and sent a left and a middle *Kampfgruppe* farther north through Luck. The division commander set up the left *Kampfgruppe* as a strong one consisting of the panzer regiment, one battalion of motorized infantry, and one artillery battalion. He set up a mobile middle *Kampfgruppe* consisting of the division reconnaissance and motorcycle battalions to link together and screen the advance of the widely separated stronger battle groups. The situation can be summarized as follows:

Advance of 13.Pz.D., 26 June '41

Left Battle Group	Middle Battle Group	Right Battle Group
Lt Col Roedlich	Maj von Hake	Col Herr
4th Panzer Rgt	13th Recon Det	HQ, 13th Moto Inf Bn
1st Bn, 66th Mot Inf Rgt	43rd Motorcycle Bn	93rd Moto Inf Rgt
1st Bn, 13th Arty Rgt	66th Moto Inf Rgt	

The division commander rode with 4th Panzer Regiment in the left battle group as it moved out at 1000 through Luck. The division Ia and operations detachment comprising the command post of the Panzer division set up in Luck but lost contact with the division commander at 1600. The Ia realized shortly after that time that the left battle group had run out of fuel and stood immobilized about half way to Rovno. By later afternoon on 26 June 41, the operations detachment of the division found it particularly difficult to piece together a clear picture of the strong enemy that confronted the division. Through reports it realized that the right battle group at about 1815, 12 km northwest of Dubno (and 40 km southeast of Luck where the operations echelon lay) was fighting against a strong enemy. The situation near Dubno was difficult also because 93rd Motorized Infantry Regiment, which should have moved out with the battle group earlier in the day had been delayed and rerouted passing only by 1620 through Luck in attempting to join the right battle group. The operations detachment, still at Luck roughly 40 km to the rear of each of the three battle groups that were fanned out to the east and southeast of it, began to move forward at 1800 to link up with the division commander and left, tank-heavy battle group. The pressure mounted on the operations detachment to keep things under control on this classic day of maneuver war when a strong Soviet tank force attacked Luck from the north preventing the division staff from leaving the city. Strong Soviet forces that had delayed the division's northern neighbor—*14.Pz.D.*—in its advance now operated in the deep rear of *13.PzD.* right up against the area of the bridge at Luck. The Ia had providentially scraped together a small force to secure Luck and it fought off the attacking Soviet medium tanks destroying nine with gunfire. With no thought of calling off the advance to consolidate the situation, the division staff set off to join the tanks about 40 km farther east at 1900.

By midnight 26 June 41, the right battle group was fighting against a strong enemy 10 km north of Dubno, the middle battle group faced resistance on "all sides" of it, and the left battle group with the tank regiment stood out of fuel and immobilized at Ploska along the main road 18 km northeast of Rovno. Arriving about 0100, 27 June 41, at the last location reported by 4th Panzer Regiment a few kilometers west of Ploska, the Ia could only locate some of the supply trains of the panzer regiment, its attached motorized infantry battalion and advanced elements of the division pioneer battalion and artillery regiment. At 0245, the operations detachment having lost touch with its escorting motorized platoon and half platoon (2 guns) of antitank cannons in the dark over difficult roads came under Soviet tank attack. The Ia, *Major i.G.* Fritz Kraemer, ordered an immediate disengagement (flight) and undoubtedly saved the division operations staff disastrous losses. At 0300, the supply trains of the motorized infantry and artillery of the left battle group, located just northeast of the division staff were overrun and "almost destroyed" by Soviet tanks attacking from the north just before break of day. The German units in the vicinity were saved by several tanks "lying around" damaged along the road whose crews mounted the vehicles and in spite of the damage to their vehicles, drove off the Soviet tanks. Soviet forces remained in and around the area, and the tank regiment still lying to the east without fuel now lost physical contact with the rest of the division.

At the same time, during the early morning hours of 27 June 41, the middle battle group began to report contact with strong Soviet forces moving against it from opposite directions namely east and west. Later as dawn broke, Soviet forces attacked the battle group from both north and southeast and "with that, 13th Reconnaissance Detachment and 43rd Motorcycle Battalion were surrounded." The battle group by this time no longer had any fuel and was unable to break out of the encirclement. The hard pressed commander of 13th Reconnaissance Detachment radioed directly to the panzer regiment asking for it to save the middle battle group. The panzer regiment was isolated itself and had been immobilized for hours previously but scraped together enough left over fuel to dispatch part of one panzer battalion by 0915 to break the Soviet tank and infantry ring around the two German battalion-level units. The German right battle group lying farthest south fought all night just north of Dubno against strong Soviet forces and would not be able to advance against Rovno until 1205 on 27 June 41.[27]

The *13.Pz.D.* engaged in as chaotic a situation in mobile war as can be imagined on the evening of 26-27 June 41. The division not only survived possible disintegration but also never seemed to vary from a will to continue the advance. What are the lessons of such a situation? The war diary states that the day was a very hard one for the division and cost painful losses. The diary then goes on to state about as much a lesson as one is able to imagine in such a record. It notes that only because all leaders had not lost their nerves and fought every action through to the end, that even greater losses had been avoided. The word, "nerves," is not used much today to describe desirable characteristics for leaders in the U.S. armed forces. The German meaning focuses on the importance of displaying detached coolness and utter determination to accomplish a mission. With the German style of general, mission-oriented orders, virtually every officer and most men in the division knew that the task of *13.Pz.D.* was to seize the bridges at Rovno. The end result: all officers sought ways even in the dark chaos of the evening of 26-27 June to advance to Rovno rather than stand immobilized in defensive perimeters.

Other factors which seem to characterize the drive from Luck to Rovno include the following. The division commander set up three battle groups to accomplish the advance with the emphasis on decentralized movement rather than centralized fire support and carefully staged advance. The point of main effort in the advance (*Schwerpunkt*) lay with Battle Group Roedlich which was built around the tank regiment and moved out with an artillery battalion attached. The division commander advanced with the tank regiment beginning at

1000 on 26 June 41 and was not back in the division command post or linked up physically with the operations echelon of the division until approximately 0700 on 27 June. Rothkirch evidently felt that he could ensure action and the movement of the division toward Rovno by his personal presence where he could see for himself the situation in his strongest and most mobile maneuver element. The Ia of the division moved with the operations echelon of the division closely behind and sometimes with the division commander. The Ia displaced the command post of the division during its drives daily and not uncommonly twice daily. During displacement of the command post when he was actually in physical movement along the road, the Ia continued to effect the staff coordination of the division from communications moving with him in the column and functioning during halts along the route of the displacement of the command post. In effect, in a German panzer division, the division command post embraced the person of the Ia and his associated operations assistants, vehicles, and communications equipment and all were often in movement.

During the dramatic rush toward Rovno, the division faced almost insurmountable problems in logistics. In the division, the Ib (quartermaster or second general staff officer of the division) coordinated logistics in the name of the commander and under the staff direction of the Ia. The Ib headed the quartermaster echelon or logistics staff of the division from a command post normally physically located near the headquarters of the division supply detachment, which, notwithstanding the name, was a strong battalion-level organization holding the division supply columns and motor vehicle and weapons maintenance and repair companies. One reason why the German division command post was so light and operationally oriented was because the Ib and his assistants and communications apparatus were in a physically separate echelon. This decentralized style worked well because the Germans affected mission-style orders that allowed the Ib to function independently of division headquarters because he knew the mission of the division which was to advance through the night of 26-27 June 41 with the task of seizing a crossing over the Usoic River at Rovno. In accordance with this general mission, the Ib labored with the division supply detachment and the trains (supply columns) of the organic units of the division to supply the required ammunition, fuel, and rations. Failure to deliver fuel to the panzer regiment during the evening and the units of the middle battle group led almost to operational disaster. By early daylight hours of 27 June, however, the division logistics services managed to get fuel through to both the panzer regiment and the middle battle group. The reason for the fuel shortage was not a defect in the German organization but rather an operational situation that involved movement over long distances on unpaved roads and in the face of strong Soviet resistance involving the "sharing" of the road system with enemy tank and motorized rifle formations deep in Soviet rear areas.[28]

During the day, 27 June 41, the division extricated the middle battle group from its encirclement and resupplied and reorganized itself to continue the advance on Rovno. The division began to advance reconfigured into a left and right battle group with the latter built around 13th Motorized Brigade, having no tanks, and being tasked to get to Rovno first. At 2215 in the dead of night, the advanced elements of the right battle group stood 6 km in front of Rovno approaching the city from the southwest. At 0838 the next morning, the motorized infantry brigade entered the city and at 1100 seized bridges intact in the center of town. At this time the motorized infantry had outstripped the left battle group and tanks of the panzer regiment and came under heavy tank attacks by strong Soviet forces directly north of the city. Without the tanks of 4th Panzer Regiment, the motorized infantry fought off the Soviet armored vehicles with the antitank guns of the entire 13th Antitank Battalion and the antitank rifles of the infantry. During this midafternoon battle, the motorized rifle brigade destroyed 75 Soviet medium tanks and broke up the Soviet attacks. Division casualties were heavy this day totaling 27 KIA, 66 WIA, and 7 MIA mostly in this violent engagement on the northern outskirts of the city. At 1500, Headquarters, 3rd Panzer Corps signaled that 25th Motorized Infantry Division (*25.1.D. {mot.}*) would relieve *13.Pz.D.* in the city at latest in the early morning of 29 June 41 and ordered the division to advance toward Zhitomir immediately upon relief.

The will to action and movement or high tempo of operations associated with *13.Pz.D.* stands out in the following chain of events. At about midnight, the division commander reorganized the division into yet two new battle groups based on the reinforced panzer regiment and motorized rifle brigade and ordered them to advance out of Rovno at 0500. At 0415, however, the Soviets attacked with strong forces again from the northwest and north, i.e., from the left rear of the division. With notable coolness and determination in the face of a strong enemy attack from the left rear quarter, an advance into the unknown, and the corps-level complexities of a relief by a following division in positions now under attack, the division commander ordered the motorized rifle brigade to fight off the Soviet attack and effect the relief in Rovno by *25.1.D. (mot.)*. He also ordered the panzer regiment to move off in the attack toward Zhitomir by 0600 with the first task to seize a bridgehead over the Horyn River 40 km directly east. At 0600, the division commander personally rode off with the panzer regiment deeper into the Ukraine.

At 0625 an operational bombshell fell. The Chief of Staff, 3rd Panzer Corps, informed the division Ia that the arrival of *25.1.D. (mot.)* had been further delayed, i.e., *13.Pz.D.* would have to continue to defend Rovno from the northwest while advancing east toward Zhitomir. Informed by the Ia that the tank regiment had already been advancing eastward since 0600, the Chief of Staff made the decision to let it go but on no account allow it to engage in a serious battle against any Soviet force. Within 10 minutes of this discussion, the Ia contacted the division commander by radio and advised him, based on the uncertain time of arrival of *25.1.D. (mot.)*, the immediate difficulties of getting fuel columns through Rovno and the continued attacks there by Soviet tank and infantry forces with artillery support, to halt the advance of 6th Panzer Regiment. With this latest information and advice, the division commander decided to halt the advance sending only the division reconnaissance battalion as far as the Horyn River to gauge enemy strength and reconnoiter crossing sites. The *25.1.D. (mot.)* arrived finally at Rovno at 1500, 29 June 41, and two hours later, 13th Motorized Rifle Brigade reinforced as a second battle group set off toward the Horyn River. By this time the operational situation had changed—the Soviets had blown up the Horyn bridges as the reconnaissance detachment probed the river area earlier in the day—and the division commander ordered the motorized rifle brigade to lead the advance to the river.and establish a bridgehead by assault with the rubber boats organic to German infantry regiments. The motorized infantry reached the river at 1940 and later during hours of full darkness on the evening of 29-30 June 41 crossed the river carrying numbers of 37mm antitank guns on the bigger boats. The division commander personally directed the advance of the infantry and pioneers across the river.

For the rest of the day, and from 1-8 July 41, *13.Pz.D.* would advance quite slowly in the face of road conditions made disastrous by unusually heavy summer rains. The division would be halted one entire day by a most interesting situation on 1 July 41 in which corps headquarters would order it to brace for an operational-level Soviet counterattack which failed to materialize. In the face of various paralyzing circumstances the division crept forward 65 km from the Horyn to the Sluc River. Several violent engagements took place during this period and the division commander continued to advance in the lead with the panzer regiment. In particularly severe fighting on 3 July 41, for example, as the division advanced approximately 25 km out of the Horyn bridgehead, the panzer regiment accompanied by the division commander destroyed 72 Soviet medium tanks and as described in the war diary, eight batteries of Soviet artillery. The Germans flourished in a "target rich" environment at this time, and the author believes that they were so tactically adept that they commonly overran compactly sited Soviet artillery positions and often reported successes in terms of gun batteries rather than individual artillery pieces. Finally, as the division moved up against the Sluc River on 5 July 41, it faced extensive fortifications that were part of the Stalin Line constructed on the east side of the river when it formed the border between Poland and the Soviet Union in the period from late 1920 to September 1939. After careful planning and with centralized control of all of its artillery, the division launched an attack on the Stalin line about 12 km south of Novograd-Volynskij at 0310 on 7 July 41. The division motorized infantry made the attack which included the crossing of the Sluc with rubber boats and successfully broke through the line by evening of the same day.

On 8 July 41, the division fought off several Soviet counterattacks, destroying 43 Soviet tanks in defensive fighting while providing cover also for pioneer troops who ran into difficulties in constructing a bridge strong enough to carry the Pz.Kw. III and IV tanks of the division. At 2100 that night, division headquarters issued orders for another distant, high tempo drive that would end with unexpected success 175 km away on the outskirts of Kiev. During the middle of the night, the division reorganized itself into an advanced detachment, *Kampfgruppe* Roedlich, built around 4th Panzer Regiment, and *Kampfgruppe* von Rost, built around 93rd Motorized Infantry Regiment. A strong advanced detachment consisting of the division reconnaissance and motorcycle battalions moved off at 0330 from positions about 10 km farther east from *Kampfgruppe* Roedlich and its panzers on the Sluc River. The tanks also moved off at 0330 soon reaching the great road to Zhitomir designated *Panzerstrasse* 1 (tank highway number 1) and headed east on it hoping to exploit the quick breakthrough of the Stalin Line. *Kampfgruppe* von Rost set out several hours later at 0725 moving toward and then along the big highway to Zhitomir.

Events unfolded swiftly. By 0825, the leading tanks of *Kampfgruppe* Roedlich had overtaken the advanced detachment and stood only 1 km away from Zhitomir. Along the road forward the German tanks and motorized infantry had run through columns of Soviet troops, tanks, reconnaissance vehicles, artillery, and an armored train on the rail line paralleling the road, and destroyed them with gunfire. Command style in real maneuver war appeared now as the Ia and operations echelon of the division moved forward. At 0930 they joined the division commander who was now riding with the corps commander, *General der Kavalerie* Eberhard von Mackensen, in the leading panzer regiment battle group of the division. In the meantime, a combat team of that battle group had moved into the city and seized intact the bridges over the two rivers flowing through Zhitomir. By 1100, the Germans had cleared the city and begun to reorganize to continue the advance on Kiev. The 4th Panzer Regiment made a determined effort to get through Zhitomir and continue the dash toward Kiev but was slowed by a strong surprise attack by remnants of one Soviet Infantry and two motorized divisions around 1855 near Korostysev on the Teterev River 30 km east of Zhitomir. The division commander personally directed the advance to Korostysev riding with the tanks of the leading battle group and under fire with the hard hit 1st Panzer Battalion. As darkness fell, the German tanks of *Kampfgruppe* Roedlich, the newly arrived motorized infantry of *Kampfgruppe* Herr, and the division commander moved forward another 30 km to Kocerov and halted for the evening (see all the cities and rivers mentioned in this paragraph on Map 3).

On the morning of 10 July 41, *13.Pz.D.* stood approximately 65 km from the outskirts of Kiev. At that moment, the division had the clear and present opportunity to thrust into the city the same day. The high command of the Army itself, however, had come to the conclusion that Kiev was not an important military objective. The commander of Army Group South agreed and the plan had become to direct south the first motorized forces arriving near Kiev to block the escape across the Dnepr River of the huge Soviet forces lying southwest of Kiev. Not surprisingly, *13.Pz.D.* received a radio message from corps headquarters emphasizing that the division would advance to the Irpen River immediately west of Kiev only on specific order of the corps commander. The war diary of the division comments that by such wording, Corps warned the division that an individual coup de main at Kiev had been forbidden by higher headquarters. Army Group South now turned 3rd Panzer Corps south to aid in the strategic-level attempt to trap the Soviet armies lying far to the west of the Dnepr and now more than 170 km to the rear of *13.Pz.D.* The Germans slowly executed the decision to move south and the division stayed for several days in the Irpen River positions until relieved by following divisions. On 20 July 41, the division advanced southwest toward the important rail communications center of Fastov entering the northern outskirts the same day but running into strong Soviet resistance. After heavy fighting around Fastov for the next two days, the division Ia noted on 22 July that the panzer regiment was down to 58 tanks *einsatzbereite* (ready for insertion in combat). The number is instructive because the war diary elaborates that with this number the division was close to running out of "striking power" as an armored unit on the offensive. This judgment illuminates technical and numerical necessities in maneuver war. Brilliant mobile style and effective combined arms action can buy only so much. The equation seems to be: too few tanks, no maneuver war.

After a day's rest on 23 July 41, *13.Pz.D.* seems to have recuperated because early in the evening, Headquarters, 3rd Panzer Corps, ordered it to advance southeast the next day in what was the beginning of another great mobile drive. German tempo shows up almost immediately with the division noting that it issued orders for "the march" in the middle of the night (2400) to the three battle groups set up for the operation. The tank-heavy battle group under *Oberstleutnant* Roedlich that included the tank regiment set off at 0500, 24 July 41, and roughly three hours afterward at 0810 moved through Grebenki 20 km to the southeast. At 1230, the corps commander appeared in the division command post and presented his "special insights for rapid advance of the division."[29] Mackensen stated that he felt the division was advancing into a gap in the Soviet defensive deployment and should accelerate southeast toward Mironovka. On 25, 26 July 41, the division ran into heavy rain and muddy roads that slowed forward movement. On 27 July even heavier rain fell and the division war diary presents the astounding comment from the viewpoint of the will to advance on the part of the Germans and the conduct of maneuver war, that headquarters weighed the dispatching forward of reconnaissance troops on small sleds (*Panjewagen*) pulled by the compact Ukrainian horses of the region. Conditions improved on 28 July, however, the ground dried rapidly in the summer sun and the corps commander ordered the division at 1545 to move out again as quickly as possible and thrust through Mironovka to Korsun, 125 km from Fastov, the starting point of the latest advance (see Map 3).

The strategic picture at this moment was both vast and challenging for Army Group South. After exploding into the area close to Kiev on 10 July 41, the Germans faced the strategic dilemma of making the correct next move to trap as many as possible of the Soviet formations lying to the south and west in the Ukraine. By 24 July 41, Field Marshal Gerd von Rundstedt had made this decision and ordered the mobile divisions to pivot southeast from Belaja Cerkov and effect an extremely challenging single envelopment far to the south of that city – eventually the pocket near Uman 130 km farther south. The German 3rd Panzer Corps and its *13.Pz.D.* were not part of that move but advanced farther east along the Dnepr River as a kind of giant strategic intercepting line to catch the Soviet formations that eluded the inner encirclement by blocking the Dnepr crossings. From the beginning then, the grand, distant focus of 3rd Panzer Corps was Dnepropetrovsk on the great southern bend of the Dnepr 440 km from Fastov. In a word, when *13.Pz.D.* set out from Fastov on 24 July 41, it had a long way to go – a vast distance that required movement, action and pull from the front rather than managing and phasing from the rear.

After beginning its advance early in the morning of 29 July 41, a special force of division motorized infantry in battalion strength seized Mironovka on the main route to Korsun at about noon on the same day. The next day, at 1310, the tank spearhead of 6th Panzer Regiment moved into Korsun but could not prevent the Soviets from destroying the bridges there over the wide Ros River. Motorized infantry of the following 66th Motorized Rifle Regiment quickly established a bridgehead south of the river, accomplishing the crossing with ubiquitous and invaluable German infantry regiment rubber boats. The destruction of the bridges was a disaster though, because the division pioneer battalion announced about midnight that it would require 24 hours (!) to build a satisfactory bridge for motor vehicles. This tactical detail highlights the almost uncanny tactical success of the Germans in seizing bridges intact one after an other in the campaign. When the Germans failed to secure an intact bridge in Korsun, it cost them an entire day in a delicately balanced race to beat the Soviets to their Dnepr River escape routes. By 0800 on 1 August 41, the division began to advance again. In a quick bound led by *Kampfgruppe* Herr, a group that was based largely on tanks, motorized infantry and attached artillery, the division moved into Gorodisce.

What kind of *Kampfgruppe* would the division set up for such a move and how would it proceed? Led by *Oberst* Herr, the commander of 13th Motorized Rifle Brigade, the group combined the combat elements necessary to march in advance of the mass of the division with effective combat power and mobility. Herr set up the group to advance in the following tactical column:[30]

Kampfgruppe Herr Tactical March Column, 1 Aug '41
6th Panzer Rgt (without 1st Bn) (approx 50 tanks).
One Moto Inf Company (from 1st Bn, 93rd Moto Inf Rgt).
1st Bn, 13th Panzer Arty Rgt.
Mass of 1st Bn, 93rd Moto Inf Rgt.
3rd Company, 4th Panzer Pioneer Bn.
1st Company, 13th Antitank Detachment.
Supply Trains, 6th Panzer Rgt.

The location of the artillery is particularly interesting. The *Kampfgruppe* commander would depend almost entirely on his attached artillery for fire support and placed it where it could intervene as quickly as prudence would allow from the tactical march column. As the column moved south along the road to Gorodisce, Herr deployed it off the road into firing positions on two occasions to "overwatch" the advance of the force. The column met significant resistance at two places along the route and disposed of it by immediate fire from the tanks combined with attack by the motorized infantry company moving with them. The Germans discovered that the right course of action in these encounters was an immediate attack with the expenditure of a lot of infantry small arms and tank gun ammunition rather than the slower deployment of a larger force. In these actions one can see an effective style of maneuver war. Additionally, in a useful lesson for today, the Germans carried larger percentages of high explosive rounds in their tanks that were effective against Soviet infantry, machine gun positions, and the numerous antitank guns and their crews encountered in delaying positions and significantly immune to armor piercing ammunition.

From 2-7 August 41, *13.Pz.D.* encountered heavy summer rains that stopped forward movement on several occasions for significant periods of time. Headquarters, 3rd Panzer Corps, also assigned the division several missions during the period to cover exposed flanks of the corps. These missions took time and energy and slowed the division in the general advance toward Dnepropetrovsk. At 1240 on 6 August, corps headquarters suddenly and dramatically ordered the division to take the great bridges across the Dnepr at Kremencug in a coup de main, but later in the day at 1600, after the division had organized a new set of battle groups to execute the mission, ordered the division to call off the operation and, of course, halt and reorient the various battle groups. The war diary of the division noted laconically "basis (for the change) unknown by the division." The next day, 7 August 41, the division met what it described as cloud bursts and its headquarters noted that all vehicles of the division remained stuck (*stecken*) in the Ukrainian black earth mud. On 8 August at 0420, corps headquarters ordered the division to attack again toward Kremencug, i.e., back to the north, and lock in tightly the Soviet bridgehead at that communications center on the Dnepr River. Division headquarters concentrated four battle groups around Pavlys 17 km south of Kremencug by midafternoon and gave them the mission to seize the south bank of the Dnepr up against Kremencug. With the support of a Stuka strike at 0545, the division attacked at 0600 on 9 August 41, led by battle group Herr now built around motorized infantry. By 1130, the battle group had reached the destroyed rail bridge at the south outskirts of the city, having already broken through the defenses near Pavlys, covered 17 km in its advance, and essentially accomplished the mission.

The advance to Kremencug is notable for several reasons. Spread out over a wide area in screening positions and oriented for further advance south, the division received orders at break of day on 8 August 41 to attack north against strong Soviet forces around a large city on the Dnepr. With the division spread over an arc of about 50 km, Rothkirch and his Ia fluidly moved the division onto the new axis of advance. The individual battle groups met their march schedules, armed and fueled, and went into assault positions for an advance that began with an air strike at 0545 the next morning, 9 August 41. Earlier at 0200, the Soviets, sensing the increase in German activity, launched a strong spoiling attack that hit some of the assembly positions for the division advance. The division commander with strong nerves ordered the Soviet attack to be beaten back and the German advance to begin on schedule. After the division had closely invested Kremencug by noon on 9 August and because of the additional task of securing the southern sector of the corps area of operations, the division still stood with a front of 50 km. In keeping with rapidly changing scenes in maneuver war, at 1545, Soviet prisoners brought in during fighting south of Kremencug revealed through battlefield interrogation that the "26th Russian Cavalry Division" was on the march towards the city. With that information, division headquarters began to concentrate its dispersed forces in the path of the anticipated attack. The Luftwaffe had assigned relatively small forces in support of Army Group South and effected a style of pre-planned strikes against important targets in front of attacking units rather than more flexible answering of distress calls. The division, therefore, braced for the attack depending largely on its own artillery for fire support. In this static situation, the division commander concentrated all of his 93rd Artillery Regiment behind the threatened front. At the break of day on 10 August 41 and for several hours thereafter, the artillery and the fire of the German "infantry guns" (75mm and 150mm howitzers in the motorized infantry regiments) broke up the Soviet attack before it got close to the German HKL (*Hauptkampflinie*) or main line of resistance. The end result by midafternoon: 455 Soviet prisoners and an unknown number of dead and evacuated wounded versus German losses of 4 KIA and 27 WIA.

Between 11-16 August 41, the division advanced southeast from Kremencug by gradually pushing forward the wide screening front it manned in that area. By the latter day, the division stood about 55 km southeast of the city, well rested, and ready for another mobile advance as German Infantry divisions began to arrive from the scene of the 8 August 41 final destruction of the Soviet armies in the Uman pocket out of which the Germans had taken 103,000 prisoners. By 17 August the division had been relieved of most of its screening missions and concentrated for further advance southeast. With a quick enough drive, the division could possibly create a moderate-sized encirclement to the southwest up against its right neighbor, 60th Motorized Infantry Division *60.I.D. (mot.)*. On 91 August 41, *13.Pz.D.* attacked, quickly gained approximately 35 km to the vicinity of Verhocevo (see Map 3), and encircled a substantial number of Soviet troops lying to its southwest by linking up with *60.I.D. (mot.)*. The division took 2,500 prisoners on 19 August and 4,265 more during fighting to destroy the remnants in the period 20-23 August. At the strategic level, it had become evident by this time that the Soviets had collapsed in the Ukraine and quick further advances were needed everywhere to move up against the Dnepr, establish bridgeheads where possible over that giant river, and annihilate Soviet forces remaining on the west bank.

At 2030, 23 August 41, sensing the opportunity to finish the war west of the Dnepr, Headquarters, 3rd Panzer Corps, ordered all available forces under its command to attack in the morning to take the great industrial and communications center of Dnepropetrovsk. In a timeless example of effective maneuver war, corps headquarters stated that the advance "must be pushed forward without regard for danger from the flanks. Every opportunity to win ground must be made good without respect for boundaries among advancing units."[31] More specifically, *13.Pz.D.* was given the mission to be ready to attack by 0700, 24 August 41, penetrate through the field positions opposite it, and seize the western railroad bridge in Dnepropetrovsk. The new division commander since 28 July 41, *Generalmajor* Walther Duevert, set up two battle groups side by side to lead the advance. In the face of strong Soviet resistance, the attack gained ground slowly but inexorably into the outskirts of Dnepropetrovsk. Given the heavy fighting against cohesive Soviet forces, the division commander consolidated positions during the night ordering the attack to be renewed at 0500 on 25 August. Duevert personally accompanied *Kampfgruppe* Radwan and at 0845 reached the great westward combined rail and road bridge over the Dnepr that the Soviets had managed to blow up just 15 minutes earlier. The Germans faced a real challenge at this moment for further operations eastward because the Dnepr is 1200m wide at this location and bridging it would be a lengthy civil engineering project.

At 0915 troops of *Kampfgruppe* Rodt, however, now on the Dnepr farther west spotted a Soviet military floating bridge upstream from the grand steel structure and reported it useable. Orders flew thick and fast at this time. Rodt ordered a crossing, formed an assault group, and directed artillery into position to support the group. Division headquarters simultaneously ordered Rodt to attack, and, at almost the same time, the corps commander personally appeared on the river bank and likewise ordered a crossing. As the Germans gathered to make the exposed crossing, a Soviet heavy tank on the east bank opened fire on them and a battle developed between it and the supporting 5th Battery of the Artillery Regiment. Then, a motorcyclist of the battle group – only noted as "a motorcyclist" in the war diary—drove out onto the bridge pulling along with him the frozen assault troop and other parts of 1st Battalion, 66th Motorized Rifle Regiment. The Soviets had placed explosive charges and motor vehicles together at four positions on the bridge, planning to destroy the bridge by burning the trucks and exploding the charges. In the rush across the bridge, the Germans succeeded in putting out all of the fires and getting around the damage from the scanty explosive charges with motorcyclists, infantry, and eventually trucks up to three-ton capacity. In a short period of time, *13.Pz.D.* pushed two motorized rifle battalions across the river and into a suitably dramatic ending to a mobile drive that had begun at Fastov on 20 July 41 and ended a little over a month later and 415 km farther into the Soviet Union.

Photo 4. A 13th Panzer Division reconnaissance tank approaches a burning Soviet T-26 infantry support tank in the Ukraine in June or July 1941. The lightly armed German tank could not engage in serious tank versus tank combat but was well suited for the advanced detachment role in the distant mobile drive of the division 900 km from the Polish border to Dnepropetrovsk on the lower reaches of the Dnepr River (Bundesarchiv Bestand).

PART ONE:
Map Section

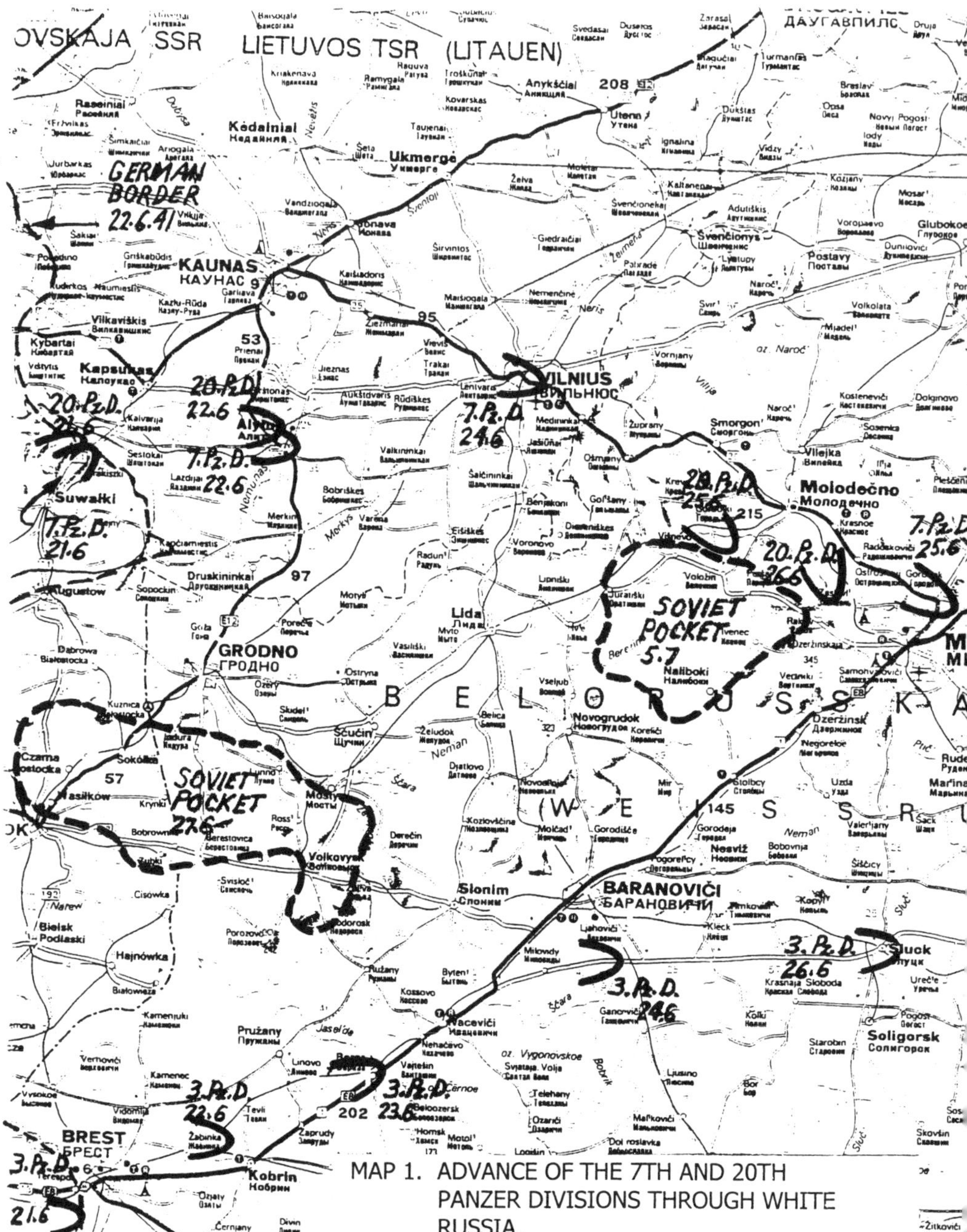

MAP 1. ADVANCE OF THE 7TH AND 20TH PANZER DIVISIONS THROUGH WHITE RUSSIA.

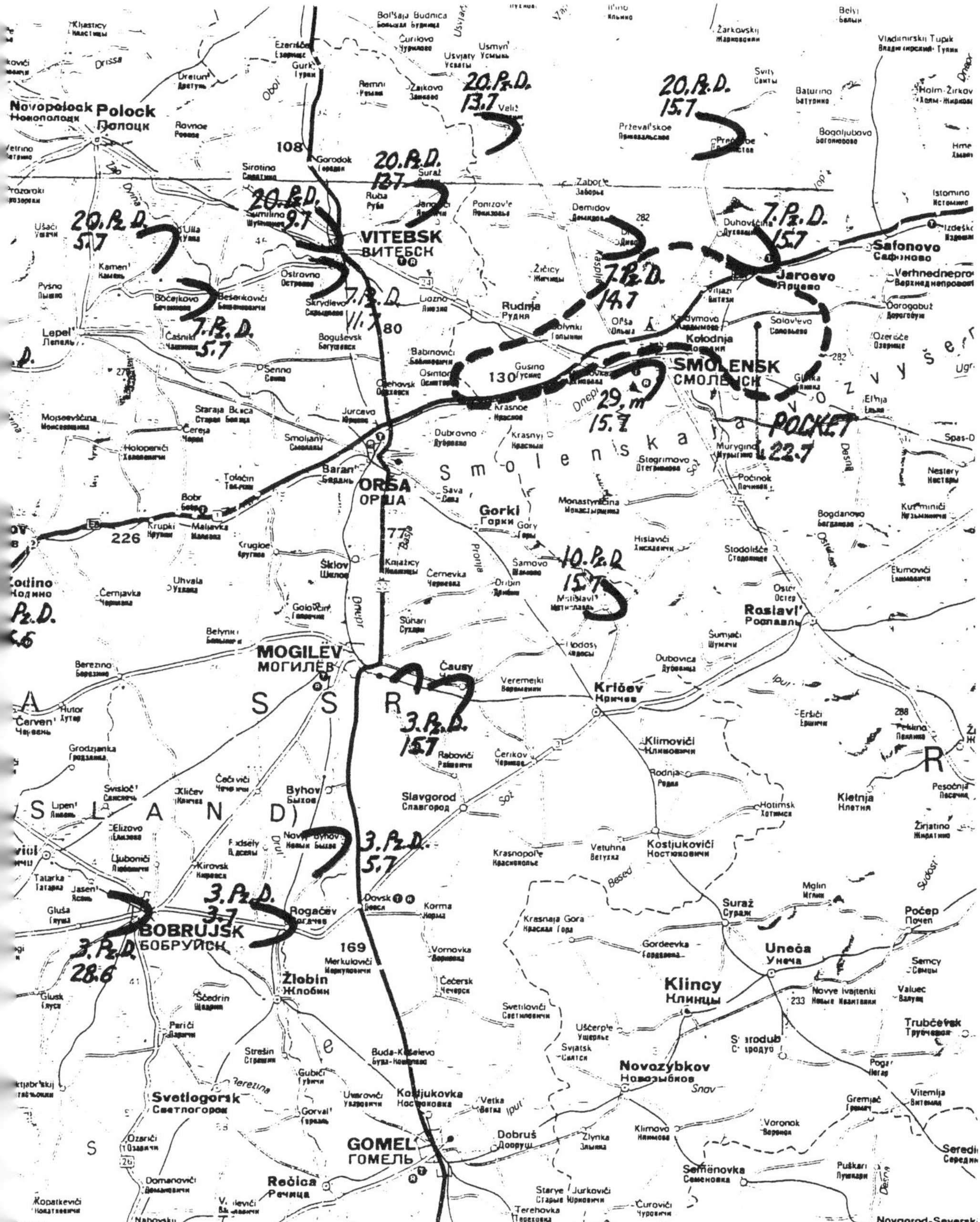
20.Pz.D. 13.7
20.Pz.D. 15.7
20.Pz.D. 13.7
20.Pz.D. 9.7
20.Pz.D. 5.7
7.Pz.D. 5.7
7.Pz.D. 11.7
7.Pz.D. 14.7
7.Pz.D. 15.7
29. mot 15.7
POCKET 22.7
10.Pz.D. 15.7
3.Pz.D. 15.7
3.Pz.D. 5.7
3.Pz.D. 3.7
3.Pz.D. 28.6
Pz.D.
Novopolock Новополоцк
Polock Полоцк
Vitebsk Витебск
Smolensk Смоленск
Jarcevo Ярцево
Safonovo Сафоново
Orša Орша
Gorki Горки
Mogilev Могилев
Roslavl' Рославль
Kričev Кричев
Bobrujsk Бобруйск
Žlobin Жлобин
Rogačev Рогачев
Klincy Клинцы
Novozybkov Новозыбков
Gomel Гомель
Svetlogorsk Светлогорск
Rečica Речица
Uneča Унеча
Smolenskaja vozvyšennost'
S S R
S L A N D
Dnepr

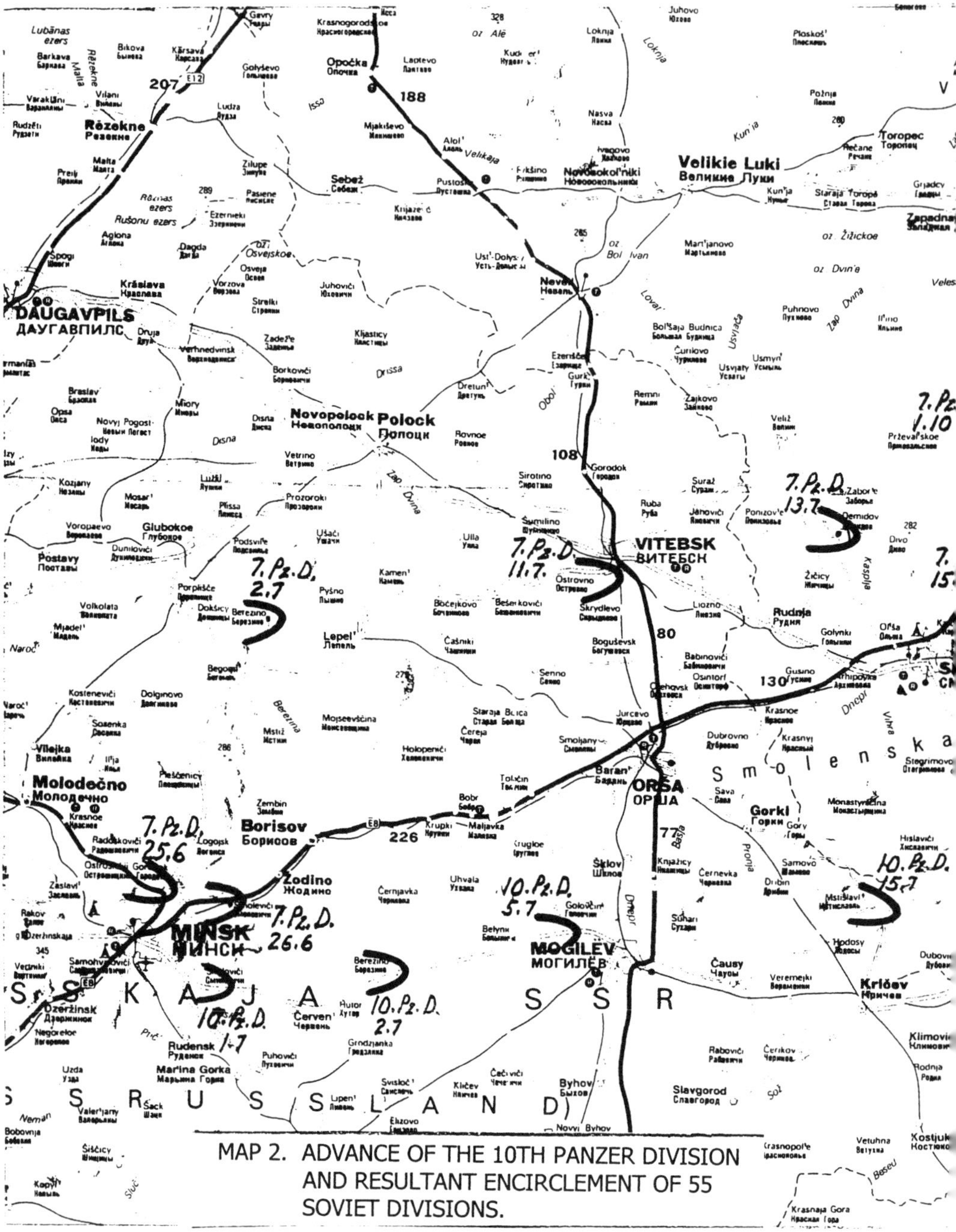

MAP 2. ADVANCE OF THE 10TH PANZER DIVISION AND RESULTANT ENCIRCLEMENT OF 55 SOVIET DIVISIONS.

7.Pz.D. 23.11
7.Pz.D. 28.11
7.Pz.D. 15.11
7.Pz.D. 15.11
7.Pz.D. 22.10
7.Pz.D. 3.10
4.10
5.10
7.Pz.D. 6.10
10.Pz.D. 6.10
SOVIET POCKET 6.10
10.Pz.D. 5.10
10.Pz.D. 4.10
10.Pz.D. 3.10
10.Pz.D. 2.10
10.Pz.D. 1.10
Konakovo
Klin
Dmitrov
Krasnozavodsk
Solnečnogorsk
Volokolamsk
Puškino
Mytišči
Ščëlkovo
Himki
Krasnogorsk
MOSKVA
МОСКВА
LJUBERCY
Žukovskij
Podolsk
Domodedovo
Naro-Fominsk
Klimovsk
Čehov
Serpuhov
Obninsk
Malojaroslavec
Možajsk
Gagarin
Vjaz'ma
Safonovo
Ržev
Nelidovo
Kondrovo
Aleksin
KALUGA
КАЛУГА
TULA
ТУЛА
Ščëkino
Kireevsk
Bogorodick
Suhiniči
Kirov
Ljudinovo
Djat'kovo
BRJANSK
БРЯНСК
Karačev
OREL
ОРЁЛ
Mcensk
R O S S I J S K A J
v y š e n n o s t'
M O S K O V S K A J A

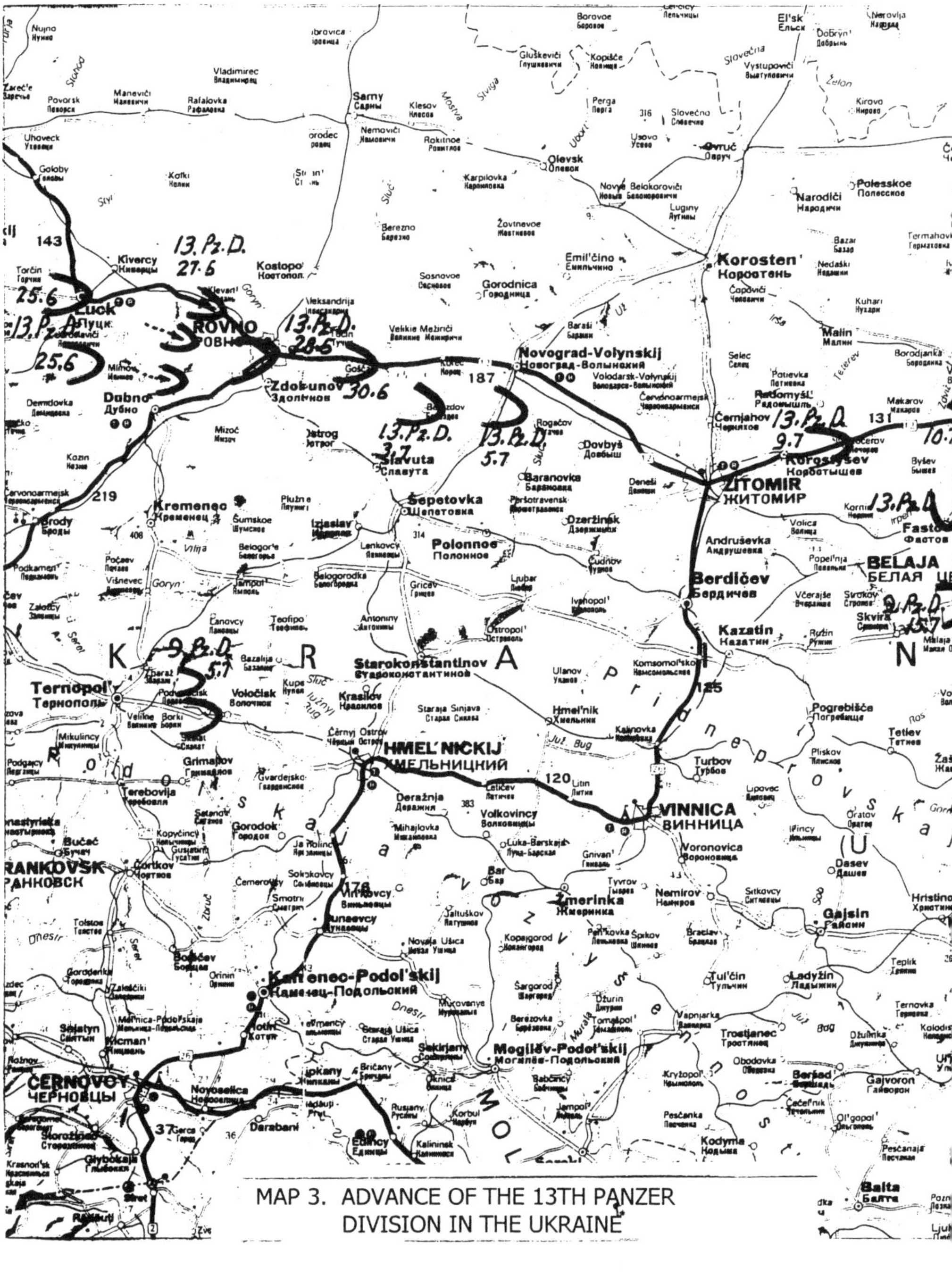

MAP 3. ADVANCE OF THE 13TH PANZER DIVISION IN THE UKRAINE

ČERNIGOV
ЧЕРНИГОВ
Konotop
Конотоп
SUMY
СУМЫ
Nežin
Нежин
Kievskoe vodohranilišče
(Kiewer Stausee)
Priluki
Прилуки
Romny
Ромны
Lebedin
Лебедин
Ahtyrka
Ахтырка
Brovary
Бровары
Borispol'
Борисполь
KIEV
КИЕВ
Lubny
Лубны
Mirgorod
Миргород
POLTAVA
ПОЛТАВА
Perejaslav-Hmel'nickij
Переяслав-Хмельницкий
Zolotonoša
Золотоноша
ČERKASSY
ЧЕРКАССЫ
Šmela
Смела
Kremenčugskoe vodohranilišče
(Krementschuger Stausee)
KREMENČUG
КРЕМЕНЧУГ
Svetlovodsk
Светловодск
Zvenigorodka
Звенигородка
Aleksandrija
Александрия
DNEPRODZERŽINSK
ДНЕПРОДЗЕРЖИНСК
DNEPROPETR
ДНЕПРОПЕТРОВ
KIROVOGRAD
КИРОВОГРАД
Novoukrainka
Новоукраинка
KRIVOJ ROG
КРИВОЙ РОГ
ZAPOROŽE
ЗАПОРОЖЬЕ
NIKOPOL'
Ordžonikidze
S K A J
U K R A I N E
13. Pz.D. 30.7
13. Pz.D. 1.8
13. Pz.D. 6.8
7.8
13. Pz.D. 8.8
13. Pz.D. 9.8
13. Pz.D. 16.8
13. Pz.D.
19.8
9. Pz.D. 4.8
9. Pz.D. 7.8
159
91
337
363

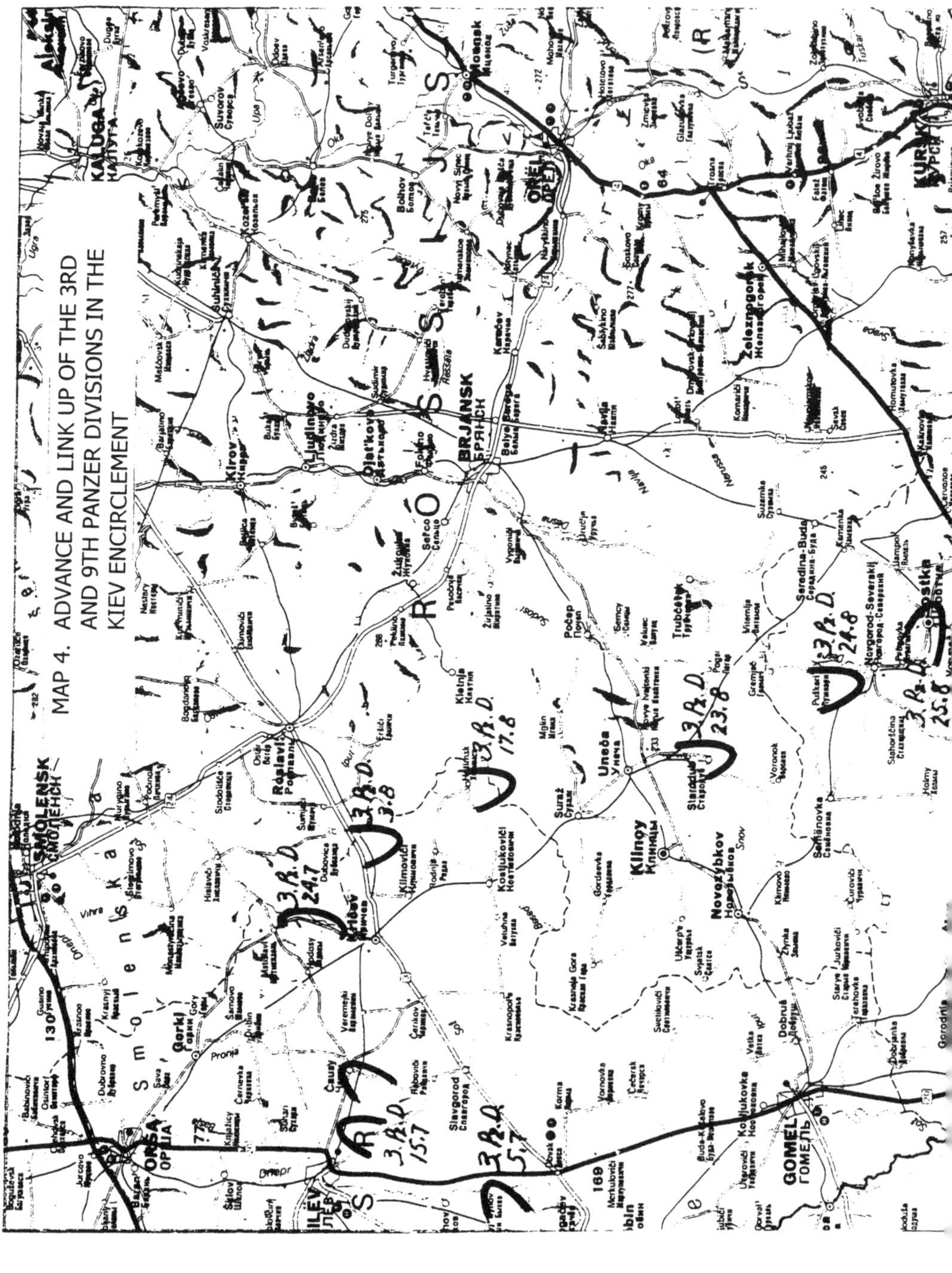

MAP 4. ADVANCE AND LINK UP OF THE 3RD AND 9TH PANZER DIVISIONS IN THE KIEV ENCIRCLEMENT

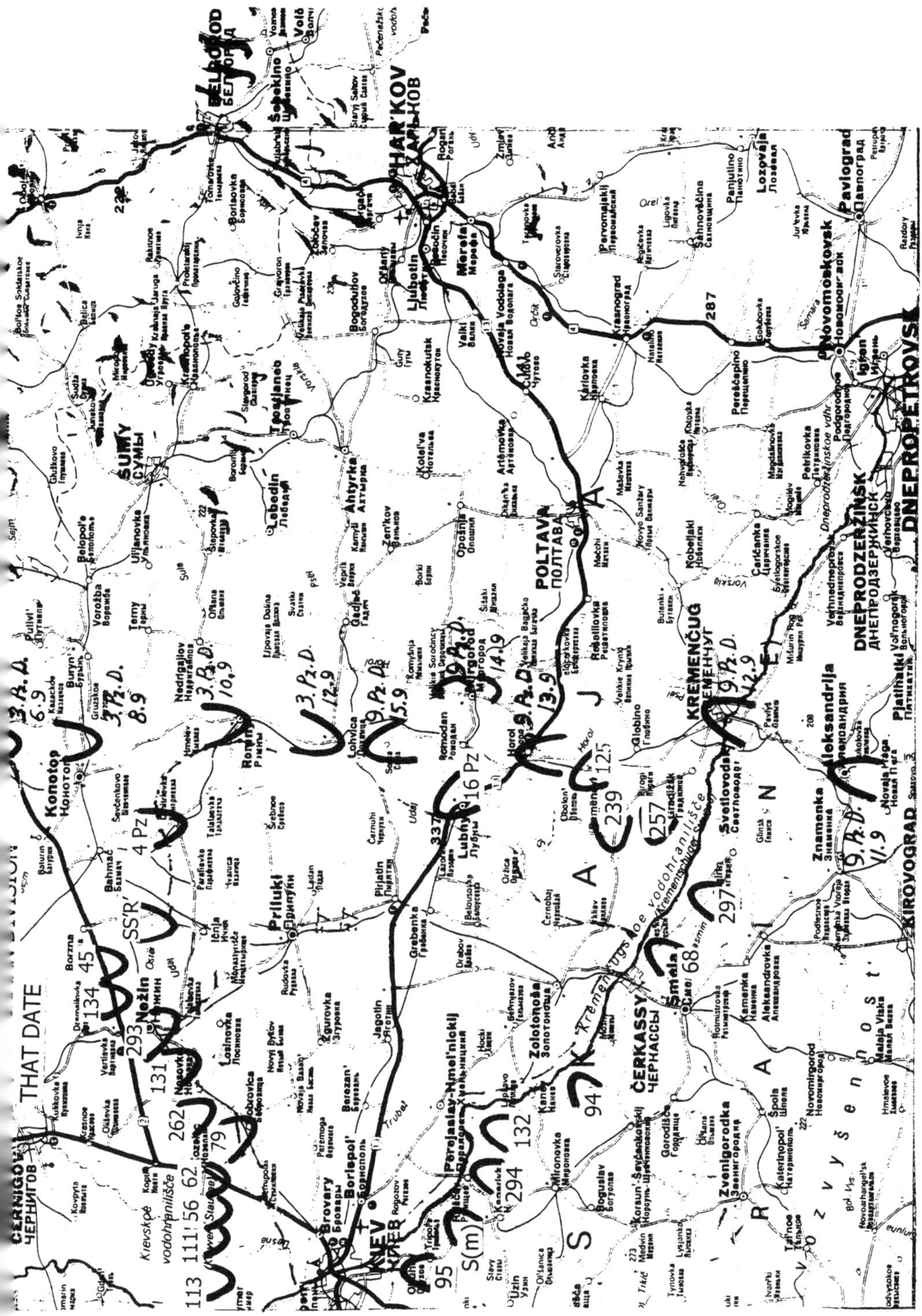
THAT DATE
ČERNIGOV
ČERNIGOV
KIEV
Brovary
Borispol'
Nežin
Konotop
Priluki
Romny
Lubny
Mirgorod
SUMY
Lebedin
Ahtyrka
Trostjanec
BELGOROD
HAR'KOV
Valki
POLTAVA
KREMENČUG
ČERKASSY
Smela
Zolotonoša
Perejaslav-Hmel'nickij
Zvenigorodka
KIROVOGRAD
Aleksandrija
DNEPRODZERŽINSK
DNEPROPETROVSK
Novomoskovsk
Pavlograd
Krasnograd
Lozovaja
Svetlovodsk
Kievskoe vodohranilišče
Kremenčugskoe vodohranilišče

5

The Kiev Encirclement: German 3rd and 9th Panzer Divisions Link Up in Central Ukraine, 15 September '41

At 0910 on 15 September 41, German troops of the 3rd Panzer Division (*3.Pz.D.*) and 9th Panzer Division (*9.Pz.D.*) established conclusive physical contact at Lohvica in the Central Ukraine trapping five Soviet field armies to the west of them.[32] This event culminated what has been described by one authority as the greatest battle of encirclement in history. The *3.Pz.D.*, that effected the encirclement with Panzer Group 2 from the north, had entered the war on 22 June 41 at Brest and moved 1,100 km through the Soviet Union across unpaved roads and in the face of determined resistance by an enemy equipped with masses of tanks to get to Lohvica. The *9.Pz.D.* effected the encirclement with Panzer Group 1 from the South, having entered the Soviet Union on 29 June 41 near Rova Russkaja and moved approximately 1,430 km through the Ukraine in the face of a more difficult strategic situation and perhaps even more difficult road conditions.

The accomplishment is monumental in terms of the distances covered in the face of the numbers and determination of the defending force. Along the route of advance of *9.Pz.D.*, the Germans were forced to thrust into the main strength of the defending Soviets in the attempt somehow to complete a single envelopment from the north of major forces west of the Dnepr River. The *9.Pz.D.* and the other German mobile divisions attacking with it faced strong Soviet forces that outnumbered the Germans in terms of men, tanks, and combat aircraft. The division not only faced Soviet formations that generally outnumbered it but also forces that proved to be skillfully led at army and army group level in terms of withdrawing behind strong rearguards and avoiding the great encirclement that the Germans were trying to effect with a single enveloping wing. The researcher has collected the following statistics from the German records that he feels substantiates the capability of *9.Pz.D.*

to advance against an enemy that was both strong and amply endowed with armor, artillery, and combat aircraft:

9.Pz.D., the Fight Against a Strong Armored Enemy (1941)

Date	**Soviet Weapons Destroyed**
29.6	12 Tanks, 2 Arty Batteries
30.6	30 Tanks
1.7	134 Tanks, 1,200 POWs
1.2	34 Tanks, 4 AA Guns

The division entered the war with a tank strength of approximately 162 tanks including 49 light vehicles weighing about 10.0 tons and armed with only a 20mm automatic cannon, and six "heavy command tanks" with dummy gun barrels to simulate main battle tanks. The data for the first four days of its insertion in the war show that the division destroyed through gunfire or captured 211 Soviet tanks, i.e., more tanks than the 162 tanks held by the division and a lot more than the 107 serious main battle tanks in it. The data show that the division was advancing against a strong armored enemy and fighting with an effective style against it.

In early August 1941, Army Group South managed finally to bring about the encirclement of major, strategic level Soviet forces around Uman 160 km west of the Dnepr at Kremencug. The *9.Pz.D.* represented the extreme point of the enveloping arm from the north which had swung down from Belaja Cerkov to link up with German infantry of 1st mountain Corps by 4 August 41 to close the Uman pocket. The following data illustrate the magnitude of the combat along the route of advance of the division as it arrived at Belaja Cerkov and then pivoted south in a movement covering more than 185 km by road to the area immediately south of Tiskovka (see Map 3):

9.Pz.D., the Uman Envelopment (1941)

Time, 24-30 July	**Time, 31 July-5 August**
Soviet Losses: 2 Tanks	Soviet Losses: 33 Tanks
8 Guns	116 Guns
15 Trucks	1,113 Trucks
747 POWs	11,100 POWs

Following the maneuver and combat illustrated by the Soviet losses above, *9.Pz.D.* advanced east through Kirovograd, Krivoj Rog, Nikopol, Zaporoze, and finally to Dnepropetrovsk a litany of significant industrial and communications centers of the Ukraine and the Soviet Union. Along this route of advance, the division cut through powerful Soviet forces that had eluded destruction south of Uman and were continuing to fight to maintain bridgeheads on the west bank of the Dnepr. The division advanced 490 km during this advance from 7-26 August 41 against resistance associated with the following losses inflicted on the Soviets:

Soviet Losses from 9.Pz.D. Advance to Dnepr At Dnepropetrovsk (1941)

7-10 Aug 41 Initial Combat	11-16 Aug 41 To Krivoj Rog	17-20 Aug 41 To Zaporoze	21-26 Aug 41 To Dnepropetrovsk
2 Tanks	2 Tanks	0 Tanks	0 Tanks
2 Guns	17 Guns	21 Guns	25 Guns
2 Trucks	51 Trucks	403 Trucks	0 Trucks
701 POWs	4,000 POWs	5,630 POWs	6,011 POWs

The figures are revealing. They show the battered Soviets with no tanks and relatively few guns remaining in the Ukraine but still fighting back. The *9.Pz.D.* advanced swiftly over a long distance, indeed a strategically significant distance even by the standards of the eastern front. The rate of advance was impressive because the division also fought engagements along the way that contributed to the establishment of German bridgeheads east of the Dnepr at three different locations – Nikopol, Zaporoze, and Dnepropetrovsk. The most significant point that stands out in terms of tanks and maneuver war is that *9.Pz.D.*, other German panzer divisions, and the infantry divisions had been so effective in tank-versus-tank combat with the tanks of the panzer divisions and antitank warfare with the antitank guns of the other divisions that the huge B-Day Soviet tank force had literally ceased to exist west of the Dnepr by August 41. In summary, the Germans not only moved fast and far with their maneuver war style but destroyed powerful enemy armored forces along the routes of advance.

Early in September 41, the high command of the Army directed Army Group South to cooperate with German mobile and foot marching infantry forces of Army Group Center that had begun to move south pursuant to a personal decision by Adolf Hitler to seize the Central Ukraine as quickly as possible notwithstanding the greater importance of destroying the main concentration of the Soviet Army now deploying in desperation in front of Moscow. As part of this strategical scene, Headquarters, 14th Panzer Corps, ordered *9.Pz.D.* on 8 September 41, to begin a march from its location north of Krivoj Rog to Kremencug. The next day, the division came under control of 48th Panzer Corps and on 11 September began to concentrate toward Kremencug and the bridges and bridgehead there over the Dnepr. The division commander, *Generalmajor* Dr. Alfred Hubicki, reconfigured the division into the usual several march groups for the concentration in the bridgehead opposite Kremencug including, for example, the division staff, 33rd Panzer Regiment, and Headquarters, 9th Panzer Brigade with a mix of tanks, motorized infantry, artillery, antiaircraft, and antitank units that made it, in effect, a combined arms *Kampfgruppe*. At 0000, 14 September 4, corps headquarters gave the division the mission to take the train station north of the Dnepr at Romodan while thrusting with *Schwerpunkt* through Mirgorod to prevent a breakthrough southeast by Soviet forces around Lohvica that were under attack from the north by *3.Pz.D.* and other units of Panzer Group 2. At 1445, corps headquarters assigned a new mission to the division ordering it to block eastward of Mirgorod, advance farther north, seize a bridgehead over the Sula River at Senca, and link up with *3.Pz.D.* at Lohvica (see Map 4). The division commander quickly reorganized the division into the following two battle groups in conformance with the new mission:

1445, 14 Sep 41, 9.Pz.D.: New Mission, New Battle Groups

1st Kampfgruppe	2nd Kampfgruppe
Hq and Part, 33rd Pz Rgt	Hq, 9th Moto Inf Bde
Hq, 102nd Arty Rgt	1st Bn, 33rd Pz Rgt
2nd Bn, 102nd Arty Rgt	2nd Bn, 10th Moto Inf Rgt
3rd Bn, 102nd Arty Rgt	4th Btry, 102nd Arty Rgt
1st Bn, 10th Moto Inf Rgt	2nd Co, 50th AT Bn

Two valuable elements of German combat style in maneuver war stand out in these battle groups. The 1st *Kampfgruppe* holds most of the division artillery and the artillery regimental commander to block eastward from static positions east of Mirgorod. The 2nd *Kampfgruppe* contains strong forces of tanks and motorized infantry but only one battery of artillery nimble enough to keep up with the other elements and go into firing positions quickly right off the road in timely support of the group and small enough to ease the challenge of artillery ammunition supply. The Germans were on to something here; they needed enough artillery immediately available to the battle group commander to beat down resistance in the battle of the imponderable chance encounter characterizing maneuver war but not too much to slow the advance and create a barrier to the seizure of opportunity in the mobile advance. As the more mobile battle group advanced toward Senca it overran large numbers of Soviet vehicles including one column with 50 trucks in it all operating as if the area were completely secure. At 0000, 15 September 41, the 9th Motorized Rifle Brigade battle group arrived around the train station at Senca and by 0745 had taken the bridge over the Sula River intact and set up a bridgehead. At 0910, troops of this strong battle group established decisive contact with elements of *3.Pz.D.* in front of Lohvica. The trap had shut on five Soviet field armies still lying in the direction of Kiev.

For the next several days, *9.Pz.D.* defended itself against Soviet attempts to break out of encirclement while simultaneously compressing the Soviet front westward near Lubny. By 24 September 41, the Soviet pocket had burned out and the Germans had come into possession of the Central Ukraine. The following data illustrates the violence of the combat and the magnitude of the Soviet collapse:

Soviet Losses to 9.Pz.D. During Kiev Encirclement Operations (1941)

Time, 14-16 Sep 41:	Time, 16-24 Sep 41:
0 Tanks	8 Tanks
6 Guns	136 Guns
456 Trucks	1,836 Trucks
3,470 POWs	35,640 POWs

Similarly to the case of the fighting in August 41, the data show that the Soviets had run out of tanks on this front in the campaign. The Soviets fought with tenacity and a kind of stubborn courage but had definite limits to their capacity to absorb punishment and maintain their equilibrium after they had been surrounded. The Germans remarked over and over again in their records about a characteristic desperation that quickly overcame the Soviets and led to profligate losses in uncoordinated attacks and finally mass surrenders. The *9.Pz.D.*

showed again the capability to reorganize and move 24 hours a day, react to orders with unique speed, operate over vast areas in decentralized battle groups, and change direction of advance almost at will.

Finally, as concerns *9.Pz.D.*, the author came across a tantalizing document produced by the division surgeon that deserves analysis. This officer put together a report, dated 8 September 41 and based on records kept by the command, that shows the breakdown of casualties in the division from 21 June – 31 August 41 by casualty producing agents.[35] The data show that in the period noted the division suffered 1,003 casualties from infantry small arms and 950 casualties from artillery and mortar fire and hand grenades, or high explosive and fragmentation effects. These data show a ratio of about 51 percent casualties to small arms in contrast to masses of data from high intensity, conventional war situations in Europe in the Second World War for American troops, for example, in which roughly 30 percent of casualties came from small arms. The author suggests that the difference is accounted for by the German style of advance in maneuver war in which brief, short-range encounters often occurred and action completed itself before large artillery forces could be massed for support. In these chance encounters, the Germans executed immediate attacks with motorized infantry or tanks often with a single German word (!) constituting the order for the attack. In such situations, the Germans used rifle and large volumes of machine gun fire to overwhelm the enemy while their own artillery moving in column with them deployed just off the route of advance to support the infantry and tanks commonly with direct fire. The Soviet combat forces subjected to this style of advance were often unable to mass and direct supporting fires against the Germans and forced to defend themselves according to the German tempo of advance rather than a more desirable set piece defense on their own part.

Unlike *9.Pz.D.*, which did not cross into the Soviet Union until 29 June 41, *3.Pz.D.* would open fire on the Soviets at 0315 on 22 June 41 with strong artillery forces directed by the corps' brigade-level 143rd Artillery Headquarters. Five minutes earlier, the division would attempt to take the bridge at Koden, just south of Brest, over the Bug River in a coup de main with a small pioneer assault troop. Five minutes later, just as the big guns sounded, the troop had successfully taken the bridge and following infantry had already moved one 75mm infantry gun across it to support the expanding bridgehead. Less than three months later, in a sudden rush in the early morning hours of 14 September 41, lighted by the gun flashes from rifle and machine gun fire, *Hauptmann* Peschke's 3rd Company, 3rd Motorized Infantry Regiment, would seize the "big north bridge" over the tributary of the Sula River running through the middle of Lohvica. Now 1,100 km inside the Soviet Union, *3.Pz.D.* would join hands conclusively with a strong battle group of *9.Pz.D.* the next day.[36] The period from 22 June – 15 September 41 is filled with similar coups de main, bold advances, fast decisions, short orders, and leadership from the front in the case of the *3.Pz.D.* of *Generalleutnant* Walter Model and his 1st general staff officer and Ia of the division, *Major i.G.* Pomtow.

The striking power of *3.Pz.D.* lay in the 6th Panzer Regiment which held the relatively large number of 209 tanks at the beginning of the campaign. This figure is deceiving because only 140 of these vehicles were serious main battle tanks—Pz.Kw. III and IV—while an additional 58 were Pz.Kw. II light tanks armed with 20mm cannons and 11 were command tanks armed only with machine guns. On any day in the life of *3.Pz.D.*, the striking power of the division could be equated with the numbers of these vehicles ready for insertion in combat. With no tanks, for example, *3.Pz.D.* would cease to be a panzer division, and, as reflected by that condition, would no longer be able to advance against a strong armored enemy. For the Germans in 1941, *3.Pz.D.* was a formation to be employed for deep, strategic advances against dangerous, powerful enemies. The Germans, accordingly, held the tanks of the panzer divisions as far back from the border as possible as they labored up to the last hours before the attack to achieve surprise all along the immense front. The 6th Panzer Regiment and its 209 tanks, as a result, lay 100 km back from the Soviet border on 21 June 41 and did not complete movement into the tank assembly areas until 0115 on 22 June 41.

The division commander set up four battle groups for the initial advance and built them around each of the two motorized rifle regiments of the division, the panzer regiment, and the combined motorcycle and reconnaissance battalions. In the big battle group under Colonel Audoersch that attacked around the bridge at Koden, the division commander combined motorized infantry, tank, antitank, pioneer and special road construction units along with a special assault detachment—*Stosstrupp*, 3rd Company, 39th Panzer Pioneer Battalion—to take the bridge. The usual artillery unit of the typical strong German battle group in mobile war is not present because of the unique conditions of the first day of the attack against the Soviet Union.

Headquarters, 24th Panzer Corps, assigned *3.Pz.D.* the mission (along with *4.Pz.D.*) to break through the Soviet border positions and advance to Sluck on the Sluc River and establish a bridgehead there (see Map 1). The assignment of Sluck as the initial objective for the division highlights the extraordinary boldness and tempo that characterized German maneuver war in this campaign. First of all, Sluck is 310 km distant from where *3.Pz.D.* crossed the Soviet border—an impressive distance for tracked vehicles to move on paved roads in peacetime—and the division faced unpaved roads literally impassable for significant periods of time after summer rain showers, and resistance from what would soon develop into the main concentration of the Red Army. Sluck was a distant first objective but its location was even more significant. *Generaloberst* Heinz Guderian, commanding Panzer Group 2, had as his highest level mission to encircle the Soviet field armies in Byelorussia by linking up with Panzer Group 3 at Minsk. Sluck, however, lies nowhere near Minsk but rather is on the direct road for the Germans to the Dnepr River southwest of Smolensk. Guderian by assigning 24th Panzer Corps and *3.Pz.D.* the mission to move along the road to Sluck was heading for the Dnepr, Smolensk, and Moscow from the first day of the war. This thinking in terms of distant objectives and the necessity to successfully exploit every opportunity offered goes a long way toward explaining the unique tempo of operations associated with the German panzer divisions of this era.

By 0845 on 22 June 41, the division commander had crossed the Bug River and was moving with the most advanced units of the mass of the division—tanks of 3rd Battalion, 6th Panzer Regiment in Battle Group Colonel Linnarz—with only an "advanced detachment" of the division several kilometers farther forward. From this position, Model was able to observe for himself "catastrophic" road and swampy off-road conditions that demanded a new route of advance. At 1430, he personally requested a change in the route forward that was immediately approved. With this decision, the division began to move forward effectively but trailed the other three panzer divisions of the Panzer Group that had crossed the Bug on the first day of the war. Close to midnight on 22 June, Model placed himself with the farthest forward elements of the 6th Panzer Regiment and ordered the whole division to move off as quickly as possible in the early morning hours of 23 June. The tanks, now lying about 20 km east of Brest, were fueled at 0430 and personally accompanied by the division commander in an advance toward Kobryn. In a telling commentary on the mobility of a panzer division command post, the operations echelon of the division with the Ia, Ic, and IIa (Personnel) rode with the division commander.

By the end of the second day of the war, *3.Pz.D.* had advanced to seize a bridgehead over the Scara River with a battle group built around the tanks of 3rd Battalion, 6th Panzer Regiment, and the motorcycles, trucks, and heavy weapons of the 3rd Motorcycle Battalion. The division now stood 165 km into the Soviet Union from where it had seized the Koden bridge in the opening act of the war. The next day, 24 June 41, the division broke into the clear advancing at 0330 with a powerful battle group that included most of 6th Panzer Regiment and the motorcycle battalion of the division. To exploit opportunity in an increasingly fluid situation, division headquarters set up an advanced detachment organized as follows:

3.Pz.D., Fluid Situation, 24 Jun 41: Advanced Detachment

1 Company, 3rd Motorcycle Bn	1 Platoon, 543rd AT Bn
2 Companies, 39th Pz Pioneer Bn	2 Twin-Barrel, 20 mm Cannon, 91st Light AA Bn
1 Bridge Column B	1 Battery, 7th Arty Rgt
Parts Bridge Column K	

Surprisingly, this advanced detachment had no tanks, but it had almost anything else that a ground force would require as a combined arms team in a mobile advance. With daring and extraordinary emphasis on rapid tempo, the Germans actually placed bridge columns with the advanced detachment. Given the tempo of operations on 24 June 41, the Ia displaced the division command post three times (!) during the day at 0815 (48 km move), 1445 (18 km move), 1930 (approximately 30 km). At 1900, while moving to the last command post site for the day, the operations echelon of the division with both the division commander and the Ia, encountered the corps commander. The corps commander ordered Model to do everything possible to establish a bridgehead at the second crossing of the Scara about 12 km farther east before the day was over. This interaction took place with all the actors in or around their vehicles on the big road to Sluck.

Earlier on 24 June 41, at approximately 1530, Model had been with the tanks of 2d Battalion, 6th Panzer Regiment when they arrived in front of the second crossing site of the Scara River. The river was only about 15m wide at this point but the bridge had been destroyed and low, swampy ground on either side made the bridge virtually impossible to bypass and difficult to approach. The tanks were forced to halt, and Model, back in the column commandeered an armored, 8-wheeled, radio vehicle of the communications detachment with the battle group and moved forward to see for himself the situation. As the armored radio vehicle halted due to incoming fire and road debris, the division commander stepped out the vehicle to keep the attack going and "at that moment an artillery direct hit blew the vehicle apart."[37] All four crew members were killed; the division commander was untouched. The incident illustrates the danger to senior commanders and high tempo in the German style of advance in maneuver war and suggests that significant opportunities continuously occur in deep advances that can be exploited by such a style.

For the remainder of 24 June, the division developed an attack with dismounted motorized infantry moving up against the river bank and to the edge of the damaged bridge whose middle span was not passable to vehicles. Finally, at 2000, the division commander personally, on the spot directing the attack, ordered 1st Battalion, 6th Panzer Regiment to insert tanks along the road to support the attack of the infantry with direct fire against the enemy on the opposite bank. First Lieutenant Buchterkirch with a tank company from the battalion moved down the road and with his tank in the lead halted at the west end of the damaged bridge. As his tanks fired down the road and across the river over the heads of friendly infantry, Buchterkirch stepped out of his vehicle and with a few riflemen around him led an infantry assault over the burning, damaged bridge. Based on this action, the division immediately began to build up a bridgehead over the river, and, still during the hours of darkness on the morning of 25 June, put in place a prefabricated war bridge over the damaged middle span for the passage of tanks. The division commander continued to direct this action and in the middle of the fighting, having temporarily exited his Pz.Kw. III command tank, witnessed it get "shot up in flames" (*in Brand geschossen*) with the resultant death of the driver. The style of fighting was action oriented with the division commander in the lead at the main point in the battle. In turn, one must suppose, the Ia was located in a movement-oriented command post not far behind, keeping the remainder of the division tracking in accordance with the general mission and coordinated with the rest of the world. This generalization is supported by the statement of the distinguished commander of the *11.Pz.D.* later in the war that he led the division personally at the decisive point in the battle while the Ia "communed with God" and coordinated all the staff work necessary to keep the division together.[38]

At 0900 on 26 June, *3.Pz.D.* reached its first big objective, the city of Sluck south of Minsk and on the direct route to the Dnepr River. Propelled by their own special style of fighting and the capture of large fuel stocks in Sluck, the Germans pressed on toward Bobruisk and the Dnepr. The next day at 1130, corps headquarters, alive to the strategic importance of maintaining the high tempo of the advance toward Moscow, radioed to division that quick movement forward to the Dnepr had decisive meaning for the entire campaign. Only an hour later, the strong leading battle group of the division, personally accompanied by the division commander and moving fast toward Bobruisk, ran into Soviet troops in a wooded area, who held their fire until the Germans were close in and among them. The Soviets inflicted heavy casualties on the battle group largely with rifle and machine gun fire at short ranges. The division commander stood upright in his open command car directing events around him and the Germans responded with fire and a physical rush at the Soviet forces. The Germans quickly overwhelmed the Soviet infantry but, shocked and sobered by the event, did not move on again until they had buried their dead. If there is a lesson in this for effective battle style in mobile war it may be the immediate sequel to the action. The division commander ordered the 1st Battalion, 6th Panzer Regiment to the spot and reorganized the battle group to move in column with a tank approximately every 100m among the wheeled vehicles. Armed now with the presence and potential firepower of the tanks, the reinforced battle group set off again at 1600, having lost little operational tempo in the face of this tactical disaster.

Events continued to move fast for the division. At 0300 the next morning, 28 June 41, advanced elements of *3.Pz.D.* entered Bobruisk on the Berezina River now farther east than any unit of the German Army. Although the Soviet High Command in the Western Military District was having severe difficulties in coordinating its own forces, it sensed danger at Bobruisk. The Germans, for example, listened in on a Soviet telephone line over which the following message was being sent: "enemy (German) armored breakthrough to be expected around Bobruisk. Put the entire air force into action at Bobruisk." The Soviets reacted vigorously to this extreme advance of *3.Pz.D.* including heavy air attacks. The division would take four days to establish a bridgehead, construct bridges, and finally break out toward the Dnepr. As a gauge of the resistance, German antiaircraft guns organic or attached to the division shot down 20 attacking Soviet aircraft on 30 June 41. After continued heavy fighting and an advance by the division on several axes toward the Dnepr. Motorized infantry and tanks reached the river at Rogachev early in the evening at 2000 on 3 July 41. The division would fight for several days around Rogachev as part of an effort to force a crossing of the Dnepr. Unsuccessful in the face of strong Soviet forces concentrated at that obvious crossing point along one of the high roads to Moscow, the division shifted north to successfully cross the Dnepr on 10 July 41. After crossing, it would battle generally on the defensive against Soviet troops attempting to break into or out of the big Soviet pocket that formed north of the division around Smolensk and out of which the Germans would take 310,000 prisoners and in which they would destroy 3,205 Soviet tanks. As the Soviets collapsed in the pocket at the end of July, the commander of Panzer Group 2 ordered the seizure of Roslavl, the road center necessary for the assembly and supply of an attack on Moscow. Assuming that the advance directly on the capital of the Soviet Union would begin soon, e.g., no later than 15 August 41, Guderian put together a force of eleven divisions to clear out the Soviets from the area around that city.

From 1-8 August 41, *3.Pz.D.* fought in the Roslavl battle and at its end began instinctively to prepare for the thrust to Moscow through whatever forces the Soviets could pull together in mid-August 1941. Adolf Hitler, however, nervous about the immediate seizure of ancillary targets on the flanks of the main attack toward Moscow, vacillated and then ordered the great German 90-degree turn south into the Ukraine. The *3.Pz.D.*, caught up in this grand decision found itself in battle south of Roslavl toward Gomel in the period 9-20 August engaged in the destruction of a strong Soviet force that would simply have been "contained" by the Germans if they had continued the march against Moscow.

From 21 August – 26 September 41, *3.Pz.D.* engaged in the great drive south into the Ukraine. At the start of the drive, the division was located near Starodub, 130 km northeast of Gomel and 280 km north of the city of Lohvica, fateful for the destruction of five Soviet field armies when the division seized it in the middle of September. On 22 August, the division fought off the last Soviet attempts to break out of the Gomel pocket and concentrated its forces for the new offensive. On that day, Headquarters, Army Group Center, directed 24th Panzer Corps in a mission-style order to advance south and "cut off" the Soviet forces lying southwest of Gomel. The army group placed *3.Pz.D.* on the extreme left of the drive forming, in effect, the extreme outer (eastern) arm of the great encirclement that was developing. The *4.Pz.D.* was placed behind *3.Pz.D.* to help to secure the left flank of the drive and add depth to the attack of the leading division. Model immediately configured the division into three battle groups for the great drive. The configuration was as follows:

3.Pz.D., Battle Groups for Beginning Kiev Encirclement, 22 Aug '41

Lead Attack Group	**2nd Battle Group**	**3rd Battle Group**
(Lt Col von Lewinski)	(Col Kleeman)	(Col von Manteuffel)
1 Tank Bn	1 Tank Bn	1 Tank Bn
1 Moto Inf Bn	1 Moto Inf Rgt	1 Moto Inf Bn
2 Arty Bns	1 Arty Bn	Div Troops
1 AT (Bn (-)	Div Troops	

Battle Group Lewinski, the lead attack group, moved out at 0500 on 23 August at the head of the division into a grand operation that several participants would refer to as the raid west of Kiev. The conceptualization of the rapid advance south as a raid suggests the presence of special mobility and command style dedicated to action, movement, and the seizure of fleeting opportunity. The word, "raid," also conjures up a vision of a heavily armed force that traveled light—certainly an accurate description of a typical battle group in a panzer division. After 40 km of movement southeast over difficult unpaved roads, the battle group passed a sign along the way with Cyrillic script standing for Ukranian Socialist Soviet Republic. The division became the first unit of Panzer Group 2 to enter the Ukraine and three hours later at approximately 1300 halted for refueling. The fueling that took place was necessary for most vehicles and shows that road conditions were to severe that the tanks and trucks moving at low speeds with heavy loads were capable of not much more than 70 km on a tank of fuel. Later in the afternoon, the battle group advanced again with 7th Company, 2nd Battalion, 6th Panzer Regiment as point for the group and the entire division. At approximately 1730 as it approached the heights along the west side of the Desna River near Novgorod-Severskij, it detected strong Soviet defensive positions and halted the battle group. As a division commander practicing German maneuver war, Model had stationed himself immediately behind the point company riding with the mass of the 2d Panzer Battalion. The battle group commander also rode with the panzer battalion and called together the battalion officers in the presence of the division commander to give an oral order for an attack against the Soviets. A soviet artillery gun crew observed this gathering and fired a projectile into the group killing one officer, severely wounding two others, and lightly wounding the battalion commander. Model again escaped untouched.[39]

Because of delays caused by primitive, unpaved roads, the approaching German motorized infantry was unable to get into position for an attack until after dark and also unable to examine the ground effectively for an advance against the Soviet defenses. Now lying approximately 7 km from Novgorod Severskij with its big bridge over the wide middle reaches of the Desna River, the division organized an advanced detachment in the middle of the night that had the mission to seize the 700m-long bridge. Under command of First Lieutenant Vopel, the advanced detachment included the following units:

Advanced Detachment Vopel, Mission: Bridge Coup de Main

1 Panzer Company	1 Moto Inf Company in Armored Three-Quarter Tracks
1 Self Propelled AT Company	1 Pioneer Platoon in Armored Three-Quarter Tracks

The detachment advanced at 0345, and through its bold move along the main highway burst through several barriers and left the prearranged Soviet artillery fires behind it. Moving rapidly along the road and forced to deploy only once out of the armored vehicles to overcome resistance at a crossroads 3.5 km northwest of the city, the advanced detachment moved right up to the west access of the bridge. The pioneer platoon leader jumped from his vehicle and followed by three of his men began to move across the nearly half mile long bridge removing the high explosive charges as he went. The tanks and motorized infantry provided covering fire. As the minutes ticked by, the advanced detachment commander, realized that the opportunity might slip away to get a bridgehead and ordered, "*Panzer marsch*," (tanks move out), leading the tank company across the long bridge past the pioneer platoon leader, who continued cutting wires and throwing charges into the river. The tank company successfully crossed and established a bridgehead about 800m deep at approximately the same time the last charge on the bridge was removed by the pioneer lieutenant and his three men. At this moment, about 1100 on 24 August 41, Model appeared on the bridge and took the report of the battle group commander who had already arrived behind the advanced detachment. He could hardly believe that the great bridge had fallen into German hands undamaged; on the spot, he ordered the immediate forwarding of the request for approval of the knights cross for the pioneer platoon leader.

As *3.Pz.D.* moved across the Desna River and attempted to continue the advance south, it ran into strong Soviet resistance based largely on the Soviet 21st Army and its commander who was just beginning to understand the vast ramifications of the latest move. He realized that the Germans, who had seemed initially to be heading southwest toward Kiev and the strong forces around it, were actually heading south southeast toward a point approximately 200 km behind the Ukrainian capital. From 25 August – 7 September 41, *3.Pz.D.* fought heavy battles south of Sostka advancing only 55 km south during that time. With the evil road conditions, the division also experienced fuel shortages and difficulties with tank maintenance and repair. The corps fuel dumps where the division fuel columns picked up gasoline lay no closer than Starodub 85 km from Sostka during this time. The distances challenged supply trucks and drivers alike over the unpaved roads, and frequent Soviet air attacks aggravated the situation.

In this difficult period in which the Germans fought to regain the momentum of the advance, two events illustrate the confusion and opportunity in the deep advances that characterized German maneuver war on the offensive in 1941. First, on 3 September, the division captured Soviet General of Engineers, Tschistoff, an officer with full and general authority of the Soviet High Command to construct a defensive wall on the Desna River with one million workers. In an astounding scene, he directed his train from Moscow into Novgorod Severski not knowing that the town had been taken by the Germans eight days earlier (!). The afternoon of the next day, 4 September, as Model sat in the division command post in a school house in Krolevec, 16 km north of the Sejm River, enemy aircraft attacked and, directly over the school house, German *Flak* (antiaircraft guns) shot down a Soviet plane. A parachute appeared and the Ic (intelligence officer) of the division laid hold of a motorcycle and immediately drove to the spot of the landing. The Soviet airman had already been shot and killed while attempting to escape from German soldiers sent to pick him up for interrogation. The Ic, however, found maps on his uniform that showed the disposition of the Soviet forces opposite 24th Panzer Corps and revealed that the division lay on the boundary between the Soviet 21st and 13th Armies and just north of a gap between them. Model presented this intelligence coup to the corps commander who ordered an advance for the next morning, 5 September, to the Sejm River directly south of Krolevec and further advance along the seam between the two Soviet armies.

For the next two days the division advanced slowly against stubborn resistance "in every village" and in the face of rain that stopped all movement for significant periods on 6 September. As the advance slowed on that day and as darkness began to fall the urgent German style of maneuver war materialized in the following scenes. Model appeared in the command post of 394th Motorized Infantry Regiment and face to face ordered its commander, Lieutenant Colonel Audoersch, to organize on the spot a battle group to advance to the Sejm River during darkness and seize bridgehead at Melnja. Audoersch put together the following combined arms battle group:[40]

Battle Group Audoersch, Evening, 6 Sep '41

1 Moto Inf Bn	1 Pioneer Plat (organic, 394th Moto Inf Rgt)
1 Panzer Bn	"Antitank Guns"
1 Pioneer Co	"Parts 75th Arty Rgt"

Organized somehow as usual almost immediately, the battle group began to advance as full darkness set in and reached the river at Melnja at 2300. As an example of the tough Soviet resistance, the leading tank of the point company was hit twice by antitank gun fire just as it entered the town killing two crew members of the light Pz.Kw. II and wounding the third. The point, nevertheless, continued on to the bridge only to witness it blow up immediately in front of the German tanks. In keeping with the accelerated tempo of the drive to exploit the seam in the Soviet defenses, the battle group commander ordered the crossing of the river in rubber boats as soon as the organic pioneer platoon could get them in the water.

For the next two days, 7 and 8 September 41, the Soviets fought hard to contain the division bridgehead. The division, however, sensed opportunity for a breakthrough and with effective air support particularly the accurate Stuka attacks, pressed the Soviets back across the great multitrack rail line running east out of Konotop (see Map 5). By the evening of 8 September, the division lay 25 km south of the Sejm River and in a position to bypass Konotop and break out southward to complete the encirclement of Soviet forces around Kiev. On 9 September, division headquarters pulled together the scattered division for a concentrated drive south. During the afternoon it organized yet another of the ubiquitous German advanced detachments consisting of the division antitank battalion reinforced by one company of medium tanks, the special light tank platoon of one tank battalion, and one motorized infantry company. The division assigned the rapidly formed battle group the extraordinarily bold and unfettered mission "to thrust forward as far as possible." Major Frank, the advanced detachment commander, led the force half way to Romney, stopping early in the evening to secure a small bridge necessary for the advance of the rest of the division. Battle Group Manteuffel moved across the bridge at midnight and then halted to get organized for a coordinated attack by the whole division at 0600 the next morning, 10 September 41. The division passed the word to every man possible that this advance meant the link up with Panzer Group 1 now advancing from the south.

Rain began to fall slowing the combat elements and preventing resupply by the wheeled supply columns as Major Frank and the advanced detachment led the division toward Romney. In spite of wet, unpaved roads, Frank reached relatively dry high ground overlooking the city and the bridge over the river Romen on its northern outskirts at noon. He observed no reaction on the part of the Soviets and realized that they were unaware of his modest advanced detachment. With the boldness that characterized German maneuver war, he determined to launch an immediate attack to seize the bridge and cross it into the northern outskirts of the city. Leading one company each of motorized infantry, antitank guns, and pioneers mounted on armored three-quarter tracked vehicles and accompanied by a battery of artillery, he advanced boldly through the Soviets who offered virtually no resistance from strong prepared positions. As the detachment moved across the undamaged bridge into the northern outskirts, Frank ordered his assault force to drive through the streets of Romney onto the big bridge over the Sula River at the southern outskirts of the city. First Lieutenant Lingk, commanding the antitank company of the assault force, led the attack in the first vehicle to cross the big bridge over the Sula and reach the east bank of the river. The Germans took both bridges intact, but as the Soviets recovered from their surprise, violent combat broke out in the city and around the bridges. The larger battle groups were close behind, however, and soon cleared the city and extended the bridgehead over the Sula. The Soviets, nevertheless, launched 25 air attacks against the division during the day which along with muddy roads conspired to cut off the division supply columns from the corps supply dumps. The Germans managed that day to get a few fuel trucks to the advanced elements by pulling them through the difficult spots with engineer tractors.

As the weather cleared on 12 September, the division reorganized into new battle groups for the final act of the encirclement. Before twilight, division headquarters put together another advanced detachment under Major Frank and his small staff from the antitank battalion of the division and ordered it to test the situation immediately to the south on the road to Lohvica. The small battle group included the following elements:

Battle Group Frank, Twilight, 12 Sep '41

Staff, AT Bn	1 Recon Co	2 Pz.Kw. II Tanks
1 Antitank Co	1 Arty Battery	2 20mm AA Guns
1 Moto Inf Co	1 Pioneer Plat	

With this newly constituted combined arms team, Frank broke through the Soviet defenses along the road just east of the Sula River at twilight. He then marched the battle group 45 km farther south in total darkness through enemy territory and seized undamaged the bridge over the Sula River 2 km northeast of Lohvica. Frank and his force took the bridge at 2115 that evening (12 September) with First Lieutenant Lingk again leading the first vehicle across the river. The battle group then defended the bridge until morning with Frank continuously calling for assistance by radio. At 1300 on 13 September, aerial reconnaissance reported a strong Soviet tank force moving in from the southwest against the bridgehead. In the meantime the division had pressed a strong battle group south to the assistance of Frank. At around 1530 shortly before the larger battle group arrived to reinforce him, the division coordinated a Luftwaffe Stuka attack against the Soviet tank formation and broke it up before it could make contact with the Germans at the bridge. The combined German ground force then fought its way during the night into Lohvica seizing the big north bridge over the tributary of the Sula River that runs through the city in yet another coup de main at 0500 on 14 September. The stunning tempo of German maneuver war succeeded again in surprising the Soviets who seemed almost always to be one step slower; for example, in this case, as the German motorized riflemen stormed across the bridge and moved 200m farther down the main street they ran through six heavy Soviet antiaircraft guns deployed wheel to wheel filling street and side walks. The Soviet crews still slept among the guns.

Photo 5. The 9th Panzer Division in the Ukraine mid-September 41. The scene shows a Panzer III command tank (dummy gun barrel, no breech mechanism, hence roomy interior for maps and radios) at left and an armored, three-quarter tracked command vehicle at right. The officer standing highest on the command track with overcoat and binocular is probably the division commander. He is talking with the two officers closest to him on the command tank, one of whom is likely a division battle group commander. The style is a telling one—oral orders, necessarily brief, not in writing, lengthy and out of date from a distantly rearward commander (Bundesarchiv Bestand).

6

The Syle and Organization of the German Panzer Division in Offensive Maneuver War

The Germans placed supreme emphasis on decision and action in battle fighting. They trained commanders to make decisions that led to immediate action. They educated general staff officers to assist commanders to make decisions, to march divisions, and to synchronize everything in them. They demanded a union between the combat soldier and his weapon conceptualized as *Waffenstolz*—a sacred bond, a splendid proudness in bearing arms. But were the Germans in touch with war as it really is?

War is an interaction among man that centers on armed violence in a surrounding climate of danger, exertion, uncertainty, and chance. In such a climate, uncertainty and chance dominate. Uncertainty paralyzes the will to act and chance demands a judgment that combines coolness and boldness in constantly changing combinations to overcome the sudden impact of the chance encounter. War demands that leaders have the character to make independent decisions under conditions of uncertainty and circumstances of unforeseen armed engagement. In war, character dominates over intelligence and is reflected in the will to act. The battle fighting commander exists to make decisions and to lead in the execution of the resultant action. The German emphasis on decision and action in battle fighting and their philosophically styled concept of *Waffenstolz* as it connected the combat soldier with armed violence, shows the Germans facing war head on—as it were, seeing war as it really is.

But what about strategy and strategic planning, and especially in modern times, weapons development, things to easily mistaken for war. If war is an interaction among man that involves armed violence, then strategic planning and weapons development do not qualify as war. No one can doubt, however, that strategy and weapons development are important for something that might be termed defense and are linked with war. The explanation for this perplexing reality would seem to be that strategic planning and weapons development are planning and preparation for war, activities that demand intelligence and scientific knowledge and are remote from the battlefield. Here we can see modern war presenting two faces—the necessary preparation for war and the conduct of war itself. Also one can ask the question: is war art or science, and arrive at an answer that connects so impressive a trinity associated with the human condition. The conclusion must be that art, which is skill in doing something, dominates in the conduct of war, while science, which is knowledge about things, realizes its greatest importance in preparations for war.

Modern offensive maneuver war is exemplified by the road march and cross country movement of motorized ground forces over passable terrain. In recent decades, because of technological advances in transport vehicles, mobile war also includes battlefield movement by forces mounted on ground effects vehicle and helicopters. The German advance into the Soviet Union in 1941 is the greatest example in modern times of offensive maneuver war based on the factors of sizes of forces involved, physical dimensions of the theater, advances per unit time on the part of the attacking Germans, and losses absorbed by the defenders. Any fundamentally couched description of war similar to that in which war is described as an interaction among man involving armed violence, demands that mobile war be fundamentally bound by the same logic. The various factors making up war will be exaggerated in importance in mobile war as demanded by more rapid, distant movement on the battlefield. Mobile war, in fact, can be seen to be war with an exaggerated climate of uncertainty and chance and with exaggerated demands on the commander to make independent decisions and take action.

The previous chapters demonstrate the performance of several German panzer divisions in offensive maneuver war and show that the German Army conducted such mobile warfare better than any other. As noted in the title of a recent historical study, the Germans exhibited "a genius for war."[41] The war philosopher, Carl von Clausewitz, writing without regard to time schedule or publisher early in the last century, remarked that the supreme principle, or recipe, or formula, in war for those who insist on having it surely must be "to do as the genius does and theory cannot do better than to show why and how this is so."[42]

In order to excel in mobile war, ground forces perhaps need only conduct mobile war the way the Germans did in their advances in the years 1939-1942. At least two problems arise here, however: the first is that we cannot all be Raphaels,[43] and the second is that it would be both difficult and presumptuous to convert modern American soldiers into German panzer troops. The German superiority in mobile war, however, is difficult to ignore, and even though it was based on the "corporate genius" of the German Army, and the performance of several individual geniuses within it during World War II,[44] the style and organization should be able to be applied as appropriate to other ground forces today.

The organization that has exemplified offensive maneuver war in recent modern times is the German panzer division of World War II. Derived from thinking of the mid-1920s and early 1930s, the division was first put together in October 1935 and then employed with great success on the strategic offensive from 1939-42 and the defensive from 1943-45. The French Army actually put together a similar complete combined arms tank division earlier in 1932, eventually fielding six similar divisions by the opening of the Battle of France in May 1940. The French, in fact, had real armored divisions before the Germans, and, by 1942, several other armies would have similar formations including especially the U.S., British, and Soviet. At present, numerous armies of the world have armored divisions similar in organization to the panzer division of World War II. In terrain favorable for the movement of tanks that includes wide areas in strategically significant parts of the world, armored divisions would dominate in high intensity conventional war.

The German panzer division scored unparalleled success in the period 1939-41. Because of that success, it became the model for the western armored divisions and similar Soviet armored formations of World War II and the period following. The success of the panzer division and its latter day emulation makes it the organization of choice for U.S. ground forces as a historical model for offensive maneuver war. The organization is important to examine not only for the structure but also for insights into command and battle fighting style. Figure 3 shows the panzer division as it was generally configured during most of World War II. The division commander, ordinarily a one-star general, stood at the top. The panzer division had no assistant division commander and no chief of staff; in fact, no German division had such billets. The panzer division had as its first general staff officer, the Ia or operations officer of the division. The Ia normally held the rank of *Major im Generalstab* or major-in-the-general-staff, signifying that he had successfully completed the two-year course at the *Kriegsakademie* (War Academy) and a following probationary period.[45] The Ia, although relatively junior and inexperienced, was the only officer who formally advised the commander on combat operations, compensating for the factors of

The German Panzer Division (esp 1941, but generally WWII)

The Elements	**Fundamental Characterization**
The Commander	The leader
1st General Staff Officer	The leader's advisor
Div Staff	The leader's assistants
Tank Regiment	Offensive striking power
Moto Inf Rgts	Offensive and Defensive Ground Combat
Arty Rgt	Fire Support
Recon Bn	Recon & advanced detachment mobility
Motorcycle Bn	Advanced detachment mobility & Recon
AT Bn	AT protection
AA Det	AA defense and ground combat
Pioneer Bn	Routes of advance & defensive barriers
Comm Bn	Radios and telephones
Supply Bn	Fuel & Ammunition; Motor Vehicle Repair
Military Police Co	Traffic Control
Medical Bn	Battle wound mitigation & sickness reduction
Food Prep Det	Rations

Associated Reinforcing Organizations

<u>Corps</u> Troops: Arty, Pioneers, etc.	<u>Luftwaffe Air Corps:</u>
	Ground Attack, Air Resupply
<u>Army</u> Troops: Arty, Pioneers, etc.	Air Movement, Fighter cover
	Air Recon

Figure 3. The German Panzer Division, Especially in 1941, but Generally in World War II

youth and lesser experience with a tough process of selection for the War Academy and completion of its course.

With a major as its senior staff officer and without chief of staff or assistant division commander, the staff of the panzer division was much more compact than that of any U.S. ground forces division today. The headquarters of the division was dominated by the Ia and contained personnel and equipment associated with the operational maneuver of the division. The vital functions of fire support control and logistics were not run out of division headquarters but decentralized. The fire support control center of other division largely comprised the headquarters of the artillery regiment, and the logistics headquarters lay in a quartermaster detachment commonly co-located with the division supply battalion that in turn coordinated all of the combat service support detachments. The relatively small and mobile division headquarters consisted of the *Fuehrungsstaffel* (operations detachment or echelon) and two other headquarters echelons that moved with it and supported it in various ways. The *Fuehrungsstaffel* normally comprised the following personnel:

Panzer Division Operations Detachment (WWII)

Div Comdr	Ic (Intel O)	Flivo (Air O)
Ia (Ops O)	03 (Asst Intel)	Hq Cmdt
01 (Asst Ops)	IIa (Pers O)	Also comm, motorcycle messenger, driver, & security personnel
04 (Asst Ops)	IIb (Asst Pers)	

In the case of *13.Pz.D.* in the Soviet Union in 1941, the operations detachment consisted of the following vehicles and personnel when on the march in a secure area on a quiet front:

Seq.*	**Vehicle**	**Personnel (plus driver)**
1.	Passenger Car	Div Cmdr, Ia, Comm Det O
2.	Command Car	01, 1-NCO, 1-E
3.	Command Car	04, 1 Orderly O, 1-NCO
4.	Truck	2-NCO, 10-E (Security)
5.	Command Car	Ic, 03, 1-E
6.	Command Car	Hq Cmdt, 2-NCO
7.	Passenger Car	2-NCO

*Seq = sequence or place in column.

The listing shows a compact body of vehicles and personnel easy to displace and having personnel dedicated to the operational functioning and more specifically the maneuver of the division. The key actors are the division commander, Ia (operations), Ic (intelligence), and their special assistants, the 01, 03, and 04. This operations detachment did not include, for example, the IIa (personnel), who although located in division headquarters, was included with one of the two additional supporting detachments that together formed the division headquarters. The operations detachment also did not include the Ib (logistics), who in the field led the *Quartiermeisterstaffel* (logistics detachment or echelon) that was located rearward of the operations detachment and close to the division supply detachment and the division trains in what U.S. ground forces would call a combat service support element. For movement in a mobile advance through unsecured areas, the Ia and headquarters commandant set up the operations detachment as noted in Figure 4. The figure displays the operations detachment in march column on the road and shows a compact body of men and vehicles capable of carrying out multiple displacements on a daily basis in pulling forward the division in a deep advance. In addition to the operations detachment, division headquarters included an adjutant detachment for personnel administration centered on the IIa (adjutant, officer records) and the IIb (adjutant, enlisted records). Division headquarters also held modest-sized supply, motor transport, motor transport repair, military police, and motorcycle messenger units. Finally, headquarters held at least one bus in which the situation maps were maintained and from which the Ia coordinated the maneuver of the division. The Ia of *13.Pz.D.* noted that the operations detachment should be as small as possible when moving near the front of the division in mobile situations and delineated the following formation as the smallest practicable:

13.Pz.D., Fuehrungsstaffel (operations detachment), Battlefield Insertion

Seq.*	Vehicle	Personnel
1.	Escort Det Combat Vehicles	Combat Crews, e.g., Pz Recon Vehicle, *Pak*
2.	Command Tank or Car	Div Cmdr & Ia
3.	Command Car	01 & Ic
4.	Armored Three Quarter Track Vehicle	Radio & other Comm Personnel
5.	Escort Det Combat Vehicles	Combat Crews, e.g., *Flak*

*Seq. = Sequence or place in column.

The listing brings German command and battle fighting style into focus about as clearly and succinctly as such a thing can be done. The hard evidence—command tank, command car, armored three-quarter track vehicle; division commander, Ia, Ic—shows the German panzer division with its ultimate command detachment dedicated to the needs of operational movement. The division headquarters shown here in microcosm was dominated by operations and its handmaiden intelligence. The German panzer division commander fought his battle from the perspective of combat maneuver and march mobility; and, the logistics detachment and even the fire support apparatus in the division were forced to make adjustments to the breaking point to support distant advances of the division.

Two additional organizational factors help to account for the domination of maneuver in the panzer division. The artillery regiment directed and coordinated all ground fire support for the division and did so from a fire support center in regimental headquarters. The fact that the division command post did not include the fire support control center contributed to a style of battle fighting that paced combat to the spirit and demands of maneuver. At the beginning of new advances in the mobile campaign, e.g., after halts at big river barriers, on lines of encirclement, etc., corps headquarters generally assigned a brigade-level artillery headquarters (*Arko*) to coordinate fire support for the next breakthrough. The *Arko* also set up away from the division command post and near the headquarters of the artillery regiment. During mobile stages of an advance, the division operated severely decentralized in battle groups with attached artillery battalions or batteries that provided fire support for

German Panzer Division
Operational Headquarters on the Move, 1941

↑ Direction of March

March Sequence	Vehicle	Key Personnel
1.	2 Pz Recon Vehicles	Combat Crews
2.	Passenger Car	Div Commander
3.	4 Motorcycles	Messengers
4.	Combat Command Car	Div Cmdr (alternate vehicle)
5.	Passenger Car	Ia
6.	Radio Hq Truck	Communications Det Cmdr
7.	4 Motorcycles	Messengers
8.	Command Car	04
9.	Command Tank	Div Cmdr (alternate vehicle)
10.	Truck	Operations Det Guard
11.	1 Pz _ Track	Radio & other Comm Personnel
12.	Command Car	Ic
13.	Cars & Motorcycles	Subord Cmdrs as Appropriate
14.	Passenger Car	Military Police
15.	Command Car	Hq Commandant
16.	4 Motorcycles	Messengers

Figure 4. The *Fuehrungsstaffel* (operations detachment) of the 13.Pz.D. Configured for Movement in a Mobile Advance (Ukraine, 1941)

each widely separated battle group. In a breakthrough, division headquarters paced operations to the heavy, concentrated fires necessary to penetrate strong enemy defenses. In a mobile drive, division paced operations to the necessity for high tempo in the advance. Division headquarters did not get involved in the technical details of providing fire support in either case.

In the panzer division, logistics was particularly challenging because of the special need for fuel and motor vehicle maintenance for a fully motorized force. In the division, the Ib, or quartermaster, supervised logistics in the name of the division commander and was also designated the second general staff officer of the division and commonly was a graduate of the War Academy with the designation after his rank of *i.G.* (*im Generalstab*). In the event of the incapacitation of the Ia of the division, for example, the Ib automatically and immediately became the new Ia. In more detail as concerns his functions, the Ib supervised supply, motor vehicle and ordnance maintenance and repair, and general administration with the heads of those services being under his staff cognizance. Most important for the German organization of the headquarters of the division, the Ib set up and operated out of a separate headquarters described in panzer division records as the Ib command post.

Figure 5 summarizes the organization of the panzer division staff and the actual arrangement and general location of the division headquarters in a mobile campaign. The top half of the figure shows a small staff by the standards of U.S. ground forces divisions. The bottom half of the figure shows though that the division headquarters, i.e., the place where the division commander was located, included only part of the division staff and thus was even smaller than a diagram of the staff organization would indicate. The division commander, however, when accompanying the leading elements of the division would often ride with only an operations assistant, radio vehicle personnel, and the combat crews of the escort vehicles. Figure 6 contrasts the panzer division general staff with that of a U. S. division today and shows striking differences in numbers and ranks.

The German Panzer Division Staff (WWII)

Fuehrungsstaffel (Operations Detachment):	**Quartiermeisterstaffel (Logistics Detachment):**
Div Commander	
Ia*, 01, 04 (Operations)	Ib, 02+ (Logistics)
Ic, 03 (Intelligence)	DNF (Supply)
IIa, IIB (Personnel)	III (Legal)
Flivo (Air 0)	IVa (Administration)
	IVb (Medical)
	IVd (Chaplain)
	V (Motor Transport)
	WUG (Ordnance)
*Ia = Operations Officer	+01, 02, 03, 04, the special staff assistants
*Ib = Logistics Officer	to the Ia, Ib, and Ic.

The German Panzer Division: Actual General Arrangement of Headquarters in Mobile Campaign (WW II)

Div Hq: (Far Forward Location)	**Ib Hq: (Rear Location)**
Div Commander	Ib, 02 (Logistics)
Ia, 01, 04 (Operations)	DNF (Supply)
Ic, 03 (Intelligence)	III (Legal)
IIa, IIB (Personnel)	IVa (Admin)
Flivo (Air O)	IVb (Medical)
Hq Commandant	IVd (Chaplain)
	V (Motor Transport)
	Wug (Ordnance)

Arty Rgt Hq: (Forward Location)
Div Fire Supt
Control Center

Figure 5. Panzer Division Staff and Actual Arrangement of Headquarters in Mobile Campaign (WWII)

The Germans organized the panzer division so that it had the capability to advance toward distant strategic level targets. The panzer division not only had immense battlefield mobility but possessed strategic mobility in the ground theater of operations. This German in-theater, strategic mobility is not the same as the global strategic mobility so important to the U.S. ground forces today and associated with the intercontinental movement of Army light or air mobile divisions by large Air Force transport aircraft and of Marine Air Ground Task Forces by naval shipping. The panzer division was fully motorized and proved capable in France and the Soviet Union of advancing in bounds of more than 300 km over periods of two to four days. Against strong resistance which jelled in familiar patterns against

(Cmdr, General Staff, and Staff Assistants)

German Panzer Division, 1941	**Marine Division, Recent Past***	
Div Cmdr (Bgen)	Div Cmdr (Mgen)	G-4 (LtCol)
Ia (Maj i.G.) (the G-3)	Asst Div Cmdr (Bgen)	Asst G-4 (LtCol)
01 (Capt)	Chief of Staff (Col)	Plans O (LtCol)
04 (1ST Lt)	Staff Secretary (Maj)	Asst Plans O (Maj)
Ic (Capt) (the G-2)	G-1 (Col)	Opns O (Maj)
03 (1st Lt)	Asst G-1 (LtCol)	Asst Opns (Capt)
IIa (Maj) (the G-1)	Asst G-1 (LtCol)	Asst Opns (Capt)
IIb (1st Lt)	Asst G-1 (Maj)	Div Adj (LtCol)
Flivo (Capt)	G-2 (Col)	Asst Adj (Maj)
Ib (Capt) (the G-4)	Asst G-2 (LtCol)	Air O (Col)
02 (1st Lt)	Asst G-2 (LtCol)	Asst Air (Maj)
	G-3 (Col)	Air Control (Capt)
	Asst G-3 (LtCol)	Air Control (Lt)
	Opns O (LtCol)	Emb O (LtCol)
	Asst Opns O (Maj)	Asst Emb (Maj)
	Asst Opns O (Maj)	Fire Supt (Col)
	Trng O (LtCol)	Asst FS (LtCol)
	Asst Trng O (Maj)	Asst FS (Maj)
	Plans O (LtCol)	Targets (Capt)
	Asst Opns O (Maj)	

*USMC T/O Check List 1986N of 14 Jan '91.

Comparable Officers

	Pz Div	**Mar Div**
	1 BGen	1 Mgen
	1 Maj	1 Bgen
	4 Capt	7 Col
	4 Lt	13 LtCol
		12 Maj
		5 Capt/Lt
Total:	11	39

Figure 6. Panzer and U. S. Marine Division General Staff and Staff Assistants Contrasted.

the Germans in their offensive campaigns from 1939-42, the panzer division proved capable of advancing against large opposing tank forces. The German had built the panzer division around the main battle tanks of the day and had organized the tanks into one panzer regiment in each of the panzer divisions in the army in 1941. The striking power of the panzer division was directly proportional to the numbers of tanks on any given day that were ready for insertion in combat. The grim point implied in this statement is that no division can be expected to advance against a strong armored enemy in terrain favoring the use of tanks without a serious tank force of its own.

The previous chapters have documented the distant advances of the panzer divisions into the Soviet Union and the terrible damage wrought on the Red Army. If mobile warfare of the day were dependent so much on the tank, just how many of these weapons were found in the panzer divisions of 1941 that were doing such damage? The single panzer regiment in each division varied hugely both in the numbers and types of tanks. The *7.Pz.D.*, for example, crossed the Soviet border with the relatively large number of 284 tanks while the *11.Pz.D.* entered the campaign with 143. Taking account of the overall numbers of tanks deployed in the east on 22 June 41, the number of panzer divisions, and the numbers of tanks in other divisions, the author believes that a figure of 180 tanks gives an accurate feel for the 1941 German panzer division in the Soviet Union. With this number of tanks organized into a single panzer regiment that normally held two panzer battalions, the German panzer division achieved spectacular results against prodigious numbers of Soviet tanks and masses of infantry and artillery. The *9.Pz.D.*, for example, in heavy fighting on a single day, 1 July 41, destroyed 134 Soviet medium and heavy tanks mostly accounted for in tank versus tank combat by the panzer regiment of the division. On the other hand, in heavy fighting on 28 June 41, *13.Pz.D.* destroyed 75 Soviet tanks. These tanks were put out of action by two companies of the division antitank battalion that were blocking Soviet counterattacks against German motorized infantry that had just seized part of Rovno in the Ukraine and the bridge over the river there.[46] These engagements show that when the Germans advanced on the strategic offensive, they destroyed large numbers of Soviet tanks in both tank and antitank combat.

A representative German panzer division would have had its 180 tanks largely in the two battalions of the tank regiment for the initial mobile drives into the Soviet Union. The division would never fight with that number because of mechanical breakdowns on the unpaved Russian roads and combat damage. Within the first two or three days of combat on the eastern front, a representative panzer division would have had approximately 70 percent tank strength based on attrition from mechanical breakdown and combat damage. The "real" panzer division, in effect, would be advancing with about 126 tanks because the remaining 54 tanks would be accounted for roughly as 45 tanks in repair workshops for mechanical damage and wear, 8 tanks under repair for battle damage, and 8 tanks totally destroyed in combat. During periods of distant movement and the heavy battles occurring at the end of such movement, the representative panzer division would be operating at about 50 percent of its original strength or about 90 tanks and this number could easily dip lower. The records and accounts of the fighting indicate that when a panzer division fell to about 25 percent of its table of equipment strength in tanks that it was no longer capable of advancing against a strong armored enemy. A point that stands out in this analysis, though is that the Germans advanced quite successfully with this representative panzer division of 1941 with actual tank strengths commonly between 50 – 70 percent of original full establishment and sometimes significantly lower. The combat reality that suggests itself here is that expertly led tank forces operating in surprisingly small combined arms battle groups maintain the capability to maneuver among and advance against strong enemy forces. There seemed to be some modest "critical tactical mass" for the German panzer division with which the Germans could operate and continue to be effective on the offensive with forces totally out of proportion to the division establishment strength.

The *20.Pz.D.*, for example, entered the Soviet Union on 22 June 41 when an establishment strength of 185 tanks. Approximately one month later on 26 July, now 700 km into the Soviet Union northeast of Smolensk, it continued to be in control of the situation in its battle area with only 51 tanks (i.e., 28 percent combat ready in terms of numbers of tanks). On that day, the division was tactically defending against Soviet forces attempting to break through to the Soviet forces in the Smolensk pocket from the northeast. The *20.Pz.D.* with only 51 tanks ready for insertion in combat that day would have to be considered to be at the borderline of being capable of a serious offensive drive. The point here though that stands out again is how low the borderline was in terms of the number of tanks ready for action in the panzer regiment. At almost the same time in the campaign on 22 July, and after a similar long drive and tough combat at the end of it farther south in the Ukraine, *13.Pz.D.* reported "*nur 58 einstatzbereite Panzer*" (only 58 tanks ready for battle). The Ia noted in the war diary that the division specifically was "impaired" for further battle with only that number of tanks, which was approximately 35 percent of its original establishment strength.[47] In summary, the German experience shows that panzer divisions with roughly 30 percent of their establishment strength and approximately 50 tanks still had enough striking power to be capable of conducting offensive maneuver war. Often, of course, these impaired divisions would be fighting against battered Soviet forces and such circumstances partly explain why the German divisions continued to be effective. Commonly, however, the German panzer divisions ran into fresh Soviet forces being thrown into combat straight out of the mobilization process, and the temporarily thinned out German divisions seemed to handle those Soviet formations just as comfortably.

The organization of the panzer division reveals a special emphasis on reconnaissance for mobile divisions. The panzer division held both a reconnaissance battalion[48] and a motorcycle battalion which had similar tactical capabilities that emphasized advanced detachment mobility and combat reconnaissance. In their discussions in the 1920s and early 1930s that eventually led to the establishment of the panzer divisions in October 1935, the German military thinkers of the day placed enormous emphasis on the reconnaissance necessities and capabilities of the new divisions. The German Army emphasized reconnaissance in its panzer divisions more than other armies in similar mobile divisions and did so with a unique style of using their reconnaissance and motorcycle troops to fight for information. Unlike most armies in which reconnaissance tends to be a process of observation and collection of information, in the German Army the process was more in the nature of advance to combat and the picking up of the pieces in order to put together a picture of the enemy. In a word, the Germans fought for reconnaissance-style information. With such instincts and style, the Germans put both a reconnaissance and motorcycle battalion in their panzer divisions and attached special importance to them. With two such battalions, the panzer division was also able to advance along two axis with adequate reconnaissance forces leading the way or covering open flanks.

The Germans organized the panzer divisions with a light antiaircraft (or, *Flak*) battalion in 1941 holding approximately 9 37mm automatic cannon and 24 20mm guns. By 1941, however, some of the divisions had been reinforced with self propelled four-barreled 20mm automatic cannon systems. The *11.Pz.D.*, for example, held two of the four-barreled (*Vierlinge*) systems as it moved across the border into the Ukraine. The Germans tended to be flexible in the arming of the antiaircraft units and *3.Pz.D.* entered the eastern campaign with 8 37mm automatic cannons and 12 20mm cannons. The Germans displayed a unique style in World War II with the employment of these light and medium Flak weapons. Under heavy air attack by the badly damaged but vast Red Air Force of 1941, the panzer divisions took punishment but shot down large numbers of Soviet single and twin engine aircraft attacking in low altitude strafing and bombing runs. In the Ukraine where the Luftwaffe was particularly weak, division war diaries often describe Soviet air "supremacy," i.e., not superiority but more decisive, supremacy, and *3.Pz.D.* reported 25 separate air attacks against it on one day in September 41. Operating for a longer period in the Ukraine, *9.Pz.D.* suffered approximately 18 percent of its casualties from air attack in the period June-September, a startling figure for an armored division on the strategic offensive.[49] Yet, in spite of the numerous and substantial air attacks, the panzer division *Flak* battalions expended about half their energy in combat against ground targets. The 3rd Company alone of the *Flak* battalion of *9.Pz.D.* in combat on 20 August 41, with a combined air defense and ground support mission fired 2,940 rounds of 20mm ammunition largely against ground targets with the resulting capture of 530 Soviet troops and the destruction or capture of 1 infantry gun, 3 antitank guns, 5 mortars, and 18 heavy machine guns.[50] These results are eye catching for an antiaircraft company. For the Germans, however, the bias towards ground missions for the *Flak* units was the rule and the style on the east front in 1941.

As concerns organization for logistics support, the Germans coordinated the so-called services – replenishment, motor vehicle maintenance and repair, post office, military police, medical, food preparation, and administration – in a division service support groupment. The Ib of the division directed and coordinated the activities of this groupment through instructions issued especially to the commanding officers of the supply battalion with its replenishment and maintenance and repair services, and the medical battalion. As the Ia attempted to keep the division command post as far forward as possible in the mobile advance, the Ib kept the logistics command post at the right distance rearward to keep the supply services balanced between the corps supply dumps and the advancing division units. The Ib worked with a division supply battalion that delivered fuel and ammunition to the division in approximately 208 trucks organized into approximately 14 columns with 10 columns carrying ammunition and other dry stores and 4 columns transporting fuel. The Germans used medium trucks each generally carrying 3 tons of ammunition or 2 tons (approximately 600 gallons) of fuel. The division supply columns picked up fuel and ammunition from corps dumps and carried it forward generally into one division fuel and one division ammunition distribution point.

The division commander issued orders as brief and general as possible and the picture in German offensive maneuver war was one of extreme decentralization in command and control. Necessary order in the extreme chaos and decentralization was effected partly by mission-styled directives containing a clear, distant objective to be taken and the mission of all commanders to drive toward that objective amid the uncertainty and change of the surrounding combat. A fairly high-level but useful example of a mission-styled directive is the following message from the appendices of the war diary of *11.Pz.D.*:[51]

From: Ia, 48th Panzer Corps Date/Time: 1540, 9.7.41
To: 11.Pz.D.
Move out immediately. Overtake enemy by pursuit. Target Belaja Cerkov.

This messenger-delivered order is a monument to succinctness, clarity and the unifying focus on a distant objective. The corps lay southeast of Berdicev, 100 km away from Belaja Cerkov, at the time the message was received by *11.Pz.D.* Within *11.Pz.D.*, the division commander issued similarly styled missions to his subordinate units with the objectives from day to day being less distant and the time for accomplishment shorter.

The most characteristic element in the battle fighting style of the Germans in maneuver war was the never ending forming and reforming of ad hoc battle groups (*Kampfgruppen*). The German panzer division in the mobile phases of a campaign fought in a different configuration daily and sometimes twice daily. The Germans often formed new battle groups at night and in significant contact with the enemy. The Germans formed battle groups and moved them out on their new missions in a process that went on 24 hours a day in the style of an operational perpetual motion machine. Fundamental questions arise of how the compact German staffs functioned continuously, how the combat soldiers and officers moved and fought with the associated sleep deprivation, and how the drivers of the hundreds of vehicles involved in thee never ending movements functioned. German division commanders, nevertheless, formed, moved, and fought with ad hoc battle groups in a decentralized style of fighting that achieved unmatched success on the strategic offensive in World War II. The German panzer division generally fought in two to four battle groups one of which was often designated also as the *Vorausabteilung* (VA), or advanced detachment. The advanced detachments could be either relatively lightly armed groups conducting reconnaissance in force or stronger groups exploiting a breakthrough and having the capability to advance in the face of heavy resistance. The following is an example of a strong advanced detachment put together in the period 1600-1800 on 1 July 41 to advance east from Minsk in a long first bound through moderately strong Soviet forces:

Advanced Detachment Lt Col Simon, 20.Pz.D.

1 Rgt Staff	1 Arty Gun Btry	3 Pz Recon Plts	1 Lt AA Btry
1 Moto Inf Bn	1 Antitank Co	1 Air Comm Plt	1 Col Ammo-Fuel
1 Panzer Bn	1 Mortar Btry	1 Radio Plt	1 Medical Plt
1 Arty How Bn	1 Pioneer Bn (-)	2 Phone Plts	

This advanced detachment was a strong one controlled by a regimental headquarters. Note the decentralized style of fire support through one 105mm howitzer battalion, one 100mm gun battery, and one 100mm smoke mortar battery attached to the force. The Germans had discovered in mobile war that a moderate amount of artillery fire applied immediately in meeting engagements disintegrated their opponents, i.e., it was always right to open fire immediately and always wrong to halt and attempt to mass distant fire support resources in the mobile advance. The subtlety in this decisive generalization is that although it was always right to attack immediately with the support of the attached artillery, the attacks were not always successful, requiring the Germans sometimes to halt and develop the attack with reinforcements. The Germans achieved great success in maneuver war with attached artillery. The German experience suggests that U.S. ground forces attachment of not only artillery but also AV8-B aircraft and attack helicopters to battle groups in maneuver war would increase changes of success in meeting engagements.

The German panzer division commander led from the front and German success in maneuver war is inextricably bound to this style of command. The Germans were uncompromising in this style, using the expression that the commander must see for himself. The style was particularly effective on the strategic offensive because the Germans would fight with the initiative under such circumstances operationally tactically. With the initiative in the battle, the panzer division commander leading from the front with his main battle group would force the critical engagement to take place in front of him, reducing the effects of uncertainty and chance and more effectively exploiting fleeting opportunity. The leadership style has application today to corps commanders and below in mobile war. A weighty objection to the U.S. corps commander as front leader would be the argument that he should be the coordinator of ground forces presence in typical U. S. overseas deployments and a kind of general director of the use of U.S. ground assets in the battle. The same objections should apply less to division commanders, making the front style of leadership preferred in maneuver war from the division downward.

German panzer divisions kept track of subordinate units, directed movement, and located targets for fire support in terms of a thrust line (*Stosslinie*). Division headquarters assigned a new thrust line daily when the division was advancing or in general movement in a mobile campaign. The line proved to be a brilliant psychological innovation because it oriented every man in the division who had to use it around a single main line of advance for the day. The thrust line was a mission-style symbol that told every subordinate commander in the division temporarily out of touch with higher headquarters and potentially frozen into immobility how to continue to advance. From a technical viewpoint, the Germans had developed a flexible and simple way of directing movement that used no place names and required no coding of numbers for security. The thrust line was simple, secure, and operationally focused and reflects a bold style of maneuver war.

Notes for Part One:

1 The Germans in 1941 considered their panzer and motorized infantry divisions to be "mobile divisions" and often used this term to describe them.

2 Heinz Guderian, *Panzer Leader* (New York, 1952), p. 204.

3 See, for example, George E. Blau, *The German Campaign in Russia, Planning and Operations (1940-1942)*, Department of the Army Pamphlet No. 20-261a (Washington D.C., 1955), p. 41, and Guderian, *Panzer Leader*, p. 143.

4 *O.K.H., Gen Sta d H, Op, Abt. (I), Nr. 1503/41 g.kdos. Chef.,Panzerlage*, U.S. National Archives, Records Headquarters Army High Command, T-78, Roll 335, Fr. 6291784.

5 Christopher F. Foss, *The Illustrated Encyclopedia of the World's Tanks and Fighting Vehicles* (New York, 1977), p. 173, figure for T-26 tanks.

6 F.M. von Senger und Etterlin, *Die Kampfpanzer von 1916-1966* (Muenchen, 1971), pp. 386, 391. Figures are for T-34 and KV tanks manufactured by 22 June 1941.

7 Colonel N.F. Azyasskiy, "On the Strategic Deployment of the Armed Forces of Germany and the Soviet Union in 1941," *Voyennaya Mysl* (Moscow), No. 8, August 1990, pp. 9-8.

8 *Generalleutnant* Hermann Plocher, *The German Air Force Versus Russia, 1941*, Harry R. Fletcher, ed. (New York, 1965), p. 33.

9 *Brigadegeneral* Rudolf Loytved-Hardegg, Interview, Nuremberg, Germany. 18 January 1980.

10 *Brigadegeneral* Rudolf Loytved-Hardegg, Interview, Nuremberg, Germany. 18 January 1980.

11 See Hermann Hoth, *Panzer Operationen* (Heidelberg, 1956), pp. 50,51.

12 See *Ia, Kriegstagebuch Nr. 3, 7.PZ.D., 22.6.41*, U.S. National Archives, Records German Field Commands, Divisions, Microcopy T-315, Roll 406, Fr. 000013.

13 The researcher will use *Kampfgruppe* and battle group interchangeably for the rest of the book.

14 See *Ia, Tagesmeldung zum Kriegstagebuch Nr. 3, Panzer-Regiment 6, Morgenmeldung, 0100, 17.6.41*, U.S. National Archives, Records German Field Commands, Divisions, Microcopy T-315, Roll 407, Fr. 000889.

15 See R.H.S. Stolfi, "Chance in History: The Russian Winter of 1941." *History* (Journal of the British Historical Association), March 1980, pp. 1-21.

16 General Franz Halder, *Diaries*, Vol. II (Washington, D.C., 1949), entry of mid-September 1939.

17 See See *Ia, Kriegstagebuch Nr. 1, 22.6.41, 20.Pz.D.*, U.S. National Archives, Records German Field Commands, Divisions, Microcopy T-315, Roll 744, Fr. 000265.

18 See *Ia, Kriegstagebuch Nr. 1, 23.6.41, 20.Pz.D.*, U.S. National Archives, Records German Field Commands, Divisions, Microcopy T-315, Roll 744, Fr. 000267.

19 See *Ia, Anlage 107 zum Kriegstagebuch der 7.Pz. Div., Feinbild vor Panzergruppe 3 vom 21 Juni – 8 August 1941*, U.S. National Archives, Records German Field Commands, Divisions, Microcopy T-315, Roll 436, Fr. 000717.

20 See *Ia, Kriegstagebuch Nr. 1, 8. und 9.7.41, 20.Pz.D.*, U.S. National Archives, Records German Field Commands, Divisions, Microcopy T-315, Roll 744, Fr. 000289.

21 See *Ia, Anlagenband c zum Kriegstagebuch Nr. 1, Gefechts-Bericht, leichte Flakabteilung 74, 8 Juli 1941, 20.Pz.D.*, U.S. National Archives, Records German Field Commands, Divisions, Microcopy T-315, Roll 744, Fr. 001228.

22 See *Ia, Kriegstagebuch Nr. 5, 28.9. – 2.10.41, 10.Pz.D.*, U.S. National Archives, Records German Field Commands, Divisions, Microcopy T-315, Roll 561, Fr. 000723-000751.

23 See these details in *Ia, Kriegstagebuch Nr. 5, 3.10.41,10.Pz.D.*, U.S. National Archives, Records German Field Commands, Divisions, Microcopy T-315, Roll 561, Fr. 000772,74.

24 See *Ia, Kriegstagebuch Nr. 5, 5.10.41, 10.Pz.D.*, U.S. National Archives, Records German Field Commands, Divisions, Microcopy T-315, Roll 561, Fr. 000788.

25 See *Ia, Kriegstagebuch Nr. 5, 24.6.41, 13.Pz.D.*, U.S. National Archives, Records German Field Commands, Divisions, Microcopy T-315, Roll 2325, Fr. 000049.

26 See *Ia, Kriegstagebuch Nr. 5, 25.6.41, 13.Pz.D.*, U.S. National Archives, Records German Field Commands, Divisions, Microcopy T-315, Roll 2325, Fr. 000052.

27 See *Ia, Anlage III, Heft 1 Kriegstagebuch Nr. 5, 13.Pz., II. Btl. Schtz. Rgt. 66, Bericht ueber das Gefecht am 26.6.41.*, U.S. National Archives, Records German Field Commands, Divisions, Microcopy T-315, Roll 641, Fr. 000033-36.

28 For this kind of detail, see, for example, *Ia, Anlage III, Heft 1, Kriegstagebuch Nr. 5, 13.Pz.D., I./ Panzer-Regiment 4, Gefechtsbericht fuer den 26.6.41*, U.S. National Archives, Records German Field Commands, Divisions, Microcopy T-315, Roll 641, 000044,45.

29 See *Ia, Kriegstagebuch Nr. 6, 24.7.41, 13.Pz.D.*, U.S. National Archives, Records German Field Commands, Divisions, Microcopy T-315, Roll 2325, Fr. 000169.

30 See *Ia, Anlage III, Heft 1, Kriegstagebuch Nr. 5, Schuetzen-Brigade 13, Gefechtsbericht Angriff auf Gorodischtsche, 1.8.41*, U.S. National Archives, Records German Field Commands, Divisions, Microcopy T-315, Roll 641, 000300-000302.

31 See *Ia, Kriegstagebuch Nr. 5, 24.8.41, 13.Pz.D.*, U.S. National Archives, Records German Field Commands, Divisions, Microcopy T-315, Roll 2325, Fr. 000278.

32 Earlier at 1620 on 14 September 41, German troops of 3.Pz.D. touched hands with pioneer troops of 16th Panzer Division (16.Pz.D.) south of Lohvica. The second, more decisive contact of 3.Pz.D. and 9.Pz.D. has been described as the "conclusive" (*endgueltig*) one. See *Geschichte der 3, Panzer-Division, Berlin-Brandenberg 1933-1945* (Berlin, 1967), pp. 180,181. See also, *Ia, Kriegstagebuch Nr. 1, 15.9.41, 9.Pz.D.*, U.S. National Archives, Records German Field Commands, Divisions, Microcopy T-315, Roll 533, Fr. 000054.

33 See *Ia, Anlagenband, Kriegstagebuch Nr. 1. 13.Pz.D., Ic Beutemeldung den 5.8.41*, U.S. National Archives, Records German Field Commands, Divisions, Microcopy T-315, Roll 533, Fr. 000354.

34 See *Ia, Kriegstagebuch Nr. 1, 14.9.41, 9.Pz.D.*, U.S. National Archives, Records German Field Commands, Divisions, Microcopy T-315, Roll 533, Fr. 000053.

35 See *Ia, Anlagenband, Kriegstagebuch Nr. 1, 9.Pz.D., Anlage 130, Divisionsarzt, Art der Feindeinwirkung, 8.9.41*, U.S. National Archives, Records German Field Commands, Divisions, Microcopy T-315, Roll 533, Fr. 000480.

36 See *Geschichte 3.Panzer-Division, p. 179.*

37 See *Geschichte 3.Panzer-Division, p. 113.*

38 *Generalleutnant* Hermann Balck, 11.Pz.D., December 1943.

39 See *Geschichte der 3.Panzer-Division, p. 159.*

40 See *Geschichte der 3.Panzer-Division, p. 172.*

41 See Colonel Trevor M. Dupuy, USA, Ret. *A Genius for War, the German Army and General Staff (1807-1945)* (London, 1977).

42 Carl von Clausewitz, *On War*, ed. Anatol Rapoport (Harmondsworth, England, 1987), p. 184.

43 Raphael (Raffaello Santi) (1483-1520) Italian Renaissance painter, An artistic genius who painted brilliantly with no apparent effort.

44 For example, Heinz Guderian, Erwin Rommel, and Erich von Manstein.

45 Some older officers would have completed the earlier three-year course of instruction of the period before World War I.

46 See *Ia, Kriegstagebuch Nr. 6, 28.6.41, 13.Pz.D.*, U.S. National Archives, Records German Field Commands, Divisions, Microcopy T-315, Roll 2325, Fr. 000063.

47 See *Ia, Kriegstagebuch Nr. 6, 22.7.41, 9.Pz.D.*, U.S. National Archives, Records German Field Commands, Divisions, Microcopy T-315, Roll 2325, Fr. 000159.

48 The German designation was "detachment," but these organizations had the strength and missions associated with battalions.

49 See *Ia, Anlagenband, Kriegstagebuch Nr. 1, 8.9.41, 9.Pz.D., Divisionsarzt, Art der Feindeinwirkung*, U.S. National Archives, Records German Field Commands, Divisions, Microcopy T-315, Roll 315, Fr. 00046.

50 See *Ia, Anlage III, Heft 2, Kriegstagebuch Nr. 6, 20.8.41, 13.Pz.D.*, U.S. National Archives, Records German Field Commands, Divisions, Microcopy T-315, Roll 64 Fr. 000364

51 See *Ia, Anlagenband 2, Kriegstagebuch, Einsatz Russland, Meldeabwurf, 48.Pz.K. an 11.Pz.D., 1540, 9.7.41*, U.S. National Archives, Records German Field Commands, Divisions, Microcopy T-315, Roll 2320, Fr. 001277.

52 See *Ia, Anlagenband zu Text-Erstschrift, Kriegstagebuch Nr. 1, 1.7.41, 20.Pz.D.*, U.S. National Archives, Records German Field Commands, Divisions, Microcopy T-315, Roll 744, Fr. 000393

PART TWO:

Panzer Maneuver War in the North African Desert, 1941-1942

7

Introduction

A thesis that the German Army fought armed battles more effectively than any of its opponents demands at least brief elaboration. In the years of sweeping social and economic change preceding World War I, the German Army developed the most impressive plan of military operations for possible war between the two opposing alliance systems that had developed between 1890-1914. The plans for military operations of the four other Great Powers that entered the war in 1914, do not remotely approach Count Alfred von Schlieffen's conceptualization in terms of boldness, decisiveness, initiative, concentration, and surprise – factors that read like a litany of the possible principles of war. In the words of probably the most distinguished historical authority on modern Germany, the Germans intended to put the armed strength of a great power (France), as it were, like a cat in a bag.[0] Just as impressive, the Germans intended then to transfer the victorious armies to the denuded eastern front and put an even bigger Russian cat in a (presumably) bigger bag. The German operations at the beginning of World War I associated with the ideas of Schlieffen reflect, in turn, the tangible German superiority in operations and tactics for the rest of the war.

The operations conducted by Helmut von Moltke (The Younger) in August-September 1914 and associated with the earlier Schlieffen "Plan" would fail to conquer France or take Paris. This failure is well known. The opening German offensive gained so much ground, however, that the Germans fought for the next four years exclusively on French and Belgian soil. This astounding general framework for the entire war in the west is rarely connected with the Schlieffen "Plan" and seldom claimed as a factor in support of German operational prowess in World War I. On the eastern front, the Germans conducted the most effective set of military operations in the entire war in the Battle of Tannenberg (August 1914) and its sequel. The Germans went on with the help of a faltering but casualty-absorbing Austro-Hungarian Empire to defeat Russia by December 1917. German expeditionary armies with deceptive ease would knock Serbia (1915) and Rumania (1916) out of the Great War. Modest German forces assisting the Austrians in the south would inflict in late 1917 the most serious defeat of the Italians in the war. The Germans would excel in gas warfare notably artillery projectile tactics and technology and the employment of mustard gas, the employment of machine guns, the construction of fortifications, and the development of "shock troop tactics."[1]

Struck by the picture above, historical authorities have quantified the relative effectiveness of the armies in World War I. Authorities have used casualties inflicted and received by each side in a battle as the most important unit of exchange in the business of war. Casualty data have been available since the modern more systematic approach to war that emerged in the nineteenth century. Authorities have been able to extract these data from medical and adjutant general (personnel administration) records of the larger European armies. These data correlated with the personnel strengths of the opposing forces in a battle and numerical factors to account for inherent advantages associated with the side on the defensive, have been used to score the effectiveness of the opposing sides in battle. Using the data as sketched out above and assigning scores, authorities note that two German soldiers in World War I were equivalent in "combat effectiveness" to three western allied soldiers, for example, French or British. On the eastern front, the combat effectiveness equations indicate that two German soldiers were the equivalent of approximately 14 Russians.[2] The effectiveness scores are tied in closely with casualties and these numbers can be generalized *roughly* as telling the reader that when the Germans received two casualties on the western front they inflicted three and when they received two casualties in the east they inflicted 14. These numbers suggest the importance of attempting to discover what made the Germans tick in war fighting.

In World War II, the German Army conducted operations from 1939 -1941 that gave it the immediate possibility of winning the war in Europe through continuation of the drive on Moscow in August 1941. The Army fought under difficult operational circumstances in Norway and the Balkans, was significantly outnumbered in men and tanks in the French Campaign, and faced the challenge of a two-front war in the Polish Campaign that demanded an immediate victory on the "eastern front." The German Army conducted the fighting in those campaigns with a style of operational moves so bold that it achieved victories in the immediate opening stages of the campaigns. In effect, during the period, the Germans won the opening stages of "campaigns" rather than campaigns as conventionally understood in the sense of the later ponderous North African, Italian, and Northwestern European campaigns of the western allies. The style of command and the methods of combat required to win so quickly and decisively characterized German war fighting on the strategic offensive.

On the strategic defensive from late 1942-1945, the German Army put on impressive performances in the three major theaters of the war in Europe. In the Mediterranean, the German Army won a defensive "victory" in Sicily, avoiding destruction, inflicting heavy casualties and escaping across water with personnel *and* equipment. In Italy, the Germans similarly won a great defensive victory punishing stronger allied forces in costly battles around Salerno, Ortona, Cassino, arid Anzio and preventing the seizure of Northern Italy until the last days of the war. In Northwestern Europe, the Germans would put up strong resistance at Normandy, defeat the allies in Operation Market Garden, and surprise them in the Ardennes offensive with damaging consequences. On the eastern front, the Germans would recover from the Stalingrad debacle so effectively as to launch a strategic offensive at Kursk in July 1943 and prevent the Soviets from reaching the fringes of the core German area until early 1945. The German Army would fight with vigor on the defensive in a style characterized by self confidence and flexibility in command and tactical coherence and counterattack esprit on the part of the combat troops.

The Battle of Kursk illustrates the tactical dominance of the German Army on the battlefield in World War II. The Soviets have continued to view the battle as the centerpiece of the Great Fatherland War and the best example of their war fighting skill. The battle can scarcely be criticized from the viewpoint of favoring the Germans as a selection for illustrating German war fighting skill. The Germans would fight the battle under circumstances so adverse that only superior tactical performance on the part of the combat troops and commanders would save the Germans from a military collapse in the east in 1943.

The Germans conceptualized the attack in early 1943 at the correct time to inflict a strategic setback to the Soviets by the destruction of the Soviet forces around Kursk in the strategically predominate southern front of that year in the war. Through the epic procrastination of Adolf Hitler in delaying the attack from April to July 1943, the German Army gave the Soviets three months to regain their composure from their substantial defeat at Kharkov in March that had resulted from disastrous overextension at the end of the Stalingrad and Middle Don operations. The Soviets would know where the attack was coming for three months, construct fortifications to a depth of 35 mi, and lay half a million mines in belts among them. The Soviets would mass men, tanks, artillery, and aircraft in numbers greater than those of the attacking Germans. Thanks to Hitler's procrastination, British warnings through breaking of the German Enigma codes, and Soviet intelligence, the Soviets would even eventually know the day of the attack. The Germans would finally launch their attack into a summer thunderstorm system that would drench the ground and independently of Soviet resistance halt German movement for about eight hours early in the offensive. Under such conditions, the German Army should have taken disastrous casualties and tank losses, gained no ground, and experienced encirclement by the vast Soviet strategic reserve massed for the battle and facing immobilized German attackers.

Authorities have examined this battle and using both Soviet and German data have calculated factors of effectiveness for the two sides. The famed Obyon sector was the area where the crucial engagement was played out. In that sector, the German 48th Panzer Corps engaged numerically superior Soviet forces organized into the Sixth Guards Army and First Tank Army and set in 35 km deep prepared defenses. The Germans achieved a score effectiveness in the resultant combat that translates into one German combat soldier having the effectiveness of approximately three Soviet. The 48th Panzer Corps attacked outnumbered in tanks and assault guns, artillery pieces, and air support sorties by factors in each case of approximately 2:1. The German force advanced 35 mi into the Soviet positions inflicting approximately 23,400 casualties and knocking out 450 tanks while suffering the loss of 4,400 men and 141 tanks.[3] How is it possible that the 48th Panzer Corps could have accomplished these tactical results under the burden of the conditions noted? This study is part of a search for the style, spirit, and weapons that gave the German Army the tactical and operational edge it held in World War II, even, for example, when engaged in what the Soviets consider their master operation of the War. The search now takes us to Rommel and the North African desert.

In North Africa in January 1941, the Italian Army stood on the brink of defeat and the loss of the last Italian territory in Africa to a motorized, well equipped and growing British field army. British forces stood near El Agheila on the Sirte Gulf half the distance from the Egyptian border to Tripoli, the capital of Libya lying a moderate distance from the Tunisian border. Faced with impending Italian collapse, the German High Command (*OKW*)[4] sent a minuscule motorized force to stiffen Italian defenses around El Agheila and prevent, or at least slow, a British advance to Tripoli. The *OKW* designated the force; German Africa Corps (*DAK*)[5] formed it on 9 February 1941, and saw to the arrival of its new commander, *Generalleutnant* (two stars) Erwin Rommel on 12 February. The *OKW* initially allotted to the Corps one panzer and one light division in process of being formed from parts of other German divisions in Europe. During the period of this study 1941 - June 1942, the *DAK* would comprise two panzer divisions and one roughly pieced together light Africa division.[6]

Between February — June 1941, Rommel and the still assembling *DAK* would dominate the fighting in North Africa. In March 1941, in a bold counterstroke, disregarding his instructions to defend and consolidate around El Agheila, Rommel would advance with a handful of German units a distance of 500 miles (along the sea) to Sollum on the Egyptian frontier. In June 1941, in conjunction with numerically strong Italian forces, Rommel and the *DAK* would repulse the British offensive designated Operation Battleaxe. The British High Command in the Middle East, pressed by the home government, launched the offensive with the optimistic intention of destroying the axis forces now concentrated between Tobruk and Sollum in Northeastern Libya. On 15 August 1941, *OKW* established *Panzergruppe Afrika* (Panzer Group Africa) and German success and prestige forced a reluctant Italian High Command to place virtually all of its field forces in Libya under the operational command of recently promoted *General der Panzertruppen* (three stars) Rommel.[7] Between August - November 1941, Rommel received enough reinforcements from Europe to put together the 21st Panzer Division and the 90th Light Africa Division. With these forces in place, the stage is set to examine the performance of a talented German commander and several German mobile divisions in action against a powerful, well equipped British field army.

Since 1945, British historical opinion has gone through several phases on the subject of Rommel and the *DAK* in North Africa. A small German force that by most accounts should have been pushed aside and destroyed along with the Italian army in Libya by the summer of 1941, in fact, survived the year and came close to defeating the British in the summer of 1942. Roughly handled psychologically by the German competence in ground warfare, the British have had a natural tendency to seek arguments that protect an image of British excellence in arms. Instead of acknowledging that the British field army had been outfought by a German commander of genius with a small but high quality corps, British commentators developed arguments that protected the image of the British army in North Africa as being at least as good as the German. Three protective arguments emerged: first, Rommel was a military genius, and a German corps no more able than the opposing British army gained more prestige than it deserved in the fighting in 1941-1942; then, Rommel was, to the contrary, not a genius but the product of historical misrepresentation, and German success was based on implied "unfair" technological superiority against which a British army qualitatively equal in all other ways to the German struggled successfully; and most recently, Rommel again became accepted as a leader of military genius, but German technological superiority received the palm as the predominate reason for the German success in 1941-42.

For purposes of this study, the above situation can be dispensed with as follows. Rommel can be accurately interpreted as a commander of genius. The *DAK* can be considered to be tangibly superior to the British field army opposing it in command and combat soldier style. The *DAK* cannot be considered to have had a significant technological superiority over the British-Imperial forces. The British argument of German technological superiority is also flawed as used to protect the image of the British soldier by claiming a non-human deficiency in the performance characteristics of the British 2-pounder (40mm) gun and Crusader main battle tank.[8] The argument fails because even the two British weapons were inferior, British military leaders stand indicted as less than effective because they developed and accepted them.

The British field army, nevertheless, stands as superbly tenacious, well equipped by any standards, numerically superior to the Italo—German forces in virtually every category of weapon and equipment, and numerically superior in the air. At sea, the British held naval supremacy seriously inhibited only by the inconsistent intervention of modest German Stuka (dive bomber) forces. Against this first class opponent, Rommel and the *DAK*, with the support of numerically strong but badly equipped Italian divisions, successfully defended eastern Libya in the extended period from February 1941-July 1942. In the latter month, Rommel and the *DAK* actually forced the British back to El Alamein, a scant 55 miles from Alexandria and now over 2,000 miles along the sea from Tripoli. The period is filled with examples of gunfire and maneuver in the desert. Many of the examples contain lessons that can be applied to ground forces today especially under conditions of mobile war in the desert.

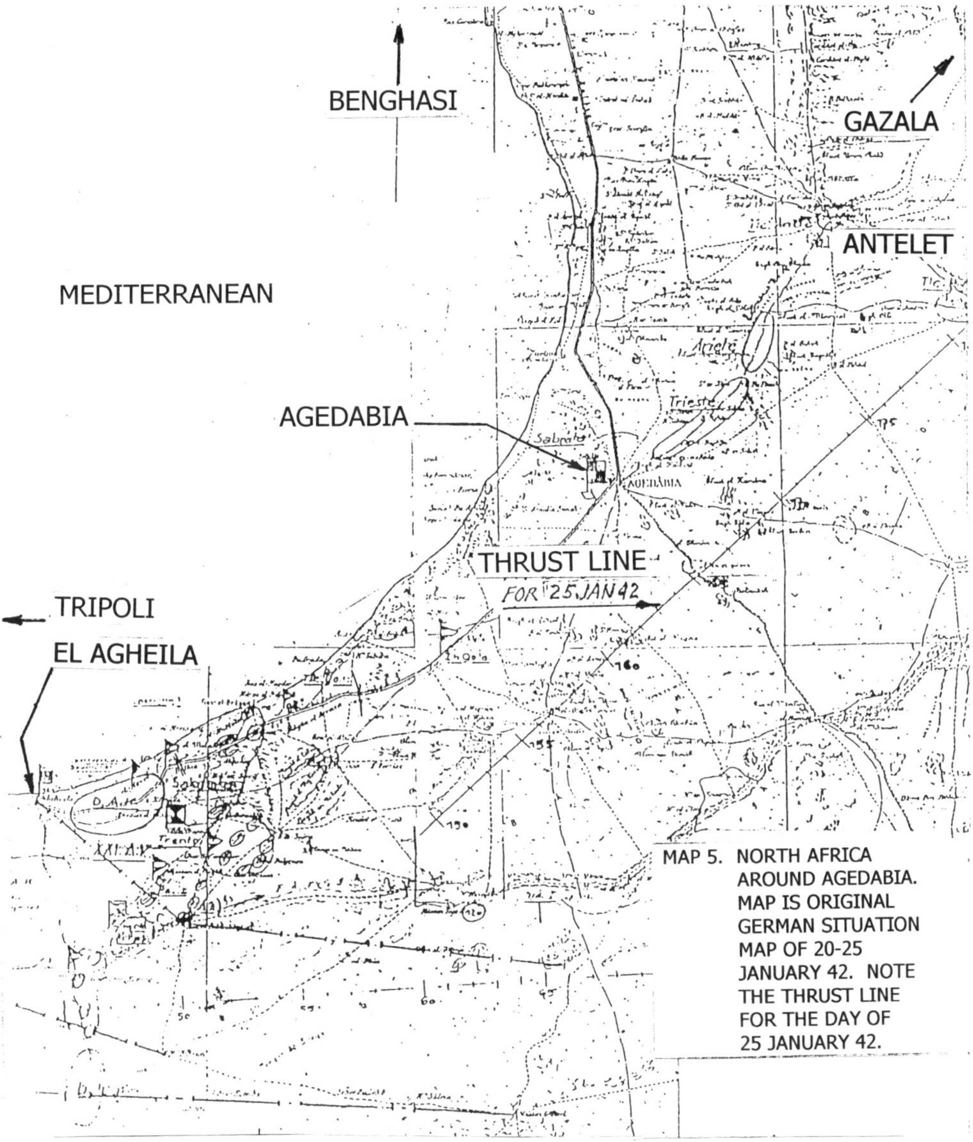

MAP 5. NORTH AFRICA AROUND AGEDABIA. MAP IS ORIGINAL GERMAN SITUATION MAP OF 20-25 JANUARY 42. NOTE THE THRUST LINE FOR THE DAY OF 25 JANUARY 42.

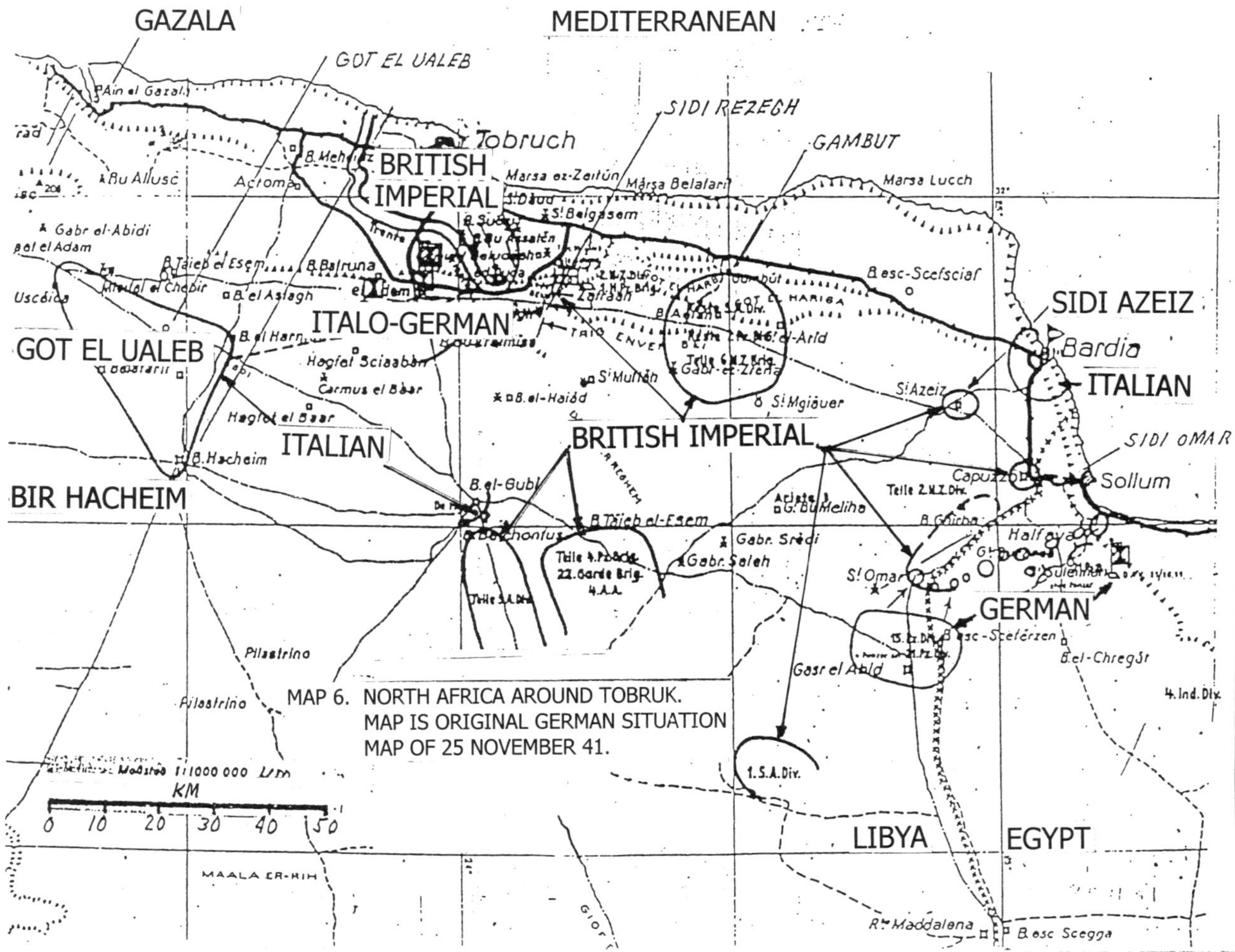

MAP 6. NORTH AFRICA AROUND TOBRUK.
MAP IS ORIGINAL GERMAN SITUATION
MAP OF 25 NOVEMBER 41.

8

Rommel

"You'll find there are always two possible decisions open to you. Take the bolder one—it's always best."
- *Generalleutnant* Rudolf Schmidt to Rommel in February 1940, on the occasion of Rommel taking command of his first panzer division.[9]

Rommel had experienced a uniquely varied and successful military career by the time of his arrival in North Africa. Born in November 1891 near Ulm in the German Kingdom of Wuerttenberg, he grew up in an area of forest and mountain in a state where the people are noted for hardheaded practicality and frugality. Rommel had little natural predilection as an adolescent for the profession of arms. His father, nevertheless, placed him in an army cadet school in the Prussian port of Danzig on the Baltic Sea in July 1910. He was commissioned in 1912 as a lieutenant in the Army of Wuerttenberg, one of four German armies that fought in World War I.[10] Between 1914-1918, he served with exceptional distinction as a lieutenant in the Wuerttenberg Mountain Battalion, earning the German Empire's highest military decoration (*Pour le Mérite*) and finding his métier as an officer unexcelled in exploiting chance situations. According to the evaluation of a senior instructor in 1931, Rommel basically remained that lieutenant, making instant decisions and acting on the spur of his battlefield impressions. War is the province of danger, uncertainty, and chance, and Rommel would exceed every division commander and higher in World War II in his capability to move within the framework of danger and to exploit the combat opportunities associated with chance. It is this mastery of the fundamental atmosphere of war that qualifies Rommel as a military genius.

At war's end, 1918, the Army promoted Rommel to captain, and after many turbulent months during the German revolution, chose him as one of an elite body of officers to remain in the drastically reduced army of the Treaty *Reichswehr*. Rommel served from 1920-1929 as seemingly permanent company commander in an infantry regiment at Stuttgart near his birthplace at Ulm in southern Germany. Rommel then served as junior instructor at the Dresden infantry school from 1930-1933 and finally as commander of an infantry battalion beginning in the latter year. In 1935, the Army assigned him as senior instructor at the new infantry school at Postdam, a suburb of Berlin. The Army recognized in him a special flair for tactics and an ebullient professionalism almost perfect for teaching. In 1937, he published a sparkling book but unlikely best seller entitled, *The Infantry Attacks*, an achievement that brought him to the attention of Hitler and resulted in his assignment as special advisor to the Hitler Youth organization in 1937 - 1938. In November 1938, the Army posted Rommel as commandant of the officer cadet school at Wiener-Neustadt in newly annexed Austria. Hitler continued to be impressed by Rommel, however, and gave him command of his mobile headquarters for the occupation of Czecho-Slovakia in March 1939 and other escort duties culminating in command of the Fuehrer's War Headquarters for the Polish Campaign.

Promoted to the rank of *Generalmajor* (one star) in 1939, Rommel was ready for command of a division after his special assignment during the Polish campaign. He presumptuously requested one of the new panzer divisions but was offered a mountain division based on a service record that was dominated by infantry assignments and war in the mountains. Hitler seems to have intervened in the assignment process and the Army ultimately ordered Rommel to command of the 7th Panzer Division *(7.Pz.D.)* 6 February 1940. Under Rommel's leadership, the division would achieve the most substantial results of any German division engaged in the French Campaign. Rommel would lead the division literally from the front and maneuver according to his personally conceptualized *Stosslinie* (thrust line). Under Rommel, the division would be first to cross the Meuse River, move consistently faster and deeper than any other German division for the remainder of the campaign, successfully repel a strong Anglo-French counterattack on its exposed right flank near Cambrai, and take masses of prisoners from respectable opponents prior to the final collapse on 22 June 1940.

Throughout World War I and while in command of *7.Pz.D.* in France in May-June 1940, Rommel led his formations from the front. He achieved extraordinary success during both periods largely through this style of command. In North Africa, as corps, and later army commander, Rommel continued to lead from the front. He achieved the great success of his life in the attack of 26 May 1942, which resulted in the defeat of the British field army in Libya and the seizure of the Tobruk fortress by 21 June. He won this victory at the army level of command as *Generaloberst* (four stars) while continuing to accompany the advanced elements of the combat forces at the point of major effort in the battle.

In surrounding chaos of battle Rommel reduced uncertainty and took advantage of chance by his personal, physical presence with the advanced elements of attacking forces. Just how far forward was Rommel during the German offensive against the British Gazala[11] positions in May and June 1942? On 31 May 1942, Headquarters, *DAK* formed Battle Group (*Kampfgruppe*) Major von Block from *15.Pz.D.* and ordered it to take the British fortified "box" at Got el Ualeb. This British box blocked the supply lines of the mobile forces of Panzer Army Africa entangled at that stage of the battle in an untenable position in the middle of strong, intact British forces. Built around 3rd Battalion, 104th Motorized Rifle Regiment, *Kampfgruppe* Block with its modest but critically poised forces, began the attack at 0715 on 1 June 1942, carrying on its slender back the hope for German success in the entire battle. The *DAK*[12] supported the attack with *Stuka* (*Junker 87D* dive bomber) sorties but the Germans made no gains until the artillery commander of the *Kampfgruppe* moved into the front line to experience personally the resistance that held up the assault force. He picked out the apparent *Schwerpunkt* of the British defenses and ordered a change of position and "new insertion" of the artillery. The *Kampfgruppe* began to bring in more effective artillery fire and coordinated another Stuka strike at 0830. At this juncture, nonetheless, the fighting seemed to be stabilizing to the advantage of the British in spite of the German exertions. If the box held another day, the German mobile force, five divisions organized into the *DAK* and the Italian XXth Motorized Corps, would likely be forced to withdraw to the area west of the vast British minefields between Gazala and Bir Hacheim.

Mid-morning at approximately 0900, the engagement report of *Kampfgruppe* Block almost casually but amply impressed with the turn of events, painted the following picture: "At this moment, the *Oberbefehishaber* (commander in chief), Colonel General Rommel appeared in the right platoon [!] of the 11th Infantry Company and accompanied the entire further attack of the battalion in the farthest forward line." [13] Attacking southward, *Kampfgruppe* Block and Rommel began to gain ground. By noon, as tank elements of *15.Pz.D.* moved alongside from the east to support the attack, the British 150th Brigade collapsed in the box. Rommel had secured the communications of his five mobile divisions east of the British mine fields. The destruction of 150th Infantry Brigade was a turning point in the battle. Rommel had effected that turning point by his physical presence in the middle of an advance skillfully coordinated by a lean staff and executed by a *Kampfgruppe* assembled late afternoon of the day before the attack. A commander at the end of a communications device miles away from the battle surrounded by a large over-ranked staff can be imagined only with difficulty to have achieved the same result.

Rommel's "lieutenant style" proved ideal for maintaining a high tempo of advance in mobile war and exploitation of opportunity in swirling mobile battle. Rommel often accompanied the leading elements of advancing forces and, on the spot, ordered tactical formations into new moves based on his immediate impressions. As commander in chief, notwithstanding his front line penchant, he acted at the operational level of war when he ordered tactical moves that contributed to the successes of the battles being linked together by him to form the operation. In a word, when Rommel ordered a tactical move, it more or less automatically became an operational maneuver based on his high-level position and outlook on the campaign.

The following incident during the 450-mile advance of late January 1942 from El Agheila to Gazala illustrates the style. On 22 January, 5th Machine Gun Battalion, *15.Pz.D.* formed another of the omnipresent German *Kampfgruppen* (battle groups) of the desert war to include a 105mm howitzer detachment, 100mm gun battery, and one company of 50mm *Pak* (antitank guns). The *DAK* ordered the machine gun battalion *Kampfgruppe* to be the advanced attachment of yet a larger *Kampfgruppe* Warrelmann and move east though the great road junction at Agedabia and the smaller but even more important road junction at Antelet farther east. German seizure of Antelet would put Warrelmann in position to outflank the strong British forces to the north around the port of Benghasi or to advance across the open desert inland to Gazala lying far away to the northeast. The Germans recognized Antelet as crucial operational terrain and an area through which they would have to move quickly in order to continue to keep the British off balance.

As the machine gun battalion *Kampfgruppe* advanced toward Agedabia, it believed itself to be the advanced element of the Panzer Group in the offensive. At 1130, 22 January 1942 as it reached the minefields in front of Agedabia, it discovered that the fields had already been breached by a neighboring *Kampfgruppe* of 21st Panzer Division personally led by Rommel who was first through the minefield [!] and now advancing on Agedabia in the lead of the Panzer Army. The machine gun battalion *Kampfgruppe* received new orders to continue the advance through Agedabia to Antelet now following the commander in chief. The *Kampfgruppe* moved through Agedabia as darkness fell and continued into the night toward Antelet. Then, six kilometers before Antelet "in the darkness along the road, the commander in chief appeared in front of the leader of the *Kampfgruppe* and ordered: 'defend Antelet and hold at whatever cost.'"[14] Rommel had already personally pressed 21st Panzer Division on to the north and now personally in an oral order set the machine gun battalion on its way to secure the communications of the advancing spearhead of the Panzer Army—in the middle of the night alongside a desert road.

In desert battles in North Africa Rommel operated out of a relatively small and mobile battle headquarters. The Germans used the terms Panzer Army High Command Operations Staff (*Panzerarmeeoberkommando Fuehrunqsstab)*, or similarly, Army Combat Command Post (*Armeegefechtsstand*) to describe this operationally-oriented headquarters. In the German Army, compared for example, with U.S. ground forces today, such a headquarters was small and normally had a security element for the protection of the commander and staff. With his penchant for intervening directly in the battle, Rommel personally developed the security element of the Operations Staff into a unique combat force described as the Panzer Army High Command *Kampfstaffel* or Combat Detachment of the Operations Staff.

After the successful counterstroke of 21 January 1942 that moved the Germans 400 miles east along the Mediterranean from El Agheila to Gazala, Rommel ordered *DAK* to form a *Beuteabteilung* (Captured Materiel Detachment, approximately battalion strength) out of captured British and American Tanks. *DAK* assigned *Oberstleutnant* (Lieutenant Colonel) Ramsauer of *15.Pz.D.* on 12 February 1942, the task of putting together the first company of the detachment.[15] Simultaneously, Rommel began to put together a strong *Kampfstaffel* for the Panzer Army Operational Headquarters[16] and took most of the British tanks and set up a *Beutepanzerkompanie* (Captured Materiel Tank Company) in the army *Kampfstaffel*. Rommel operated in this situation with a style that illustrates the ingenuity, imagination, and practicality of the man. He saw two things: first, the special possibilities of a small *masse de manoeuvre* available to him personally at the Panzer Army Operational Headquarters, and second, the necessity for a strong combat element to protect a headquarters that he characteristically projected in and among the opposing British forces in the fluid desert combat. He knew such an element would need tanks and with his practicality and frugality, he could not justify taking German tanks from the two relatively thin panzer divisions. The answer was a *Kampfstaffel* with a British tank company. Similarly, but with a somewhat different general purpose, the Israeli Army organized an entire captured tank brigade of approximately 139 tanks after the June 1967 War, and, in soldier's vernacular, referred to it as The Russian Brigade.

In March and April 1942, Rommel and his staff pieced together a *Kampfstaffel* to meet the demands of mobile operations against a first class motorized enemy in permissive terrain for movement and little cover or concealment from air attack. To the *Beutepanzerkompanie* of 12 British Mark III (16 tons, max 65mm armor, 40mm guns) and two Mark VI (20 tons, max 40mm armor, 40mm guns) tanks, Rommel added a special 1st Company consisting of a wild but effective melange of weapons for protecting the Army Operational Headquarters. Shortly before the Gazala offensive of 26 May 1942, Rommel added a regular company of motorized infantry called Company von Koenen and designated it 2nd Company of the *Kampfstaffel*. Rommel also attached a strong antiaircraft (*Flak*) battery, 3rd Battery, 43rd Antiaircraft Regiment, that held light and heavy weapons capable of engaging both armored ground targets and aircraft. These units comprised the Rommel *Kampfstaffel*—Rommel's combined personal defense and mobile combat element. They held the following men and weapons:

ROMMEL KAMPFSTAFFEL
(May – June 1942)

Element	Personnel[17]*	Heavy Weapons
1. *Kasta*+ HQ and 1st Company	9/37/179	8 20mm *Flak*; 4 40mm *Pak* (e)**
		3 50mm *Pak*; 1 57mm *Pak* (e)**
		1 75mm *Pak*; 1 86mm Arty (e)**
2. 2nd Company	4/18/106	3 80mm mortars
3. 3./143	4/17/156	2 20mm *Flak*; 8 88mm *Flak*
Kasta Totals	17/72/441	See above. Mostly *Flak*, *Pak*.

* Officers/NCOs/Men.
** e or englisch or English
\+ *Kasta* or *Kampfstaffel*

Ironically, Rommel ordered the company of captured British tanks away on a special mission two days before the attack. He held the strong force noted above as his personal combat detachment on the day of Operation Venezia. In typical German Army style, Rommel placed *Hauptmann* (Captain) Kiehl in charge of a mixed 500-man force that would demand a lieutenant colonel on the part of U.S. ground forces today.

In the chaotic combat of armored forces among the fortified British "boxes," the *Kampfstaffel* provided security and launched attacks of its own. By 27 May 1942, Rommel's sweep with his five mobile divisions around Bir Hacheim at the southern end of the British defenses had miscarried. The Panzer Army found itself being forced back through the British mine seas and fortified boxes by an enemy field army whose tank forces outnumbered its own. In a situation filled with uncertainty and dominated by chance encounter, Rommel moved with his Battle Headquarters and *Kampfstaffel* as a four-star general directing the maneuver of four Axis army corps with approximately ten divisions. The following combat illustrates the fluid conditions of maneuver war in the desert, the leadership style of a successful commander, and the value of a strong headquarters battle detachment.

Moving northeast since 0600 through desert terrain crisscrossed by marching friendly and enemy combat forces and supply columns, the Battle Headquarters and *Kampfstaffel* ran into a deployed British artillery battery and antitank guns. Rommel ordered the handful of German tanks he had within the Battle Headquarters as a small *Panzerstaffel* (tank detachment) to attack the enemy force. Rommel did not call for assistance from some nearby German combat force but rather immediately attacked the enemy with his own personal resource. In this attack, the tanks of Battle Headquarters forced the British to withdraw but suffered heavy losses: The detachment of five German tanks lost one *Panzer III H* (21 tons, max 50mm armor, 50mm gun) through direct hit by *Pak*, one *Panzer IV Fl* (23 tons, max

50mm armor, short 75mm gun) through direct hit by artillery, and two *Panzer IIIs* to engine breakdown during the maneuvering. The *Kampfstaffel* held the ground at the end of the fight and a German *Panzerwerkstattkompanie* (tank repair company) aggressively operating in the middle of the combat retrieved the four tanks and successfully repaired them.[18]

Shortly after this encounter, Rommel with his personal *Begleitstaffel* (Escort Detachment) of the *Kampfstaffel* continued farther to the front to find 33rd Reconnaissance Battalion, *21.Pz.D.* At 1245, "it bumped into" three British cruiser tanks (15 tons, max 30mm armor, 40mm guns), which "shot up" the captured British radio vehicle accompanying Rommel. The main protection for Rommel in the escort echelon was a platoon of four captured British 40mm truck-mounted *Pak* which fought off the British tanks forcing their retirement. Fifteen minutes later, the *Kampfstaffel* closing up behind Rommel ran into a British artillery battery on the march similarly to the Germans. The *Kampfstaffel* attacked scattering the more surprised British unit capturing one gun and its towing tractor while destroying another gun and three trucks and taking 29 prisoners including two officers. This level of combat action around the Battle Headquarters of an army commander in a mobile desert engagement suggests a special dimension in desert warfare different from beach assault and insurgency warfare.

Combat around the *Kampfstaffel* intensified later in the day. At 1430, British aircraft made low level attacks on the column with machine guns and bombs and hit one 8-wheeled armored radio vehicle with a light bomb. Only two hours later, as the Battle Headquarters column halted to set up the Army Command Post, a strong British force attacked out of the north and northeast. The scene again represents elements of cultural shock for military forces inexperienced in maneuver war in permissive terrain. The battle headquarters of the four-star commander of a German field army was in the middle of a British attack aimed quite by chance at it—the British, of course, did not know that they were attacking the Headquarters of Panzer Army Africa. In the battle that followed, the *Kampfstaffel* using its *Flak* battery and 1st Company with their 88mm *Flak*, towed 50mm *Pak* and one 75mm self propelled *Pak*, knocked out nine British cruiser tanks, two armored reconnaissance vehicles and two trucks. The British attack forced the Battle Headquarters to change position a short distance to the west where it remained fixed for the next several days 3km south of Bir el Harmat and 12 km to the north northeast of Bir Hacheim, the southern bastion of the British defenses. The next day, 28 May 1942, illustrates the *Kampfstaffel* in defense of the temporarily static Battle Headquarters of the Panzer Army. The 3rd Battery, 43rd *Flak* Regiment set up a "linear" front of its weapons defending to the northeast. After intermittently firing at British armored reconnaissance vehicles, the *Flak* battery experienced a "sudden" tank attack from about 15-20 British cruiser tanks which had moved around the battery positions from the southeast and immediately attacked the surprised Germans. In an intense gunfire engagement that lasted 20 minutes, the mixed *Flak* battery destroyed 13 British cruiser tanks including three that had advanced to within 50m of the German 88mm and 20mm *Flak* firing positions protecting Rommel's Battle Headquarters. The fight was brutal. The *Flak* battery combat report noted laconically that the British "commander, another officer, and six other crew personnel were taken prisoners. The rest of the crews died in the tanks."[19] The *Kampfstaffel* lost one man badly wounded and expended 132 rounds of 88mm antitank and 60 rounds of 20mm antitank ammunition in repulsing the British surprise attack and achieving an annihilating tactical result. The *Flak* battery held the battlefield at the end of the fight and its brief note on British losses can be taken as accurate.

In the days following 28 June 1942, Rommel used the *Kampfstaffel* in two additional thought provoking ways. Located in the middle of strong British mobile units, he several times used *Kampfstaffel* units to support neighboring German mobile formations against anticipated. British attacks. The Free-French and British fortified box at Bir Hacheim held out tenaciously until 11 June 1942, and Rommel used 2nd Company of the *Kampfstaffel* with additional *Flak* and *Pak* actually to launch an attack against the fortress alongside of other strong German forces. Later on 19 and 20 June 1942, Rommel again inserted the *Kampfstaffel* into an attack this time against Tobruk. Rommel seems to have envisioned the formation not only as a strong security element for his exposed Battle Headquarters against both air and ground attack, but also as a unique maneuver element immediately available to him as a forward-oriented commander to take advantage of chance in battle.

Rommel introduced the *Stosslinie* (thrust line) into use in *7.Pz.D.* after he assumed command in February 1940 and used it during the French Campaign. The technique proved to be superior to the use of map coordinates or geographical features as means of designating locations on tactical and operational maps. After Rommel left 7th Panzer division, its next commander *Generalmajor* Hans Freiherr von Funck, used the thrust line throughout 1941 in the Russian Campaign. In North Africa, Rommel enforced the technique in Panzer Army Africa and the records give almost innumerable examples of its use.

Just what advantages did Rommel sense in placing a line—generally a single straight line but sometimes one with a single turning point in it—on a map, around which he would direct movement and demand the location of subordinate units? During the French Campaign (May-June 1940), he stated that the thrust line had the special advantage of security over designation by map coordinates or geographical features. An alert enemy with captured maps can detect map coordinates even when encoded and, of course, easily through radio listening in the event of encoded coordinates sent over the air. The Germans sometimes encoded numbers used with thrust lines, but generally they simply gave the numbers calculated for the designated locations. With thrust lines changed often, there was virtually no way that an enemy could reproduce it. Halfway through the Gazala battles, Rommel's Battle Headquarters ordered the 33rd Armored Reconnaissance Battalion to move to new positions west of Bir Hacheim to block any escape of the Free French Brigade in that unlikely direction. The Panzer Army order reads simply "To block Bir Hacheim to the west, 33rd Armored Reconnaissance Battalion is attached (to Panzer Army) and ordered to set itself in at 175.5 right 31.5... " No enemy seizing that document or hearing the order transmitted in the clear could locate that point.

Although the thrust line was uniquely secure, security was not the main reason for its creation by Rommel. He undoubtedly saw the *Stosslinie* as an ultra quick way of moving and locating forces and giving his own location in the clear without even the necessity to encode a single number. As employed by Rommel, the thrust line gave the Germans one of several edges that they displayed over their opponents in the desert. Map 3 illustrates the thrust line for the German offensive planned against Tobruk for late November 1941. The German sketch on the map shows one elegantly simple line heading into the British position around which all commanders and combat soldiers could concentrate their efforts.

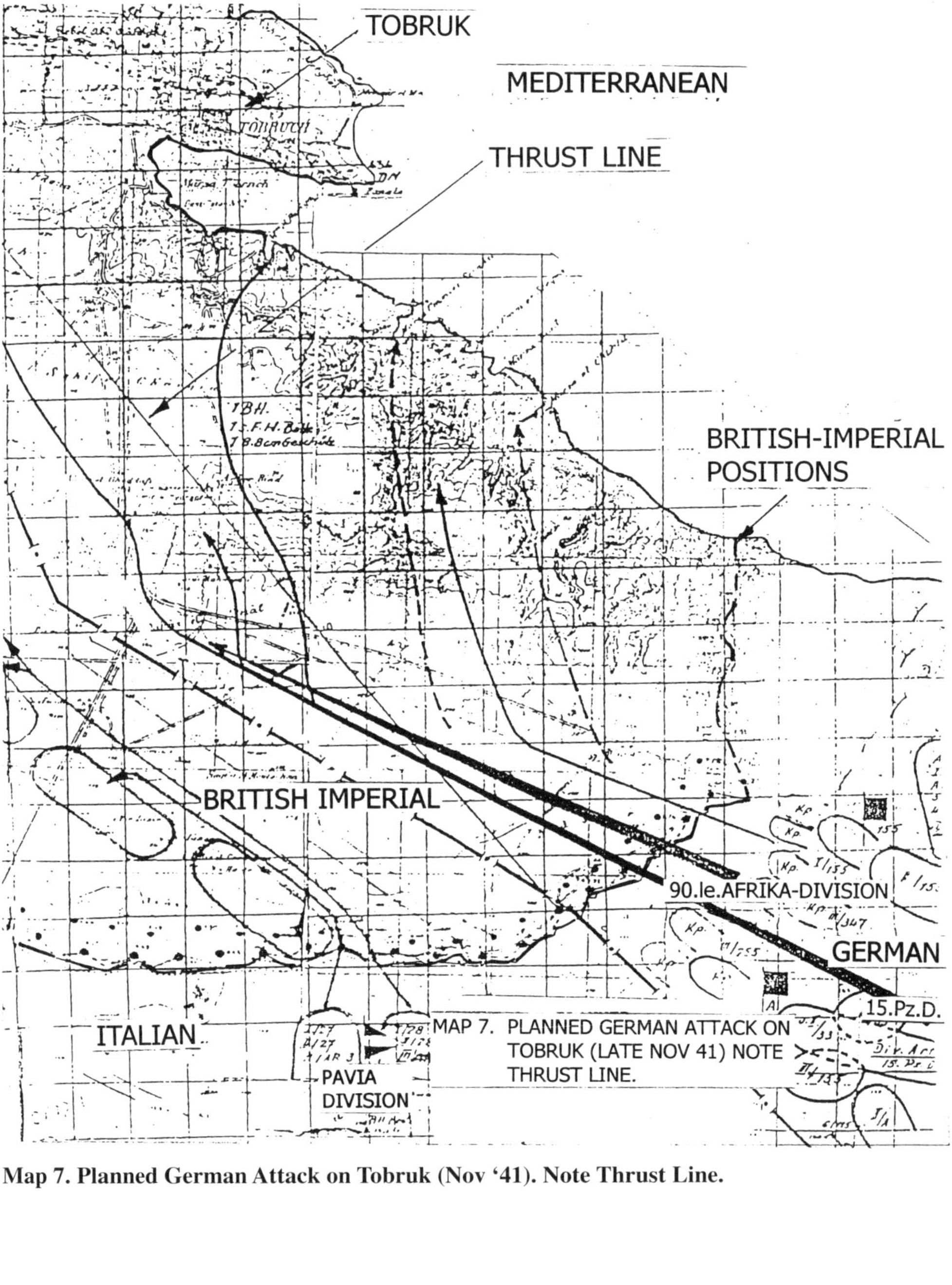

Map 7. Planned German Attack on Tobruk (Nov '41). Note Thrust Line.

9

The German Style in Mobile War

In preparing themselves for the next move in mobile combat, German military units of appropriate size, for example, divisions, instinctively organized themselves into *Marschgruppen* and *Kampfgruppen* (march groups and battle groups). In mobile campaigns like France (1940), Russia (1941), and North Africa (1941-42), German divisions rarely fought as divisions but rather maneuvered into contact with the enemy and fought as a tactical conglomerate of several self contained *Kampfgruppen*. In ongoing battle, the German divisions reorganized and reconcentrated daily for the next day's combat. This process of reorganization and reconcentration was omnipresent in mobile warfare. The German Army in World War II organized different *Kampfgruppen* and concentrated them nightly for the following day's battle more effectively than any other Army in the mobile stages of the various European campaigns.

The German Army commanders, staffs, and combat soldiers seemed to possess some special instinct in reforming *Kampfgruppen* and fighting in them. In analysis of European combat in World War II, British commentators have noted the superiority of the Germans fighting in what the British characterized as "ad hoc" units (i.e., "for the sake of this case alone"). The British based their estimate on studies later in the war with the Germans on the defensive. They stated that in disastrous defensive situations, the German Army threw together forces to overcome individual, one-time crises with special success. The British recognized this skill but associated it with remarkable expertise in improvisation that served the Germans well in the defensive stages of the war.

In the grand German offensives of the first part of World War II, however, and the mobile battles in North Africa in 1941-42, the Germans similarly and with the same technical and tactical skill, put together *Kampfgruppen*. On the defensive, the German Army put together *Kampfgruppen* largely to survive immediate, overwhelming pressures from a numerically and materially superior enemy. On the offensive, the Germans observed a different rationale. They formed them when attacking in mobile warfare to seize crucial ground and to defeat strong enemy concentrations. German commanders and staffs showed a flexibility in putting together the innumerable *Kampfgruppen* that characterized the German style in mobile war. German combat soldiers showed special qualities of "teamwork" in constantly shifting in and out of different *Kampfgruppen*. They also showed some difficult to define but nevertheless tangible esprit in attacks with these battle groups.

The *15.Pz.D.* reacted to the far-reaching British Crusader Offensive in a way that illustrates the *Kampfgruppe*-style of combat in war in the desert. The British began the Crusader operations on 18 November 1941 with the surprise move of the mass of the armor of the 8th Army around the southern end of the German fortifications anchored near Sidi Omar 45 km from Sollum in Egypt on the Mediterranean Sea. The massive British force moved during the night and projected itself far behind Panzer Army Africa. Rommel and his headquarters did not realize the full magnitude of the danger and on 19 November 1941 sent *21.Pz.D.* Division piecemeal (i.e., without its running mate, *15.Pz.D.*) to engage British forces that if seriously engaged together would probably have destroyed it. Fortunately for the active Germans, both sides groped in the dark for each other until the first big engagements of 22, 23 November 1941 in which the Germans fought concentrated.

The *15.Pz.D.* did not begin to make serious contact with the British mobile force that had driven close to the Tobruk fortress to link up with its British garrison until 21 November. With a successful linkup, the British envisioned destroying the surrounded *DAK* now lying to the east. Panzer Army Africa envisioned simultaneously hunting down and destroying the British *masse de manoeuvre* while maintaining the siege lines around Tobruk. Such intentions represent the mutually opposed wills of opponents in war that breed uncertainty and friction in battle and lead to the quick obsolescence of long written orders. At 2015 on 21 November, *DAK* ordered *15.Pz.D.* to concentrate south of Gambut for a coordinated blow with *21.Pz.D.* against the British mobile force lying to the south. In characteristic German style, *DAK* ordered the concentration and necessary regrouping at a time that required *15.Pz.D.* to reorganize and move during the middle of the night.

The *DAK* order not only necessitated a night movement of the entire division but also required disengagement from British forces up against it. The division set up a rear guard to hold its early evening position of 21 November until 0300 the next morning. The rear guard consisted of a strong detachment of 1st Battalion, 115th Motorized Infantry, artillery, and *Pak*. The division commander did not march *15.Pz.D.* to its new concentration area as a single force. He ordered the setting up of three *Marschgruppen* (march groups), that under the conditions of impending combat were in fact three large *Kampfgruppen*. *Generalmajor* (one star) Neumann-Silkow was able to move the division along two axes in three self standing maneuver elements. Between 2100-2400, 21 November 1941, at night and in contact with enemy forces, *21.Pz.D.* reorganized itself into the following groups:[20]

***Kampfgruppe* Lt Col Cramer (*Marschgruppe* A)**
Panzer Rgt 8
3rd Battery, *Flak* Rgt 33
1st Bn, Arty Rgt 33
Staff, Arty Rgt 33
3rd Bn, Arty Rgt 33
Div Staff
78th Armored Comm Bn

***Kampfgruppe* Col Menny (*Marschgruppe* B)**
Staff, 15th Moto Rifle Bde
115th Moto Rifle Rgt
33rd *Pak* Bn
33rd Armored Engr Bn
2nd Bn, Arty Rgt 33

***Kampfgruppe* Lt Col Geissler (*Marschgruppe* C)**
Staff, 200th Moto Rifle Rgt
15th Motorcycle Bn
2nd Machine Gun Bn

In spite of the fatigue of the combat and movement of 21 November, difficult road conditions, night movement, and British control of the air, Groups A and B moved out promptly at 2400 and Group C at 0100 22 November 1941. The rear guard followed at 0300. The *15.Pz.D.* was not a small unit. March Group A, for example, moved out with 144 battle and command tanks. The movement proceeded with little internal friction, and Neumann-Silkow radioed *DAK* at 0730 that the division had reached its concentration area.

During this same period of time, *21.Pz.D.* fought largely in self standing *Kampfgruppen* that were constantly reorganized. At 1210 on 19 November 1942, the division commander ordered the formation of *Kampfgruppe* Stephan in the face of the somewhat premature *DAK* order to seek out and destroy the British mobile force between Tobruk and the Egyptian border and now lying south and west of *DAK*. The *Kampfgruppe* was typical of the stronger German battle groups and consisted of the fo1lowing:[21]

***Kampfgruppe Stephan* (After 1210 19 Nov 41)**

8th Panzer Rgt (that moment w/124 operational tanks)
2nd Bn, Arty Rgt 33 (approx 12 105mm howitzers)
3rd Battery, *Flak* Rgt 18 (mixed, 2 20mm and 4 88mm guns)

Generalmajor Johannes von Ravenstein, the division commander, directed the *Kampfgruppe* to isolate and destroy a British motorized force located by 3rd Panzer Reconnaissance Battalion and estimated initially to hold approximately 200 *tanks* and numerous other vehicles and guns. *Oberst* (Colonel) Stephan moved south with his *Kampfgruppe* at 1420 and soon located the British force now estimated at 130 tanks and numerous other armored vehicles, guns, and trucks. In a fight lasting about two hours until the approach of darkness, *Oberst* Stephan engaged the powerful British force and threw it back to the southeast toward the Egyptian border. The *Kampfgruppe* claimed 21 British-held American tanks as destroyed and remaining on the battlefield mostly by the guns of the attached 3rd *Flak* Battery. German records show the following friendly losses:[22]

***Kampfqruppe Stephan Engagement* (Afternoon 19 Nov 41)**

Tanks: Catastrophic Kill by Gunfire - 2 *Panzer III.*
Tank: Damaged, Repairable but lying in enemy country -1 *Panzer II.*
Tanks: Damaged, Repairable, Retrieved by Panzer Maintenance Company off battlefield but lost to 15th Panzer Division by evacuation rearward - *4 Panzer III*
Tanks: Mechanical Breakdown -*1 Panzer III*

The Germans put together *Kampfgruppe* Stephan in the brief period from 1210-1430 with movement to combat beginning at the latter time. In spite of this short notice, the group fought a coordinated action with the *Flak* maneuvering effectively enough with the German tanks to get credit for knocking out most of the British tanks. The Germans also achieved a favorable exchange ratio—8 tanks damaged in various degrees compared with 21 permanently lost by the British—a circumstance supporting a view of some special German tactical efficiency in the battle.

The Germans put together these battle groups in innumerable shapes and forms. Later in the campaign, in March 1942, *DAK* ordered *21.Pz.D.* to conduct a reconnaissance in force designed to clear ground in front of it in order to move the *DAK* and Italian XXth Motorized Corps into more favorable positions for the eventual offensive at Gazala. The new division commander at that time, *Generalmajor* Georg von Bismarck, decided to set up *Kampfgruppe* Bismarck under his personal leadership to conduct the foray.[23] Bismarck received the order on 13 March 1942 with the requirement to move on the morning of 16 March. To accomplish the mission he put together a medium-sized *Kampfgruppe* that concentrated itself for the foray by 2000 15 March. He built the force for an advance across open desert against an enemy with strong armored reconnaissance forces and the danger of air attack. The *Kampfgruppe* looked suspiciously like a *Panzer* division in microcosm. Figure 2[24] shows a force with just about anything necessary for combat but with special emphasis in the open desert on weapons rather than men, e.g., the force held only one platoon of motorized infantry. The Figure also shows a somewhat awkward organization with Bismarck as a senior commander with only one modest-sized maneuver force. Bismarck prob-

Kampfgruppe Leadership Element

Cmdr, 21st Panzer Div (*Generalmajor* G. von Bismarck)
Part of Div Command
Part of 2d Co, 200th Panzer Comm Bn
Three Recon Troops, 33d Panzer Recon Bn
Div Recon Platoon

Kampfgruppe Troop Element

Cmdr, IId Bn, 104th Motorized Inf Rgt and Staff
One Panzer Co (Reinf), 5th Panzer Rgt
One Battery, 155th Arty Rgt (105mm Howitzers)
One *Pak* Co (minus one plt), 39th Panzer AT Bn*
One Motorized Inf Plt, 104th Motorized Inf Rgt
One Pioneer Plt. 200th Panzer Pioneer Bn
One *Fla* Plt, 617th *Fla* Bn**
Part of Supply Troops, 21st Panzer Div

*_Pak_ or *Panzerabwehrkanone* or antitank gun.
**_Fla_ or "Army antiaircraft cannon" in contradistinction to *Flak* or "Air Force antiaircraft cannon."

Figure 7. _Kampfgruppe_ Bismarck (15, 16 Mar '42)

ably envisioned the relatively strong reconnaissance assets in the leadership detachment as another maneuver element.

It is difficult to overemphasize the German use of night time to regroup into new *Kampfgruppen* for the next day's mission and to be on the move into combat by *Morgengrauen* (break of day) – a term used by the Germans in their orders over and over again to indicate the time at which the next offensive maneuver would begin. After a day of considerable movement and moderate combat on 26 November 1942 in the area behind the Sollum front, *15.Pz.D.* went through the following evolution that illustrates German style in the middle of a big operation. In night rest positions finally by midnight on 26 November, the division received the order from Rommel himself at Panzer Group to attack the British behind the Sollum front from the rear. Shortly after the midnight hour, in an example of the flexibility demanded in mobile war, the division received a new order to move in the opposite direction directly toward Tobruk to retrieve the situation, a move which demanded the reorganization of the division during darkness and advance toward the enemy before daybreak. In full darkness, the division reorganized itself into four *Kampfgruppen* with missions to move as follows to the desert road leading west to Sidi Azeiz and Tobruk and then along it toward the enemy:[25]

> ***Kampfgruppe* |1|** - 33rd Armored Engineer Bn with one company 33rd Antitank Bn, and followed by IIIrd Bn, 33rd Artillery Rgt. Task: Reach the road and proceed west at 0430.
>
> ***Kampfgruppe* |2|** - 2nd Machine Gun Bn with one platoon 33rd Antitank Bn. Task: Reach the road and proceed west at 0440.
>
> ***Kampfgruppe* |3|** - 8th Panzer Rgt with 1st Battery, 33rd *Flak* Regiment, one platoon, 33rd Antitank Bn, with staff 33rd Antitank Bn, and Div staff. Task: Reach the road and proceed west at 0445.
>
> ***Kampfgruppe* |4|** - 115th Motorized Infantry Rgt, with one platoon, 33rd Antitank Bn, and IId Bn, 33rd Artillery Rgt organized in among the infantry battalions. Task: Reach the road and proceed west at 0500.

In spite of interference from march columns of *21.Pz.D.* also moving at night in the same area, the division reached the road on schedule. Once the division was on the road, the division commander moved 8th Panzer Regiment to the front to lead the march west. By shortly after the break of day, the first element of tanks lay on the road just east of Sidi Azeiz and heading into it. At that moment, approximately 0600 27 November, it received artillery fire from the area around the village.

The Germans reorganized and moved at night with a style and tempo of action that led to shattering tactical victories during the war. On the move, alert, and advancing with an urgent, distant mission, the panzer regiment immediately deployed and attacked supported by a battery of four 105mm howitzers that had been moving in column with it. The division commander recognized the British force as a "strong enemy" and ordered all of the division's artillery forward and into action to support the panzers. The heavy artillery battalion (150mm howitzers and 100mm field guns) was farthest forward and added its fire to that of the medium battery at short range of about 3,000-4,000m. The British force was immediately smothered by German artillery fire which continued to be reinforced. Supported by this fire and the advance of the division pioneer battalion, the tanks in a brief 15-minute fire fight broke into the village area and forced the surrender of the headquarters of 5th New Zealand Brigade and other units encamped around it taking 800 prisoners. The German artillery regiment commander remarked that the battle ended before he could get the artillery into action out of the rear *Kampfgruppe* in the division column. The Germans excelled in surprise encounters like this one in World War II.

As the circumstances above show, the Germans excelled because of the sense of urgency and tempo in their operations. As the British slept in their laager around Sidi Azeiz, the Germans reorganized and moved through the desert in the night. As the Germans advanced out of the edge of darkness onto Sidi Azeiz they moved to the urgent drum beat of yet another offensive thrust that they had worked through the hours of darkness to generate. The special energy reflected in continuous operation through night and into day maintained the initiative for the Germans and gave them the edge in surprise encounters characteristic of mobile war.

In command of *7.Pz.D.* in France (1940), Rommel led the division from the front often placing himself physically in the leading column in a division advance. In command of Panzer Army Africa in 1941-42[26] Rommel led with the same style during similar periods of high intensity mobile war. During the considerable periods of quiet in the ground campaign, he visited subordinate commanders or frontal positions of the combat troops on almost a daily basis.[27] Other German mobile force commanders similarly led from the front during the French Campaign and most of Rommel's subordinate commanders in Libya affected the same style. The German Army in the development of its mobile forces encouraged the commanders to lead from as far forward as possible. It is difficult to estimate the balance between the influence of the German Army in general and Rommel in particular on the minds of the German commanders in North Africa. Suffice it to say, that German commanders led from the front in a style encouraged by the Army and with the powerful additional stimulus of the example set by the commander in chief himself in North Africa.

Positioned forward in the battle itself, the commander of an attacking force has the best opportunity through his direct impressions of the fighting to clear up uncertainty. Located in the same position, he has similar opportunity to master chance surprise encounter and other unexpected fire and maneuver on the part of the enemy. With the continuous regrouping and movement at night, the German commander also tended to keep the initiative on the battlefield. In possession of the initiative in a battle, he established the offensive *Schwerpunkt* in the fight and led the *Schwerpunkt* formation. Placed forward in the battle, the commander would have impressions necessarily limited to the area around him, but those impressions would be from the center of the battle and in touch with reality.

Earlier in the Crusader battles, for example, 8th Panzer Regiment, 15.Pz.D., had greater success in a meeting engagement than that related above at Sidi Azeiz. Success was based on the same factors plus the German commander being located literally at the front of the unit. On 22 November 1941, in full darkness at 1900,[28] the panzer regiment received the mission to move out immediately to the northwest to seize ground lying 14km from Sidi Rezegh. After moving 4km through the night, the 1st Battalion, 8th Panzer Regiment ran into a tightly bunched concentration of vehicles. At 10m distance, the panzer battalion commander moving in the lead vehicle of his unit recognized the equipment as British. He continued to drive straight through the British laager and while doing so radioed his following 1st Company to move to the left and the 2nd Company to the right in and among the British vehicles. The battalion commander then ordered the headlights on the German tanks to be turned on and the tank commanders to use the machine pistols in the vehicles on foot to force the surrender of the surprised British tank crews in the laager. Not a single shot was fired until one British tank moved to get away and was shot up in flames by the German tank crews remaining in their tanks. A British officer managed to set one more tank on fire furnishing additional light for the Germans to take more prisoners. The panzer battalion had captured the commander of the British 4th Tank Brigade, 17 officers, 150 men, 36 tanks and numerous other weapons and pieces of equipment.[29]

In a directive circulated to his subordinate commanders during the deployment to Libya early in 1941, the commander of *15.Pz.D.* pointed out the following about the "location of the leader:"[30]

"All leaders must

(a) see for themselves,
(b) have a lead so far to the front of their troops that they are in a position to provide the troops with orders without them having to stop (a command friendly orders style). The location of the leader as far forward as possible (the leader of the point company behind the point, the leader of the rear guard behind the most advanced company, etc.). Special protection most necessary for the leader!"

In Panzer Army Africa, German commanders operated largely in accordance with the spirit expressed in these words. Rommel personally exemplified the style and his headquarters *Kampfstaffel* mirrored the practical necessity to protect him and provide an additional maneuver element. German division commanders accompanied their advanced units on the march and in the attack. Typically, for example, in his order for the movement of *21.Pz.D.* closer to Bir Hacheim for impending Operation Venezia, Bismarck noted in the last paragraph of the movement order: "I ride alongside of the commander of the 5th Panzer Regiment (the lead element). My Operations Detachment and Quartermaster behind the panzer regiment."[31]

In combat, the division commander stood in the same advanced position. At 1620 23 November 1942, the commander, *15.Pz.D.*, stood physically in the middle of the combat of the 8th Panzer Regiment near Sidi Rezegh on the verge of the substantial German victory that day. The war diary of the division noted that "the division commander standing in the most advanced line where it is always necessary to be, recognized an enemy attack coming in on the left flank of the division. Enemy tanks including heavily armored Mark II tanks began an attack. The division commander personally snatched up an 88mm *Flak* and a heavy field howitzer (150mm) and directed the location of the firing position. Under the fire direction of Captain Fromm, commander, 1st Battery, 18th *Flak* Regiment, the attack was repulsed."[32] This account is a little classic. The division commander in the middle of the combat with his panzer regiment, personally detected a strong enemy attack with tanks impervious to German tank and *Pak* fire. Cutting through any uncertainty about what was happening by his presence in the path of the enemy attack, the division commander also mastered chance disaster in the presence of the Mark II tanks by personally finding and siting two weapons heavy enough to break up the attack. This same division commander, *Generalmajor* Neumann-Silkow, would be wounded by shell fragments in an advanced position next to his armored command vehicle on 7 December 1941 and die of his wounds two days later.

Photo 6. A 15th Panzer Division battle group in Libya in the winter of 1941. In foreground two Panzer III main battle tanks followed by command car, trucks, and 88 mm *Flak* facing forward towed by a large three-quarter tracked vehicle. This German anti-aircraft cannon was capable of direct fire with its optical sights against ground targets while still on the wheels of its four-wheeled trailer. With these capabilities it was an impressive weapon for use in the tank escort role to counterbalance British numerical superiority in tanks (Bundesarchiv Bestand).

10

The German Conduct of Maneuver War in the Desert

Commentators often break down the conduct of war by military leaders into strategy, operations, and tactics. From such a view, strategy stands as a high level, cerebral art that defines the goals of war in theaters of military operations and is susceptible to analysis in terms of principle or rule. In a war, the strategic goals can be gained only by the armed violence associated with the military operation and the battles comprising it. Military operations and the inclusive battles are less susceptible to control in terms of principle and rule. Lying in the realm of armed combat, they march to the drumbeat of the climate of the armed violence of war. In such a scheme, the military operation comprises the battles strung together in given space and time to achieve a set of strategic goals. Operational art becomes the art of stringing together those battles to achieve those goals. Battles—armed encounters, engagements, raids, and strikes—are the realm of tactics. In the conventional arrangement of strategy, operations, and tactics, the latter stands out as the art of fighting battles.

In North Africa in 1941-42, Rommel and the staff of Panzer Army Africa practiced operational art with a style that can be characterized by the words quick tempo, decisive objective, and continuous movement. In contrast, for example, with Russian operational art today in which the Russians use a systematic approach and various recipes involving correlation of forces for success, the Germans recognized the uniqueness and danger in every operation and practiced a style characterized by the observation of one German general[33] that in danger there is always opportunity. If Russians and others attempt today to take uncertainty and chance out of the conduct of the military operation by systematic, quantifiable, rule-book addressal to every contingency, the Germans overcame the same factors by making quicker decisions from more advanced positions seeking opportunity in the province of chance and taking advantage of it. The Germans were painstaking and thorough in the putting together of their operations when in possession of the initiative on the offensive. The Germans systematically (i.e., always) employed *Planspielen* or command conferences in which they calculated the difficulties of an anticipated operation but never confused the game with the reality of the violence and uncertainty of war.

During the time covered by this study, Rommel and his staff orchestrated their first operation in the period 18 November - 7 December 1941 as a reaction to the British Crusader Offensive. This German "operation" was not planned by Rommel and his staff, but rather it was forced on Panzer Army Africa by the British. Under surprise attack by an enemy numerically superior on the ground and in the air, Rommel had the clear strategic goal to avoid the destruction of his own army and thereby prevent the seizure of Libya and the ending of the war in North Africa. Rommel and his staff faced the sudden prospects of linking together several battles—one around Tobruk, another farther east on the frontier defenses, and the largest of all among the opposing mobile forces in the area between the siege lines of Tobruk and the defenses on the frontier between Sollum and Sidi Omar. Just what style of operations did the Germans reveal in coordinating these battles in the desert against a superior enemy?

First of all, for two days, 18, 19 November 1941, Rommel and his staff mistook the purpose of the strong British reconnaissance forces that had driven close to the Tobruk siege lines by the evening of the latter day. Rommel optimistically dismissed the activity as a reconnaissance to clarify German intentions relative to the impending German attack on Tobruk. The Panzer Army staff estimated the situation as late as the evening of 19 November as one in which the British were attempting to disrupt the German preparations. Rommel and his staff did not accurately gauge the situation until the afternoon of 20 November when it became "apparent that the enemy had not only set out on a relief thrust to Tobruk but on a great general offensive."[34] In effect, the German command did not react to the actual great offensive of the enemy until the evening of the third day. Rommel showed considerable energy during this period, however, approving the *DAK* order to commit the 21st Panzer Division alone on 19 November against the vastly underestimated British mobile force. Fortunately for the Germans, 21st Panzer Division did not contact the main strength of the British tank forces. The next day, 20 November, the *DAK* finally concentrated 15th and 21st Panzer Divisions. The same day, Rommel realized the presence of a grand British offense and began the operation from the German side.

During the first several days, 18-20 November 1941, of the British advance, the Germans groped for a British mobile force of uncertain dimensions. The Germans groped in open, level desert for the British moving with a mobile force that had a pool of approximately 500 cruiser-type tanks and 250 armed reconnaissance vehicles available for the advance. It is a notable point that the British motorized forces in desert terrain rather than being vulnerable to detection were extremely difficult for the Germans to find. Panzer Army command had three Panzer reconnaissance battalions under its direct operational control, elements of two panzer divisions, and other forces including aerial reconnaissance assets airborne in spite of substantial British air control and skilled radio intercept units all dedicated to finding the British but none having decisive success.

Rommel and his staff began to practice operational art on 21 November 1941 by stringing together three battles forced on them by the British attack. Panzer Army Command sent out orders daily from this point on to the two static battles developing around Tobruk and Sollum. The orders came out in a consistent, firm, succinct pattern, for example, on the evening of 21 November: "XXth Army Corps hold Tobruk front," just as simple as that.

Rommel knew that a collapse of his predominately Italian forces either at Tobruk or around Sollum would jeopardize full success in the unsolicited operation developing around him. Well aware of the danger surrounding him by 21 November, Rommel, as his actions show over the course of the operation, sensed that the opportunity offered itself to defeat the British field army in fluid maneuver war. In effect, Rommel began by 21 November to link together the battles into a German operation that had the strategic goal to defeat the British mobile force (i.e., the tank formations) and drive into Egypt with the possibility to collapse the British in North Africa.

After directing hard fighting on the morning of 22 November 1941 in the Tobruk battle that kept the British contained in the fortress, Rommel made the bold decision to drive the *DAK* concentrically into the main concentration of British armor in North Africa now lying southeast of Tobruk. In the resulting maneuver that took place around Sidi Rezegh, the *DAK* and the Italian XXth Motorized Corps blocking from the southwest inflicted heavy losses on the British mobile force. On the evening of 22 November 1942, pacing his whole operation to the maneuver battle with the British mobile force, Rommel ordered the *DAK* to continue the attack around Sidi Rezegh with the specific intention to encircle the armored forces and destroy them. On 23 November, the two German panzer divisions continued to show tactical superiority over the opposing British, and won another great victory inflicting heavy losses on the British armor and forcing the intact elements to the southeast away from Tobruk. At the same moment the Italo-German force outside of Tobruk had successfully fought its battle to contain the British, and the Italo-German force between Sollum and Sidi Omar although hard pressed in its battle but still successfully blocked any British advance along the sea westward to Tobruk. Rommel believed in the evening of 23 November 1942 that he had won the operation. He believed he had done so through his success in the maneuver battle against the British armor and stabilization of the fronts in the two defensive battles.

Studies on German battle fighting on the offensive in World War II emphasize maneuver as the key element in German success. Studies of a bold, successful commander such as Rommel in North Africa tend to describe his genius also in terms of maneuver particularly in open, level desert. This study detected a special German skill in tactical maneuver in agreement with the conventional wisdom. As the author continued to examine the records, he also came across an unmistakable, perhaps unique, German preoccupation with weapons in North Africa. He had already observed in earlier study of the offensive battles of a panzer division in France (1940) and Russia (1941) a similar special emphasis on weapons. In North Africa in 1941 and 1942, however, the German forces showed a sensitivity to the numbers and qualities of their own weapons that was exaggerated beyond that shown on the European continent. The reason for this is probably that in the open desert, the Germans witnessed that the gun tended to dominate the man and to protect against the tank. In a return to past observations now largely disappeared from the literature, the author could not help but notice the similarity between war at sea where weapon and machine dominate man, and war in the desert in similar open, trafficable "terrain" where armored forces and associated guns dominate the rifleman.

The Germans identified the tank as the key weapon and the panzer division as the key war fighting organization in North Africa. In its engagement report on the Crusader battles from 18 November - 7 December 1941, 5th Panzer Regiment, *21.Pz.D.*, gave daily accounts of each tank lost and the strength in tanks ready for insertion in battle (*Einsatzbereit*). On 17 November, for example, 5th Panzer Regiment had ready for action the following tanks representing the entire strength of *21.Pz.D.*:[35]

5th Panzer Rgt, 21st Panzer Div (17 Nov 41)

a. Panzer II	35	
b. Panzer III	68	
c. Panzer IV	17	A total of 124 recon, battle,
d. Panzer III (Bef.)*	4	and command tanks

**Bef.* or *Befehlswagen* (Command Vehicle).

On 17 November 1941, the German Command—the commanders and staff of the Panzer Army, *DAK,* and the 21st Panzer Division—based its estimates of the "striking power" of *21.Pz.D.* almost exclusively on the 124 tanks held by 5th Panzer Regiment. The same division could defend itself effectively in the open without a single tank through use of its complement of artillery, *Pak* and *Flak* and also while fighting from field fortifications. To be a factor of significance in mobile war, however, *21.Pz.D.* required tanks. The Germans had invented the first modern combined arms team in their panzer divisions of 1935 and were dedicated to the concept notably in terms of the ad hoc *Kampfgruppen* that they put together so often in World War II. Tanks, in fact, even in the open desert, could not be expected to advance effectively against opposing forces with strong artillery, *Pak*, and pioneer assets without combined arms tactics. Knowing all of this, the Germans also knew that the Panzer Army could not conduct mobile warfare without the tank and that the capability of the army to maneuver and advance in North Africa could be measured both tactically and technically in terms of the number of tanks *Einsatzbereit* (ready for insertion in battle).

Rommel, for example, conducted the great multi-battle operation of 18 November - 7 December 1941, based largely on the maneuver of *DAK* and its two panzer divisions. The two panzer divisions functioned, in turn, according to the number of tanks available for maneuver by skilled commanders and combat by skilled crews in combination with other arms. The acute German sensitivity to the importance of the tank shows in the daily accounting of the standing in tanks. The Germans recorded three bits of information about their tanks that allowed Rommel and Panzer Group Staff to gauge both the tactical and operational possibilities of the Crusader situation. In *21.Pz.D.* the Germans painstakingly identified the numbers of tanks totally lost, the numbers of tanks not ready for action but under repair and in process of being returned to service, and the number of tanks at any point in time ready for action (*Einsatzbereit*).

The German situation in tanks was the most decisive measure of German exertion in the Crusader fighting. The situation allows the reader as well as it allowed Rommel and his commanders and staff in 1941 to gauge the course of the fighting and to relate the tactical situation with the remaining operational possibilities at any point in time. Beginning with 124 tanks on 17 November 1941, *21.Pz.D.* lost tanks as follows from 18-23 November

1941, the period in which the German mobile force groped for the British and at the end of which it fought a great tank battle that Rommel believed gave him victory in the operation:

21st Panzer Division

Tanks Totally Lost (accumulated 18—23 Nov 41) (catastrophically destroyed or immobilized and lying in enemy territory)	42
Tanks in Repair (situation 2200 23 Nov 41) (complex picture with approx half due for return from 1-48 hours later)	50
Tanks Combat Ready (situation 2200 23 Nov 41)	*32*
Tanks Total	124

As a result of the tank battles of 22, 23 November 1941, *21.Pz.D.* stood on the evening of the latter day with only 32 tanks ready for combat on 24 November. The German situation was even more disastrous than it appears. Of the 32 remaining tanks, 5th Panzer Regiment could use only 18 in tank versus tank combat because 11 of the operating vehicles were lightly armored, 10-ton *Panzer II* tanks armed with 20mm cannons and three additional vehicles were command tanks with dummy wooden gun barrels and armed only with two machine guns. Early on the morning of 24 November 1942, Rommel nevertheless became convinced that he had defeated the British mobile force. As a result he faced the grand operational problem of how to transform the victory in the great maneuver battle into victory in the operation forced on him by the British offensive. In a move unequaled in boldness by any army-level commander in World War II, Rommel determined to thrust to the Egyptian border with the two German panzer divisions under his personal command. With only 32 tanks in *21.Pz.D.* and 65 tanks in *15.Pz.D.* and prospects of rapidly dwindling numbers as he outstripped his overburdened repair companies, Rommel had little possibility of finishing off the British mobile force and destroying the British field army in Libya.

On 26 November 1941, after a fruitless three days of march, countermarch, and moderate combat south of Sollum along the Egyptian frontier, Rommel under the prompting of the Panzer Group staff directed the two panzer divisions back to Sidi Rezegh. The staff made it clear to Rommel that the Tobruk battle had turned critically to the disadvantage of the Germans and the nearly beaten British mobile force had begun to recover southeast of Tobruk in the open desert. On the morning of 27 November 1941, back in the area of the earlier great mobile battle, Rommel found himself in possession of an army whose striking power lay in 30 combat ready tanks of the returning *21.Pz.D.* and 54 tanks of *15.Pz.D.* From 27 November - 7 December 1941, Rommel directed numerous engagements and encounters in the closely linked battle southeast of Tobruk and the great battle with the recovered British mobile force in the desert. As the tank numbers indicate, Rommel did not have the strength in tanks to bring the German operation to a successful conclusion by a second more decisive defeat of the British armor. When Rommel began to withdraw on 7 December 1941 toward El Agheila 500 miles away, *21.Pz.D.* reported 20 tanks ready for combat and *15.Pz.D.* 30 tanks. Panzer Army Africa specifically held the following tanks on that day ready for combat:[36]

Panzer Group Africa (7 Dec 41) Combat Ready Tanks

a. Panzer II .... 10 (Recon Tanks)
b. Panzer III 28
c. Panzer IV 8
d. Panzer III (Bef.) .... 4 (Command Tanks)
Total 50*
*A total of only 36 battle tanks.

With only 36 German battle tanks remaining, Rommel and Panzer Group Africa had no realistic chance of operational victory in Eastern Libya. Rommel now sought the operational goal of successful withdrawal of his shattered Italo-German force based on rear guard battles strung along from Tobruk all the way to El Agheila. Rommel would employ rear guard *Kampfgruppen* built around small tank detachments combined with strong *Flak* and *Pak* elements to prevent the British from breaking directly through his forces or outflanking them to the south out of the open desert. He had enough tanks remaining after 7 December 1941 to conduct this operation but little more.

Rommel and Panzer Army Africa faced heavy odds in open desert terrain in 1941-42. The British field army, the famed 8th Army, drastically outnumbered the German forces in the Italo-German Panzer Army in almost every weapon. British numerical superiority included greater numbers of tanks, antitank guns, field artillery pieces, antiaircraft guns, and combat aircraft including fighters, low-level attack aircraft, and medium bombers. The British field army significantly outnumbered the *combined* Italo-German forces in the same categories of weapons. As concerns the question of technology and specifically weapons performance characteristics, the British field army held weapons that were similar in performance to those of the Germans and superior to those of the Italians. Argument continues to rage on the question of technology, but the generalization above holds even in the face of the complex technological picture. The British complain that their 40mm tank cannon was smaller that the German 50mm and 75mm tank cannon with implied technical superiority for the Germans. The British had designed, however, a smaller cannon that was so good technologically that it matched the armor penetration capabilities of the larger German tank cannons. Most of the technological analyses end similarly in closely balanced characteristics such as those between the British and German tank cannons.

Rommel and the German elements in Panzer Army Africa faced an uncomfortable situation in which they were drastically outnumbered and held no counterbalancing advantage in technology. The Italian elements in the Panzer Army reduced the numerical inferiority but added an element of technological inferiority that reduced the effect. In the fighting during the period covered by this study, the two German divisions of the *DAK* would do the bulk of the fighting in both the great defensive battles of Crusader (November - December 1941) and the offensive operation of Venezia (May-June 42) because of their superior mobility. The following listing illustrates the adverse balance for the Panzer Army and the heavier responsibilities of the *DAK* in the mobile battles:[37]

Adverse Balance for Germans 18 Nov 41, Crusader Battles

	Weapon	**German**	**Italian**	**British**
a.	Tanks	260	154	648
b.	Pz Recon*	33	24	646
c.	*Pak*	94	195	312
d.	*Flak*	128	112	300

*Armored Reconnaissance Vehicles.

The listing shows that the Italians, who had approximately three times as many men as the Germans in North Africa, would not be able to do a proportionate share of the armored maneuver warfare that would dominate the theater. The Germans would conduct maneuver war significantly to the exclusion of the Italians based on the relatively small numbers and weak performance characteristics of the Italian armor and other weapons of the Italian XXth Motorized Corps that was formed a week before the British Crusader Offensive. Based on this analysis, the author suggests an operational picture in North Africa in which a German armored force with 299 tanks and armored reconnaissance vehicles assisted by a smaller, tactically and technically deficient coalition force, faced a British armored force of approximately 1,112 technically similar vehicles. Rommel and the German forces of the Italo-German field army had faced similar adverse numerical situations from the beginning of their deployment to North Africa. The adversity was compounded by British air superiority in open, level desert. The Germans became preoccupied with *Flak* from the beginning of the campaign in North Africa to redress this situation.

As early as April 1941, Rommel sited a handful of the 88mm *Flak* in the German Africa Corps[38] in static strong points between Sollum and Sidi Omar on the Egyptian frontier. With his front line instincts and imagination, Rommel sensed the value of the cannon as a heavy antitank weapon (*Pak*). The British at this time also had an infantry support tank, the "Matilda" Mark II, a relatively heavy tank at 26 tons with 80mm of armor liberally distributed over the fronts and sides of the hull and turret. The Germans had no *Pak* in the middle of 1941 that could penetrate the 80mm armor on this tank. By the beginning of the Crusader Offensive, the Germans had placed 23 of the total of 35 88mm *Flak* in North Africa with the Italo-German forces on the Sollum front. By the same time, the Germans realized that the gun system with its three-quarter tracked towing vehicle and four-wheel gun carrier and trailer from which it could be fired, was mobile enough to accompany the tank formations in battle. During the Crusader battles, the Germans would employ the 88mm *Flak* in support of numerous *Kampfgruppen* in what the Germans called the *Panzerbegleit*, or tank escort, role.

In the *Flak* regiments of the day, the Germans had both 88mm and 20mm guns organized into batteries. In combat in the desert, the Germans used the 88m *Flak* batteries predominately in the antitank role. The 20mm *Flak* batteries in contrast provided most of the *Flak* air defense for the German mobile divisions - specifically *15.Pz.D.* and 90th Light Africa Division during the period. The Germans also had mixed batteries of 88 and 20mm *Flak* which they used predominately as antitank units. The Germans found quickly by experience that the 20mm guns were nimble weapons systems with high rates of fire that proved to be effective against the low-level air attacks that were most dangerous to the mobile formations. The Germans also found that the 20mm *Flak* firing the armor-piercing round was capable of knocking out any of the British armored reconnaissance vehicles and other similar light armored vehicles. The 20mm *Flak* firing the high explosive round also proved to be extremely effective against trucks and similar unarmored vehicles and also against infantry. The Germans, as a result, commonly employed the 20mm *Flak* batteries to screen and fight off British reconnaissance units and similar light forces.

Beginning in 1930, the Germans developed the 88mm *Flak* used by the Germans in World War II and thoughtfully put together a family of ammunition and fuzes that permitted the *Flak* to fire effectively against air, ground, and heavy ground armored targets. As a result, the German *Flak* batteries in North Africa could fire two types of projectiles and fuzes against tanks, and several additional types of high explosive projectiles and fuzes against ground and air targets. The Germans used high explosive projectiles with instantaneous and delay nose fuzes and clockwork nose fuzes for various effects against ground targets. They used exclusively clockwork fuzes with 88mm high explosive projectiles against aircraft. The Germans could shift direct fire among different targets immediately simply by loading the appropriate ammunition and using the appropriate sights. The gun could also be fired from its four-wheel trailer-carrier. Towed by an 8-ton, three-quarter tracked vehicle, and organized generally into 4-gun batteries, the 88 mm *Flak* had the off-road mobility in desert terrain to move with the German tank regiments and support them with direct fire.

By 1942, the Germans had a succinct set of guiding principles for the insertion in battle of the heavy 88mm *Flak* batteries. Headquarters, *DAK*, advised on 22 May 1942 that German forces should consider inserting the heavy batteries as antiaircraft units, tank escort units, or ground firing units, the latter especially for shooting at ranges between 8-14km. The German directive noted the flexibility of the batteries in shifting targets and missions commenting specifically that an 88mm *Flak* battery set up to fire at air targets could shift "immediately" to fire against armored and ground targets.[39] HQ, *DAK* continued in characteristic German-style to state that the heavy *Flak* batteries should be inserted in combat together notwithstanding the target—air, armored, or ground. The directive warned that the temptation must be resisted to provide single 88mm *Flak* for the hard fighting and hard begging motorized infantry units because the guns would end up as targets too far forward and too big to escape losses from enemy infantry. The directive continued that the heavy *Flak* batteries did not have the mobility necessary to keep up with the reconnaissance battalions and should be used only sparingly with them. The directive ends on the tantalizing generality that "the insertion of the 88mm tank escort battery succeeds as a rule on a wing of the tank force by achieving flanking fire against the enemy."[40]

With their mobile divisions, the Germans had considerable success with the self-propelled 20mm *Fla* (Army designation for *Flak*) companies of the army. Army columns were difficult to protect with truck towed 20mm *Flak* against low level air attack because the guns took time to get into a firing mode. In stationary positions, either towed or self-propelled 20mm *Flak* could fire immediately against air attack. The Germans found that the light *Flak* batteries (and army companies) were effective against the British armored reconnaissance vehicles at ranges below 800m. The Germans as a doctrinal procedure in North Africa had the towed 20mm *Flak* go into firing positions during the halt of mobile columns.

With forces on the move in combat, the Germans placed the guns of the light *Flak* battery on the outside of the combat formations whenever possible.

Fighting against a numerically superior enemy with strong air forces, Panzer Army Africa was forced to use *Flak* to protect its mobile force from excessive damage and casualties and to maintain its capability to maneuver in the face of low-level air attack. The Germans had strong air forces in North Africa but not enough to provide full cover over their marching columns or engaged forces. Between 19 November-15 December 1941, the Commanding General, *15.Pz.D.* used his attached 5th Battery, *Flak* Regiment 33, to support several organic battalions of the division in combat against the British during the Crusader battles. The battery was a light one armed with 20mm *Flak* and would support, for example, the division machine gun and motorcycle battalions and some of the artillery battalions. The battery fought numerous actions during this time period that illustrate the necessity for light automatic cannon with mobile forces operating in the desert today against strong opposition.

On 19 November 1941, 15th Panzer Division began to move into its "alarm areas" (*Alarmraeume*) and the *Flak* battery moved in support of a marching column. At 1630, six British Bristol-Blenheim light bombers began attacks on the column. Two platoons of the battery went into firing positions to fight off the bombers and fired 370 rounds of high explosive, nose-fuzed instantaneous projectiles against them. Faced with this moderate *Flak* fire from the ground, the British did not press home their attacks effectively and caused little damage or delay to the Germans.[41] This pedestrian action is similar to numerous other fights in the German records and suggests that moderate *Flak* defenses based on light automatic cannon with their spectacular tracer effects as well as real damage capabilities can generally provide adequate defense against air attack.

The 5th Battery, *Flak* Regiment 35 had its hands full during the Crusader battles and its actions also illustrate the extent to which an opposing air force can intervene on the ground even when friendly air assets remain intact and fairly strong. On 20 November 1942, two platoons of 20mm *Flak* in support of the marching columns of the division motorcycle and machine gun battalions went into firing positions twice in the morning and once in the afternoon firing off 445 rounds of high explosive ammunition against British fighters armed for ground attack. The next day, 21 November, the 2nd Platoon of the *Flak* battery and the machine gun battalion it was supporting came under attack by 16 British armored reconnaissance vehicles. The Germans drove off the British in a late afternoon action but the *Flak* platoon lost one 20mm gun and its towing truck. Other columns supported by the battery came under low-level air attack three times during the day. In a substantial success, the battery shot down one British Hurricane fighter armed for ground attack. The battery fired 716 high explosive and 56 armor piercing rounds in support of the division moves.[42] The action on 21 November was less pedestrian and shows a 20mm *Flak* battery flexibly engaging light armored targets on the ground and successfully engaging more determined enemy fighter bombers.

The 5th Battery, *Flak* Regiment 33, fought actions in a similar pattern during the rest of the period of the Crusader battles. The *Flak* battery met its biggest challenge on 23 November 1941 in a day of violent fighting and chance encounter involving combat against British infantry, tanks, and attacking aircraft. At 0930, 4th Platoon, in a sudden chance encounter with British infantry in trucks destroyed one armored machine gun carrier, several trucks, and took 20 prisoners. Later in the day, the 20mm *Flak* of two of the platoons supported attacks of the machine gun and motorcycle battalions against British infantry, machine gun and antitank gun positions. At 1745 in the afternoon, in a wild melee among the mobile forces engaged in the desert, the 20mm *Flak* faced British cruiser tanks at close range. The battery commander himself pulled the 4th platoon around to one flank of the local British tank attack and immobilized one Mark IV cruiser tank with 20mm armor piercing rounds fired through the sides and rear. Fifteen minutes later, the platoon engaged two Mark IV cruiser tanks which suddenly appeared from another direction and catastrophically destroyed one with 20mm armor piercing projectiles that caused a fire and explosions inside the tank. The battery also engaged infantry in trucks, and deployed on the ground in and among the British tanks, and had taken by 1900, 250 prisoners. In one of the last engagements of the day the battery commander with the 12th gun of the battery engaged a British armored reconnaissance vehicle and another Mark IV cruiser tank at short range, immobilized both with gunfire, and took the crews prisoner. During this same busy day, the battery defended against air attack three times during the late afternoon by a total of about 17 British Bristol-Blenheim light bombers. The intensity of the fighting and the flexibility of the battery is exemplified by the expenditure of 2,240 rounds of 20mm HE and 570 rounds of AP ammunition, and the expenditure of 150 rounds of machine gun ammunition and 60 rounds of machine pistol ammunition by the *Flak* crews.

During the same period, 3rd Battery, *Flak* Regiment 33, a heavy battery with 4 88mm and 4 20mm *Flak*, supported the 1st Battalion, Panzer Regiment 8, of the division. Attached to the tank regiment, the battery was employed in the tank escort role rather than air defense. The battery commander would employ his guns with great flexibility often firing at ground targets of opportunity. On 23 November 1941, the battery commander deployed two 88mm *Flak* on the left and two additional on the right flank of the panzer regiment in support of a morning attack against concentrations of British tanks, truck columns, and infantry. The battery fired both impact-fuzed and time-fuzed airburst rounds against British truck and infantry targets and armor piercing rounds against tanks, immobilizing four Mark IV cruiser tanks and destroying approximately 20 trucks.[43] Later, in the afternoon, the battery advanced on the left flank of the tank regiment but so close to the British that it could not set up to fire because of British rifle and machine gun fire. Toward the end of the day, the panzer regiment disengaged the battery and inserted it into a gap that had developed on the left between it and the neighboring Italian Ariete tank division. In the blocking role, the *Flak* battery destroyed 5 British Mark IV cruiser tanks with the firing of 66 rounds of AP ammunition as the enemy tried to exploit the gap. The battery lost two men killed and eight wounded and suffered the total destruction of a tracked towing machine and a carriage for one of the 88mm guns.

In the fighting on 21 November 1941, the heavy *Flak* battery effected a tactic worth noting. The battery was in positions in and among the tanks of Panzer Regiment 8 that was engaged with strong British tank units. After about one hour of combat, the German tanks found themselves short of ammunition and forced to break off the battle. The British sensed the German disadvantage and pressed their attack as the German tanks began to withdraw. The *Flak* battery commander recognized the situation also and on his own initiative kept his four 88mm guns in firing position and brought to bear enough fire to halt the British tanks. The battery commander had established spontaneously a "*Flak* screen" behind which the friendly tanks could disengage and take on ammunition.

Faced with British numerical superiority in tanks from the day of their arrival in Africa early in February 1941, the Germans needed every antitank gun they could lay their hands on. During the first several months, the German Forces in Libya would have a relatively small number of *Pak* weapons and more than half would be the modern looking and exceptionally agile 37mm *Pak*. By 1941, however, based on their experience in the brief but tough French Campaign in which they had suffered 156,000 casualties, the Germans knew that the gun was outmoded. In France, the German 37mm *Pak* crews had not be able to knock out virtually any of the French light, medium, or heavy tanks, all of which had large surface areas protected by 40mm or somewhat greater thicknesses of armor. The Germans met in France near Cambrai for the first time on 21 May 1940, the British Mark II (Matilda) infantry support tanks whose 80mm armor was completely impervious to the 37mm AP projectiles. In Africa, the *Pak* battalions of the panzer divisions would again meet the Mark II (Matilda) and Mark III (Valentine) heavily armored infantry support tanks with little or no prospects of damaging these vehicles. Against the more numerous cruiser tanks in the British tank brigades, the 37mm *Pak* would be more effective in getting through the 30mm to 40mm frontal armor of the vehicles at short range but would still be a marginal weapon. German *Pak* crews during the French Campaign had already begun to refer to the 37mm *Pak* as "the Army's doorknocker"—the doors would be just as solid in 1941 against the British in the desert.

Earlier, in 1938, the Germans had already begun to develop a replacement for the light *Pak* designated ultimately the 5cm *Pak* 38 and considered by the Germans in 1941 to be a "heavy" *Pak* weapon. The 50mm *Pak* was a vast improvement but still only a partial answer to the British armor. With an armor perforation capability at 1,000m range of 61mm at a 30-degree angle of obliquity, the 50mm *Pak* dominated all of the British cruiser tanks at 1,000m, the Mark III Valentine to approximately 800m, but continued to have little effect against the Mark II (Matilda) at any range. Rommel and his staff worked feverishly to get the heavier gun into Africa. They pressed the Army High Command (OKH) for additional imaginative stop gaps and successfully supplemented the gradually arriving 50mm *Pak* with the 47mm *Pak* built in Czechoslovakia and innovatively mounted on a German *Panzer I* light tank chassis. For use as antitank guns, Rommel and his staff also managed to extract from *OKH* numbers of Soviet 76.2mm field guns that had been captured along with huge stocks of ammunition in the summer of 1941. The Germans even converted significant numbers of the famed but ancient French model 1897 75mm field guns into antitank guns by cleverly placing the barrels on various available 50mm *Pak* carriages and using French ammunition. Working in this manner, Rommel and his staff had managed to scrape together the following array of *Pak* on the eve of the great test of the Crusader battles:

Panzer Group German Pak (16 Nov 41)[44]

	Weapon	Number
a.	37mm *Pak* 35/36	36
b.	47mm *Pak* (Czech)(Self Propelled)	27
c.	50mm *Pak* 38	94
d.	75mm Model 97 (French)*	0
e.	76.2mm 36/39 (Russian)*	0
f.	88mm *Flak* 36	*35*
	Total	192

* Not deployed at this date.

Soon to be attacked on 18 November 1941 by approximately 750 British tanks (including 100 out of the Tobruk fortress), the Germans faced hard questions of survival from the viewpoint of antitank defense. How would the Germans avoid decisive defeat in November and indeed come close to winning the operation?

The answer comes from several directions. The Italians contributed a large number of *Pak* weapons although the bulk was located around Tobruk and Sollum and never able to be used against the tanks of the British mobile force. The Italian XXth Motorized Corps contributed substantially to the mobile battle and held around 120 Italian 47mm *Pak* with moderate armor perforation capabilities. The German 88mm *Flak* proved to be outrageously effective based on some combination of technical excellence and bold, uninhibited tactical handling. Although the *DAK* fought with *only 12* of these guns, the 88mm *Flak* goes a significant way toward explaining the survival of the Panzer Group. The Germans also handled their own *Pak* in ways that help to explain their successes in the battle.

Similarly to the thoroughness and tactical awareness in the design of the 88mm *Flak* 36, the Germans developed a high explosive round for the 50mm *Pak*. They also developed a sophisticated antitank round with a delay fuze that set off a small charge in a heavy-walled penetrator that exploded behind the armor, i.e., often inside the enemy vehicle. Armed with high explosive ammunition, German 50mm *Pak* units could engage British infantry in the open, in field fortifications, and manning machine gun and mortar positions. Armed with such ammunition, 50mm *Pak* units could more effectively destroy British trucks and also knock out British armored reconnaissance vehicles. The *Pak* units even forced the shifting of British artillery positions in some engagements through use of high explosive rounds. The Germans also had large quantities of high explosive projectiles for the large number of 106 Russian 76.2mm *Pak* that had been converted from the Russian field gun and inserted in North Africa by May 1942.[45]

Early in 1942, the Germans continued to press for antitank guns and Rommel requested the outfitting of each of the six motorized rifle companies of the motorized infantry regiments of the panzer division with six 50mm *Pak* 38. The statistic is impressive. Rommel and his staff saw the war in the desert dominated to such a degree by the tank and armored reconnaissance vehicle that they decided to place six 50mm *Pak* in each German infantry company. The *OKH* approved the new outfitting of the companies on 12 May 1942. Two months later in July 1942, as the Germans began to put together a fourth division for employment in Africa—the 164th Infantry Division—*OKH* and Panzer Army Africa agreed on an outfitting level of 196 50mm *Pak* 38 for the new organization.[46] These are heady numbers of antitank guns. The Germans seem to be telling the historical observer something about the necessities of mobile warfare in the desert.

The Germans inserted their *Pak* units in combat with a style illustrated by the following combat action. In full withdrawal by mid-December 1941 after the Crusader battles, Rommel and his staff organized *Kampfgruppe* Colonel Menny as a strong rear guard to prevent the encirclement and destruction of the remaining forces of the Panzer Army. The Germans combined the panzer regiments of 15th and 21st Panzer Divisions to form a single tank force of 34 combat ready tanks—the entire number of combat ready German tanks in North Africa—and built the *Kampfgruppe* around them. Other elements included one battalion of 33rd Artillery Regiment, 2nd Machine Gun Battalion, part of 1st Battalion, 33rd (Army) *Flak* Regiment, and 3rd Company, 33rd Antitank Battalion. At this moment, 15 December 1942, a British force had moved around the south flank of the Panzer Army into positions between the Italian XXIst and XXth Army Corps and threatened to break up the Panzer Army and block the retreat of Italo-German forces positioned to the east. *Kampfgruppe* Menny had the mission to destroy this British force ensconced around height 181 which lay 15km west of Gazala. The 12 50mm *Pak* of 3rd Company, 33rd Antitank Battalion fought in this action.

Oberleutnant (First Lieutenant) Tocue, the *Pak* commander, placed himself and one platoon of four 50mm *Pak* with the leading elements of the machine gun battalion. He deployed one additional platoon on the flank of the battalion, and the remaining platoon on the right flank of the panzer force. Rather amazingly for an antitank gun commander, Tocue described his mission to include destruction of enemy ground targets "as well as especially to suppress enemy *Pak*, machine gun positions, etc., with high explosive shells and to furnish fire support for the attacking infantry."[47] Given the dangerous operational situation for the Panzer Group, *Kampfqruppe* Menny attacked with determination and in a short, intense battle essentially annihilated the dangerously positioned British force. *Oberleutnant* Tocue noted in detail the eclectic success achieved by the tactically flexible German *Pak* force. The 50mm *Pak* knocked out one heavy armored reconnaissance vehicle, two Mark IV cruiser tanks, one artillery tractor "shot up in flames," four 40mm self-propelled antitank guns, nine trucks also shot up in flames and 12 additional trucks damaged by the *Pak* crews. Tocue noted that his guns destroyed (or captured after the action) 30-40 British machine guns in the "very numerous machine gun nests" though use of high explosive shells.[48] In additional convincing detail, he noted that one of the British Mark IV cruiser tanks that he claimed for his company had in fact been immobilized by some other German weapon but was still firing and was finished off by a direct hit by a 50mm *Pak* AT round low on the hull. The antitank gun crews also brought in 234 prisoners including seven officers out of the British positions that had been physically overrun by the Germans. From the viewpoint of weapons effects, he noted finally that the two British 87.6mm field guns claimed by him had been knocked out by direct hits with AT rounds that wounded (but not killed) the crews.

One more combat action should suffice to illustrate the flexible handling of German antitank gun units in the desert and the potential application of ground antitank weapons to desert war today. Early in the Crusader battles on 21 November 1941, *15.Pz.D.* continued to search in a southwest direction from Sidi Azeiz for strong British tank forces operating deep in the rear of Panzer Group Africa and heading for Tobruk. The division commander deployed two companies of his 33rd *Pak* Battalion on the flanks of the 115th Motorized

Infantry Regiment that was in tactical march column behind the leading 8th Panzer Regiment. The division commander assigned the remaining 1st Company, 33rd *Pak* Battalion, to a separate *Kampfgruppe* Major Oberent formed for another mission. War is filled with friction, however, and 1st Company lost *Kampfgruppe* Oberent in the darkness of the evening of 20-21 November and at break of day was assigned to secure the right flank of 115th Motorized Infantry Regiment behind 2nd Company already deployed there. The motorized infantry regiment advanced westward seeking contact with the British.

As the march continued, strong British armored reconnaissance forces began to move in from the south, and the commander, 115th Motorized Infantry Regiment shifted the 2nd and 3rd Companies, 33rd *Pak* Battalion, to screen the regiment's south flank. In an instructive lesson in the fluid nature of desert war, the *Pak* battalion commander took over the two *Pak* companies and moved them 3km farther south into what he described as the best firing positions according to the lie of the land. As the two *Pak* companies moved into the firing positions, they found themselves engaged by large numbers of British armored reconnaissance vehicles which they checked momentarily by "shooting up in flames" two accompanying trucks. The two *Pak* companies continued to engage the British while the motorized rifle regiment already 3km distant continued, to march west. The *Pak* battalion commander decided to break contact with the British but continue to screen the regiment's south flank by "leap frogging" his two companies from firing position to firing position parallel with the advance of the regiment. Acting according to this plan, 3rd *Pak* Company "limbered up" and moved west into new positions. As 2nd *Pak* Company attempted to break contact with the British and leap frog forward it found itself strafed and bombed by part of a force of 20 British Hurricane fighter-bombers attacking the south flank of the motorized infantry regiment.[49]

Approximately an hour later, at 1100 22 November 1941, the motorized rifle regiment slowed and halted in the face of strong British tank forces and a major battle began to take shape. The 1st *Pak* company had continued to move on the north flank of 115th Motorized Rifle and as strong contact developed with the enemy, the *Pak* commander, Lieutenant Walters, on his own initiative advanced to the point of the regiment and went into the best firing positions he could find. The tactical situation seems unreal—a *Pak* company in position alone as the most advanced front of a motorized rifle regiment. The company observed British tank forces massing for an attack about 1,200m away and knocked out one of several tanks which had moved closer to the front of the motorized rifle regiment. At this juncture, mid-afternoon, strong German tank forces moved out from the front of the motorized rifle regiment through the 12 50mm *Pak* cannons of the company and engaged the British tank force. After tank-versus-tank combat, the German tanks short of fuel and ammunition broke contact with the British and rolled back toward the front of the motorized rifle regiment and through the *Pak* company. Sensing an advantage, the British tanks pressed forward and ran up against the advanced *Pak* screen. The guns had lain largely undetected by the British for what they were—a full-strength company well deployed in good firing positions. The company commander opened "surprise fire" with all 12 guns simultaneously when a large number of the advancing British tanks were at 800m range. The company commander observed that one tank immediately burst into flames and others stopped with smoke pouring from them.[50] The British halted their advance and engaged the *Pak* cannons with tank cannon and machine gun fire. When darkness fell, the *Pak* company still lay in its firing positions.

This historical incident can be used to make some important generalizations about war in the desert and the German style of fighting it. There is a frontless quality about war in the desert between two motorized opponents. The motorized rifle regiment moved long distances through open desert hunting for an equally mobile opponent but unable to locate him. There is a long range quality about desert war. Endangered by an enemy lying somewhere to the south, the motorized infantry regimental commander did not secure his flank with a motorized infantry company but rather with two antitank gun companies. The infantry company did not have enough weapons with long enough range to keep a strong motorized opponent from closing with and destroying it. In desert war, the tactical realities are far different from those in hilly country with vegetation and built up areas. The antitank gun battalion commander set up his screen of guns 3km off the flank of the motorized infantry regiment whose commander continued to advance away from the guns. What about the security of the flanks of the antitank gun line? What about the expanding several-kilometers-wide gap between the motorized rifle regiment and the *Pak* companies?

The following factors seem to explain apparently ill-considered and dangerous tactical moves. In open, level desert, motorized forces in movement cannot be concealed in daylight. The relatively large (compared with men) vehicles can be seen when moving and often raise clouds of dust that can be seen even farther. The regimental commander in the incident above could see from the flank of the regiment that the gap between the *Pak* and the infantry was empty and knew that the *Pak* companies had long range weapons that could dominate large areas of the gap in the event a maneuvering enemy force appeared in it. In contrast to a moving unit in open, "level" desert, the 1st *Pak* Company that deployed at the front of the motorized infantry regiment and apparently exposed itself to destruction, once stationary in its firing positions virtually disappeared into the desert.

One of the great undiscovered battles fought in the desert that pivoted around the tank was the battle of retrieval and repair. The number of combat ready tanks available for battle day to day always depended on the original number available for action minus attrition through (1) tanks totally lost, and (2) tanks temporarily lost and in process of retrieval, evacuation, repair, and return to action. The *DAK* had no tank reserves and in the relatively brief Crusader battles received no replacements through the supply line to Africa. The *DAK* began the Crusader battles with 260 battle, reconnaissance, and command tanks and with that number comprised a mobile force capable with skill and reasonable luck of defeating the larger British tank forces. Separately from tactical skill, however, the *DAK* would win, survive, or be annihilated based on how many of that original number of tanks it would continue to have available for battle day to day.

The Germans lost tanks in combat in the desert from causes that included combat (gunfire, mines, etc.), terrain hazards, and mechanical breakdown. The balances among these causes could be surprising and one must understand the realities of this situation in order to come to grips with maneuver war involving tanks. In Korea, for example, from 1950-53, the United Nations forces lost more tanks to "terrain hazards" than they did to enemy action. The difficult terrain for tanks and entrenched warfare largely explain the result. In the desert in 1941-42, the Germans lost tanks mainly to gunfire from British tanks and antitank guns, but they also suffered significant losses from mechanical breakdown. The following distinctions help in the understanding of the tank strength of mobile forces at any point in time:

Tank "Losses" During Combat*

Tanks Lost (Combat: Gunfire, Mines, etc.)	**Tanks Lost (Non Combat Cause)**
1. Catastrophic Kill – Perm. Loss	1. Terrain Hazard – Perm. Loss
2. Immobilization – Perm. Loss	2. Terrain Hazard – Temp. Loss
3. Immobilization – Temp. Loss	3. Mech. Breakdown – Perm. Loss
4. Firepower Damage – Temp. Loss	4. Mech. Breakdown – Temp. Loss

*Perm. or permanent. Temp. or temporary. Mech. or mechanical.

The listing shows that mobile forces in combat can expect daily to suffer "losses" that can be characterized as either permanent or temporary. The listing suggests thereby that the permanent losses cannot be recouped during critical, brief periods of high intensity combat by resupply and are particularly devastating. The listing also suggests that losses can be returned to combat by a process of retrieval and repair that is a uniquely important factor in maneuver war in the desert.

In the period 18 November - 7 December 1941, the *DAK* faced a situation in which it would attempt to conduct a mobile operation with its original striking power as intact as possible but would be ground down in battle by tank losses characterized as permanent or temporary. The *DAK* would begin to suffer numbers of tanks totally lost and have to take steps to keep those numbers as low as possible. The Germans could not do much about the catastrophic destruction of their tanks by gunfire, mines, etc. They were constrained by the existing designs of the vehicles and the realities of armed violence. In the category of total loss, however, the Germans lost most of their vehicles to retrieval problems on the battlefield. Typically, panzer forces would observe immobilized German tanks at the end of engagements lying irretrievable on British ground. On their own ground, unless the tanks were burning, the Germans would tow immobilized vehicles immediately with the tractors of the tank repair company (*Panzerwerkstattkompanie*) organic to each panzer regiment. Repairable tanks would then be evacuated to the workshops of the organic repair company. In some cases, the Germans would move the repair companies to concentrations of tanks in process of evacuation. The Germans suffered many tanks as total losses because they were unable to retrieve them from the battlefield as soon as they were immobilized in German-held territory. The "retrieval battle" fought above was one of the most important in the mobile engagements of 1941-42.

The *DAK* would also begin to suffer numbers of tanks immobilized through combat damage, terrain hazard, and mechanical breakdown during combat and remaining on ground under German control. In the case of tanks immobilized but capable of repair, the Germans had to evacuate the vehicles on tank transport vehicles as quickly as possible to the repair companies for work and return to combat. If the tanks could be repaired in two days shop time, the Germans did the work in the maintenance companies and returned them to the panzer regiments as dictated by the tactical situation. Tanks requiring more than two-days work were evacuated to Army-level workshops farther to the rear. Once in that cycle of evacuation, the German tanks had little chance of return to combat in a fight of the duration of the Crusader battles.

During Crusader, the Germans fought the following "battle" of retrieval and repair. With 124 tanks on 17 November 1941, 5th Panzer Regiment, *21.Pz.D.* suffered its first losses on 19 November. On that day the panzer regiment lost two tanks catastrophically killed by British gunfire and six others lost permanently through other damage and loss mechanisms. By the end of the day, 22 November 1941, the panzer regiment had suffered permanent losses of 24 tanks including five catastrophically killed by gunfire and 19 permanently lost mostly as damaged vehicles unable to be moved during forced shifts of the panzer regiment's repair workshops, or left behind at damaged-tank concentration areas in the cut and thrust of the mobile battle. On 23 November, 5th Panzer Regiment fought its biggest battle of the operation with a substantial number of tanks - -approximately 80 ready for combat. The 5th Panzer Regiment scored along with the tank regiment of the other panzer division, the biggest German victory in the Crusader battles and one that brought them close to victory in the whole operation. The panzer regiment suffered heavy losses that day though that ran as follows: 17 tanks catastrophically killed by gunfire or permanently lost through other means, 51 tanks temporarily damaged and under repair (including a substantial number from previous days' actions), and 32 tanks ready for insertion in combat. The remaining striking power of Panzer Group Africa can be equated with those 32 tanks and a somewhat larger number in the other German panzer regiment in North Africa. Rommel would practice maneuver war on the morning of 24 November 1941 constrained by the offensive capabilities of that small number of operable German tanks in North Africa.

German tactics for tank retrieval included the aggressive towing of vehicles under fire. The Germans developed these tactics in order to prevent the capture or destruction of friendly tanks occasioned by sudden shifts in location by opposing forces in the desert. The Germans pushed their regimental tank repair company as far forward as possible to reduce evacuation and return times. It is difficult to exaggerate the importance of these tactics because of the direct correlation between the number of tanks in Panzer Group Africa and the operational possibilities open to its commander. The Germans did these things well, for example, note the total of 51 tanks having been successfully retrieved off the battlefield and evacuated to the regimental tank workshops by the evening of 23 November by a single regiment. In contrast, the Germans had permanently lost 41 additional tanks including 23 tanks left behind due to chance shifts in the mobile battle and resultant overrunning by the British.

After the Crusader battles, 5th Panzer Regiment, *21.Pz.D.* put together a report of its battles in the period 17 November-31 December 1941. In the report, the regimental commander painstakingly pieced together the picture in tank losses suffered during the high intensity mobile battles. The Germans provide a valuable picture of the distribution of losses by various causes and the importance of the tank retrieval and repair company in armored combat. The picture was the following:[51]

5th Panzer Regiment
Mobile Desert War: Distribution of Tank Losses

Tanks Lost	Description of Loss
29	Gunfire: Burned or Completely Destroyed.
28	Gunfire or Mech Breakdown: Some Permanently Lost Others Successfully Retrieved.
5	Immobilized. No Tow Available. Blown Up in Place.
2	Unknown Fate
12	Immobilized. Towed to Repair Companies Both Panzer Rgts. Then Abandoned During Tactical Displacements.
16	Immobilized. Towed to First Assembly Area. Then Abandoned During Tactical Withdrawal.
92	Tanks Damaged Out of Original 124 in Panzer Regt.

For ground forces today, the listing gives a rough idea of the distribution of losses that could be expected in a high intensity armored engagement in the desert against a first class enemy. Even more usefully, the listing shows the importance of battlefield retrieval in maintaining numbers of tanks and armored reconnaissance vehicles and similar armored combat vehicles in the category of "ready for insertion in battle." The Germans also suffered painful losses due to displacements of the tank repair companies and the abandonment of the initial assembly area for retrieved tanks. The 5th Panzer Regiment permanently lost the staggering total of 28 tanks through its displacements compared for example with the permanent loss of only 17 tanks in the biggest engagement of the Crusader operation on 23 November 1941 around Sidi Rezegh. Tank retrieval has always been known to be a serious business. The German experience indicates that it is so important that special tactics and techniques are necessary to be developed to secure tanks lying in retrieval assembly areas and in the tank workshops themselves.

The Commander, 5th Panzer Regiment came to the conclusion that the Retrieval Platoon of the Repair and Retrieval Company needed radios and accompanying combat vehicles to reduce the losses to salvageable vehicles. This experienced commander pointed out also that higher headquarters must assure a secure basis for the retrieval of damaged armored vehicles, for example, a protected area for the assembly of the vehicles away from the immediate battlefield. He noted also that the motorized rifle regiment must be tasked to provide a reserve combat force to protect the damaged but repairable tanks of the panzer regiment and to protect the retrieval platoon during towing off the battlefield.

11

German Logistics in the Desert

Rommel and the Germans in North Africa conducted operations that had a striking similarity to the great allied amphibious campaigns of World War II in both Europe and the Pacific. Panzer Army Africa depended almost entirely on sea lanes of communication between Italy and North Africa. The *Luftwaffe* supplemented those lines by flying all of its aircraft and most of its personnel to Africa and also most of the German Army personnel that moved between Italy and Africa as replacements and evacuated wounded. Rommel and his staff practiced coordination with the large Italian and small German naval forces responsible for seaborne logistics. Rommel faced operational disaster in the Crusader battles because of the breakdown of the sea lines of communication in the months prior to the British offensive.

With the importance of seaborne logistics demonstrated by November 1941, Rommel and his staff, and the High Commands of Italy and Germany took steps in the Mediterranean in the first half of 1942 to secure the logistics of the Panzer Army. German supplies flowed freely during that period and Rommel was able to supply his forces by sea more effectively than the British. As a result, he was able to put together forces strong enough to conduct offensive operations around Gazala in eastern Libya in May-June 1942 with the strategic goal to defeat the British field army. With its defeat, the Italo-German forces planned to continue the axis strategic offensive by the conquest of Malta and securing of the sea lines of communication to Libya. Based on the extent of the defeat of the British field army, the Germans also had the alternate option to continue the attack into Egypt with the remote but tempting possibility of immediately driving the British out of North Africa. In the actual event, Rommel demanded the continuation of the drive into Egypt. In spite of his unique brilliance in seizing chance opportunity and maintaining a fierce tempo of operations, he was unable to advance beyond Alamein. Two factors largely explain his failure - the continued general weakness of his sea lines of communication which limited the strength of the

Panzer Army just below that necessary to push on to Alexandria and the chance British seizure of a German enigma coding machine in 1934 and the eventual capability to read high level German message traffic in the Mediterranean theater.

Ashore, in Libya, within the Panzer Army, the Germans organized effective logistics operations. Under the German Army system, the Panzer Army held the Service Troops and delivered supplies into dumps at corps level in support of the divisions.[52] Each German division had an organic Service Echelon that paralleled the Panzer Army Service Troops. The 21st Panzer Division, for example, had one division-level panzer workshop company while the Panzer Army had a similar company with capabilities to accomplish higher levels of repair. The division would also have two ambulance companies, two medical companies, and a division hospital. The Panzer Army in turn had several higher level hospitals—two army, one field, and one war hospitals—to which the division evacuated casualties as appropriate to the wound, road conditions, and distances. For the Germans fighting a mobile war, however, the logistics challenge in supplying a battle was provision of fuel, ammunition, water, and rations. In *21.Pz.D.* the commander had the division *Nachschubdienst* (Supply Service), a battalion-level organization also often referred to as the division *Trosse* (trains) for resupply. In the German division of World War II, the division Ib, or quartermaster, normally a general staff officer, directed the resupply in the name of the division commander. The Ib accomplished this resupply largely through the columns and companies of the division trains and orders issued to the commander of the trains.

In *15.Pz.D.*, the division commander provided service support for the division through means of his Ib and the trains organized as sketched out in Figure 3. The Figure, which has been extracted directly from a division order on organization, shows the Ib with a Quartermaster Echelon co-located with the commander and "staff" of the division trains. The Ib resupplied the division largely through 13 numbered columns each with a 30-ton capacity for appropriate supplies. Columns 8-10, for example, carried fuel, one numbered column carried water (*Wasser*); and another unnumbered column (*Ers.* or *Ersatz*) carried replacement tanks. The division trains also included three automotive repair companies with capabilities to handle both wheeled and tracked vehicles. The number of trucks in a 30-ton column varied according to the capacities of the trucks used.[53] Most commonly, the Germans put together the columns with ten vehicles. With the columns, the Germans had a resupply system that was redundant and flexible with what can be likened to interchangeable transportation building blocks.

In a panzer division, the Ib co-located the Quartermaster Detachment with the commander and "staff" of the division trains in order to be in touch with the actual situation in fuel and ammunition, and intervene as necessary to maintain resupply. As such, he often found himself with lightly armed service troops, e.g., drivers and assistant drivers of the numerous trucks in the division trains and personnel of the workshop companies. With a significant concentration of vehicles in a theater where the enemy had a strong air force, the Ib in *15.Pz.D.* had a little *Kampfstaffel* with 8 20mm *Flak* for defense against low level air attack for both the quartermaster staff personnel and the parts of the division trains often around the headquarters. The Ib faced another more dangerous characteristic of warfare in the desert in the ultra-mobility of the opposing forces. The British in the Crusader battles advanced with several hundred armored reconnaissance vehicles, truck-borne infantry, and large numbers of tanks. Formed into numerous battle detachments large and small that often freely roamed the open desert in a frontless mobile war, they constituted potentially mortal danger in sudden, chance encounter with the Ib, the commander of the trains, or individual columns.

For its own protection and for the defense of the commander of the trains arid the trains themselves, the Quartermaster Detachment had six truck-towed 37mm *Pak* in addition to the eight 20mm *Flak* weapons. The Ib personally deployed a force that could fight off fairly strong British units on the move in chance encounters. The 37mm *Pak* was a marginal weapon against the British cruiser tanks at ranges over 500m, but, at shorter ranges, its projectiles would perforate the armor of the numerous older cruisers with their frontal protection of approximately 40mm and lighter armor elsewhere. With its armor piercing shells, the 37mm *Pak* could easily knock out the British armored reconnaissance vehicles at longer

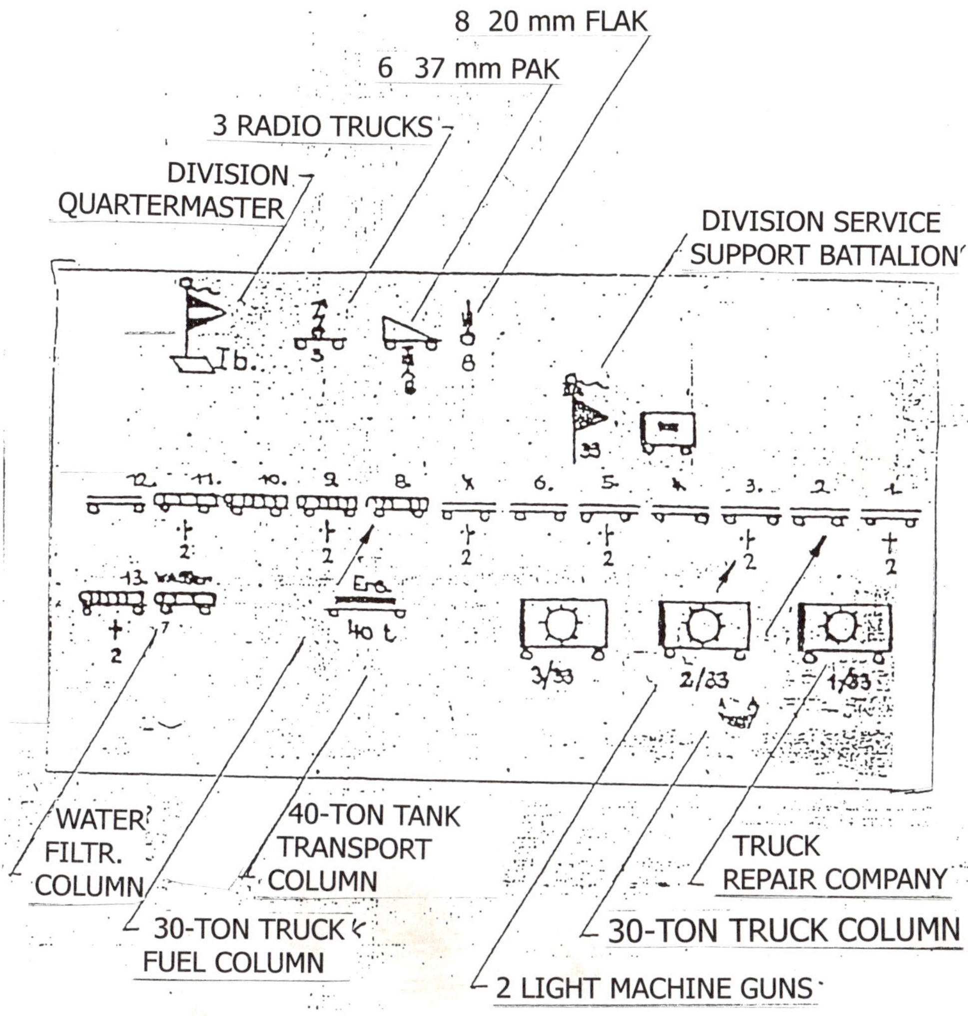

Figure 9. 15th Panzer Division, *DAK*, Panzer Army Africa, 3 Jan '42: The Ib (Quartermaster) and the Division Trains.

ranges, and, with its high explosive shells, it was effective against trucks, infantry, various infantry weapons, and antitank guns. The Ib could use the 20mm *Flak* in a ground firing role against the British armored reconnaissance vehicles and knock them out with the two types of antitank ammunition developed for the weapon—the conventional AT round and the tungsten-cored AT round. German test firings showed that the antitank rounds had similar performance at 500m range[54] with armor perforation of about 17.5mm at 30 degrees angle of obliquity. These figures translate into knocking out armored reconnaissance vehicles at ranges somewhat over 500m. At shorter ranges of approximately 100-200m, the 20mm *Flak* could perforate the frontal armor of the early British cruiser tanks with low obliguity impacts over wide areas of the sides. The 20mm *Flak* also had high explosive projectiles that were particularly effective against trucks.

The Germans recognized the detached and exposed situation of the division quartermaster and the trains and provided him with a *Kampfstaffel* (battle echelon) to defend the quartermaster echelon and the trains near it. For the fluid combat situations of mobile war in the desert the Germans were on the right track. The quartermaster *Kampfstaffel* should probably have been even larger so that the Ib could send out escort forces with columns when required and defend the division workshop companies from disastrous displacements and the abandonment of crucial weapons forced sometimes by small British forces. The Germans should probably have increased the *Kampfstaffel* to include an infantry platoon reinforced by medium mortars and machine guns and as many captured weapons as could be put together conveniently. The 15th Panzer Division had begun to develop a division trains organization with an integral combat force strong enough to fight off enemy mobile forces, escort its more important columns, and form strong points for self defense.

By February 1942, Panzer Army Headquarters, concerned by the harassment of supply columns by light British forces and by a relatively small numbers of British-recruited Arab *franc tireurs* (guerrillas), put out orders that required a driver and assistant driver in every supply truck on the move individually or in columns. The Panzer Army required that the two men in every truck each have a firearm specifically loaded and accessible for action. For each column of the supply trains on the move, Panzer Army orders required a security troop armed specifically with automatic weapons and hand grenades in addition to the rifles or pistols of the drivers and assistant drivers. Sensitive to air attack, the Germans designated members of the security troops as *Spaeher* (or, lookouts) for British low level aircraft and mobile ground forces.[55]

In May-June 1942, Rommel conducted the Venezia operation, orchestrating three separate battles toward the strategic goal of the destruction of the British field army lying between Gazala and Tobruk. With the German plan revealed to the British in advance through Ultra decoding, Rommel faced a difficult operation that lasted longer than expected and was characterized by an extremely complex crisscrossing of opposing combat formations. He also experienced a disastrously dangerous situation for the almost unarmed German supply columns terribly exposed in the middle of the deep enemy defense system and harassed by British light troops operating out of the desert from the south. With the service support situation near collapse, he issued the following order on 31 May 1942, as the operation was beginning to unfold:

> "All service support columns and supply convoys are to attach the fundamentally necessary antitank weapons for self defense. Further, all supply convoys are to be outfitted with radio communications by which means they can be escorted by radio and be in a position to request prompt support."[56]

Rommel issued this order while deeply embedded in the British Gazala defenses. At that moment, he and his mobile force depended for their survival on supplies moved by truck columns. The truck columns of the German divisions, for example, had to move from the combat areas of their divisions back to *DAK* dumps to pick up supplies and deliver them forward to the combat units and division dumps. Panzer Army truck columns simultaneously delivered supplies to the *DAK* dumps and constituted additional logistics traffic in the rear area. In the first two days of the offensive, Rommel hoped to have roads opened through the British minefields and past the fortified British boxes directly into the mobile force. Unable initially to get through the British minefields or reduce the static defense positions, the Panzer Army depended on long routes for their truck columns south of the British defenses around Bir Hacheim that held out until 11 June 1942. The situation was chaotic with the German divisional truck columns and even Panzer Army truck columns farther to the rear under attack by British armored reconnaissance forces and various other raiding detachments. The German truck columns once among their own divisions came under further attack in the extremely fluid conditions of mobile combat among the opposing tank forces.

The situation was similar to one of the factors often assigned as unique to warfare at sea. The supply lines of naval forces are subject to attack by enemy submarines and surface raiding forces unlike the situation on land where army supply lines, as a rule, are not menaced anywhere by opposing ground forces. The naval situation in the open, level "terrain" of the sea demands special protection for supplies afforded by convoys which sometimes may be so strong that they are naval battle groups in their own right based on the organization and mission of the protecting naval vessels. In the open, level terrain of the desert during the mobile battles among the opposing tank forces, for example, in November-December 1941 and May-June 1942, the German supply truck columns shared the same terrain with opposing combat forces and their supply columns. In the directive quoted above, Rommel does not order the use of combat units to convoy supplies. Rommel does order the service support truck columns to attach the necessary "antitank weapons for self defense" and have the means to call for help immediately. The German command arrived at the conclusion that the truck columns on an ad hoc basis required their own combat defense force. In effect, the Germans converted their truck columns into little *Kampfgruppen* with missions to protect themselves and assure the delivery of supplies.

12

German Staffs: Small, Modestly Ranked, Action Oriented

In the first half of 1942, Rommel held the rank of *Generaloberst* (four stars) and command of the field army in an entire theater of war. A ground forces staff today for a general commanding a similar field army would be a large organization comprising roughly one hundred officers in the immediate staff sections of the headquarters. The staff would have a formidable rank structure with approximately four generals in the commander, deputy commander, chief of staff, and operations officer billets respectively, and numerous colonels. The staff of Panzer Army Africa was much smaller than the picture suggested above for a similar ground forces staff today. The staff was so much smaller and its ranks so much lower that is worthwhile to present some of the details of the organization. American readers today may be hard pressed to believe that so trim an organization could run so large and complex a campaign. Suffice it to say that the Panzer Army staff and its pugnacious commander ran the Axis operations in North Africa as a model of bold decision making through the fog that characterizes war.

The Germans organized their staffs in three groupments namely a *Fuehrungsabteilung* (Operations detachment), *Quartiermeisterabteilung* (Quartermaster Detachment) and *Adjutantur Gruppe* (Adjutant Group). For various reasons often in combat, the Germans placed the adjutant or personnel administration officer in the Operations Detachment. Organized into two staff echelons for operations and service support, the High Command of Panzer Army Africa presented a trim and uncomplicated picture. In the Operations Detachment, the Panzer Army had a chief of staff with rank of brigadier general, an operations officer (designated Ia) with rank of lieutenant colonel, an intelligence officer (designated Ic) with rank of major. The quartermaster (designated OQU) of the Panzer Army and head of the Quartermaster Detachment was a major. In terms of the principal staff officers, the High Command, Panzer Army Africa presented the following picture in February 1942 (equivalent U.S. ranks):[57]

Field Army Commander (four-star General)
Chief of Staff (one-star General)

Operations Detachment	**Quartermaster Detachment**
Operations (Ia) (LtCol)	Quartermaster (OQu) (Maj)
Intelligence (Ib) (Maj)	
Personnel (IIa) (Maj)	

The *OKH* in setting up this headquarters earlier in August 1941, placed highly qualified general staff officers in the key positions—Chief, Ia, Ic, and OQu. These were the only general staff officers in the High Command of the Panzer Army. Painstakingly selected, based on character and intelligence for attendance at the *Kriegsakademie* (War Academy) general staff officers such as these had completed either the two or three years course at the academy and held the critical staff positions in the German Army.

With his front line style, long absences from the Army Command Post and Operations Detachment, and unusual predilection to take his chief of staff into the front line with him, Rommel placed a heavy burden on the less than a handful of general staff officers left to keep the Panzer Army together. As the two general staff officers remaining in the Operations Detachment, Lieutenant Colonel Siegfried Westphal and Major Friedrich Wilhelm von Mellenthin were often forced to make decisions in the names of the absent commander and chief of staff that one would not expect staff officers of any rank or experience to make. Westphal and Mellenthin made decisions under these challenging circumstances so effectively that one must suspect that there are special advantages in two such men (and no more) making decisions in the surrounding absence of debate, inertia, and frictions associated with the weighty staffs of present ground forces.

The following example illustrates the effectiveness of the staff of the Panzer Army. Convinced on the evening of 23 November 1941 that he had defeated the British in the Crusader operation, Rommel set off the morning of 24 November in personal command of the two panzer divisions of *DAK* in a bold advance to the Egyptian frontier intended to defeat the major forces he expected to find there and stampede the commander of the British Army into a precipitous retreat out of Libya. Although badly shaken, the British command determined not to retreat and Rommel missed finding any important force that he might have defeated with final decisive effect. Moving with insufficient communications by 26 November, Rommel had lost effective contact with the Army Command Post and the two divisions under his command and was no longer able to control the battle outside of Tobruk or bring about a decisive result on the frontier. During the whole period 24-26 November, Westphal and Mellenthin conducted the battle around Tobruk and had the clearest picture of the overall operation. As disaster began to approach in the form of the collapse of the Tobruk front on 26 November, Westphal, out of contact with Rommel and Headquarters, *DAK*, ordered the 21st Panzer Division, then under the personal control of the army commander, to halt the advance eastward turn about and advance west to save the situation at Tobruk. Westphal, in effect, ordered Rommel, Headquarters *DAK*, and the two German panzer divisions out of Egypt and back to Tobruk in a grand operational decision. When Rommel returned the following day, he did not like what had happened but approved everything Westphal and Mellenthin had ordered.

What is the connection between the small and modestly ranked German staffs and the decision-making noted above? Consistently in World War II, the characteristically small German staffs produced effective results with the commanders that they advised. Small staffs seem to have special efficiencies both in peacetime and in war. Large, over-ranked, and redundant staffs isolate the commander, block his access to subordinate commanders, and, as classical bureaucracies, inhibit action rather than encourage it. With Rommel and the chief of staff absent, the miniscule but competent and action oriented staff—essentially Westphal and Mellenthin—accomplished the staff work necessary in keeping track of the tactical situations and strung together the three major battles into a coherent operation. A lesson seems to be that small staffs work and that they work more effectively than large ones. The operating theorem may be that small staffs with little internal frictions take action while large staffs with probably disproportionately larger friction tend to produce internal debate rather than external action.

The Germans did not "adopt" the small staff of World War II as a result of some contemporarily styled study in which masses of instantaneous, present day data are analyzed statistically and used to effect change. The Prussians labored for two centuries to understand war as it really is. They discovered through historical experience that effective command in war pivots around taking action and developed a staff officer who could relieve the commander of the details of staff work and advise him on taking action. The Prussians demanded a few competent staff officers not numerous senior ones gathered around their commanders. The result was a lot of staff work accomplished, little bureaucratic obfuscation, and a single responsible advisor to the commander. The Prussian-German staff reflected a German preoccupation with operations and the winning of battles. The contemporary staff organization in the U.S. Armed Forces continues to reflect a preoccupation with planning, logistics and set piece, fire support battles.

Similar to the cases of the panzer divisions in France (1940) and Russia (1941), the two panzer division of Panzer Army Africa had staffs that effectively ran the divisions and advised the commander in combat but were a small fraction of the size of a U.S. ground forces staff today. The *15.Pz.D.* was similar in size to a U.S. ground forces division with approximately 14,000 men, 140 tanks, and numerous trucks and heavy weapons. Three officers ran the operational staff work of the division—one major in the general staff who also advised the division commander on the conduct of battle, one captain, and one lieutenant. These officers were not only responsible for keeping track of the combat maneuvers and actions of the 15th Panzer Division and its neighbors in a mobile war in the desert, but also had pieced together in late 1940 the division from elements of the 33rd Infantry Division and various motorized formations of the German Army. These officers then moved the newly formed division from Germany across the Alps into Italy and then by sea and air to Libya. With the assistance of the Ib (Logistics) and IIa (Personnel) they planned and executed movements and loading probably as complex as the similar actions required to deliver a U.S. Army or Marine Corps division to a distant seacoast in an amphibious operation. Modestly ranked as they were, the division' general staff officers spoke all the more clearly in the name of the division commander and had neither the time, nor the inclination, nor the excess numbers to engage in bureaucratic debate or insulate the commander from the rest of his organization. The following listing shows the general staff positions in the 15th Panzer Division and illustrates the streamlined nature of the staff of a German division in World War II:

The General Staff
Positions in 15th Panzer Division (16 Feb '42)

Staff Operations Detachment	**Staff Quartermaster Detachment**
Ia (Maj. I.G) (Opns)	Ib (Capt) (Logistics)
01 (Capt) (Asst Opns)	02 (1st Lt) (Asst Logistics)
04 (Lt) (Asst Opns)	
Ic (Capt) (Intel)	
03 (Lt) (Asst Intel)	
IIa (Maj) (Personnel)	
IIb (1st Lt) (Asst Pers)	

With lesser combat formations than divisions, the Germans affected the same small staffs. The Germans had staffs so small at regimental and battalion levels that the battle of opposing military cultures between the German Army in World War II and U.S. ground forces today comes into sharper focus than in a panzer army or division. The greatest shock in this brief comparative survey, of staff organization is in the infantry battalion. The Marine Corps infantry battalion today, for example, has a staff comparable in size and rank to the staff of the *15.Pz.D.* of 1941-42 in North Africa. In contrast, the staff of the German motorized infantry battalion was so small that it suggests a fundamentally different approach to fighting battles.[58] The U.S. staff is so large that it seems to have been designed for planning and organizing rather than assisting its commander in fighting battles. Such a staff inhibits a commander, slows his decision-making, and blocks access between the Commander and the leaders of his combat maneuver elements. In contrast, the small German staff was just able to run the day-to-day business of the battalion, write brief orders and pass on oral ones, and keep track of the fighting units. Such a staff could scarcely inhibit a commander or slow him. In such a system, the battalion commander had nothing to do but take action (i.e., fight). With such a system, the Germans engaged in battle and moved to the next battle site rather than plan to engage in battle and prepare to move to the next battle area. The staff positions were the following:

USMC and German Infantry Bn Staffs

USMC (Today*)		**German (1942**)**
Bn CO (LtCol)	Bn XO (Maj)	Bn CO (Maj)
S-3 (Maj)	S-2 (Capt)	Adjutant (1st Lt)
S-3 Asst (Capt)	S-1 (Capt)	Asst Adj (Lt)
S-3 Asst (Capt)	S-1 Pers (Lt)	Supply O (Lt)
S-3 Asst FAC (Lt)+	S-4 (Capt)	
S-3 Liaison (Lt)	S-4 Asst (Emb) (Lt)+	
S-4 Asst (MMO) (Lt)		

*Approx 1,000 officers and men. + FAC = Forward Air Controller
**Approx 750 officers and men. EMB = Embarkation

Some of the reasons for the gross disparities in the sizes of the two battalion staffs are the following. The U.S. ground forces experience in high intensity war has been characterized by strategic deployment by sea over long distances and infantry attack against fortified positions in relatively static situations. The U.S. infantry battalion has been dominated by the historical demand to embark in conjunction with another service, activity requiring planning. Once ashore, the Army infantry battalion and especially the Marine has been dominated by initial tactical situations in which powerful supporting arms have been available to coordinate in relatively static situations against entrenched enemy forces. The resulting battalion and staff are admirably suited to plan, to embark, to land, and to coordinate supporting arms. Once ashore and projected into a fluid situation against a strong motorized enemy, the U.S. battalion is less likely to be effective with such a command and staff style because the advantage must be with the maneuvering force with enough fire-power to exploit the fleeting opportunity at the crucial point in the battle. Perhaps the key to effective tactics here is the balance between movement and firepower. In direct contact with his company commanders, the German motorized infantry battalion commander moved them characteristically in *Kampfgruppen* put together with an artillery battery and *Flak* and *Pak* admirably suited to intervene directly in the unstructured and decentralized mobile battle.

13

Maneuver War in the Desert: Conclusions and Applications

Rommel was a noteworthy modern commander who fought with weapons similar to those held by U.S. ground forces today and with a style that fundamentally reduced uncertainty and exploited chance in war. Rommel directed his battles often from among the leading vehicles of his advancing columns. He accompanied on foot the leading platoons of his dismounted motorized infantry in combat engagements he determined to be crucial to the operational level of war that he conducted as an army commander in North Africa. Rommel created a *Kampfstaffel*, or strong combat echelon, to accompany him and the headquarters of Panzer Army Africa in battle. Rommel used the *Kampfstaffel* to ensure his "battlefield mobility" and to serve as a unique personal *masse de manoeuvre* for him as commander in chief. Rommel created the *Stosslinie* (thrust line) in France and applied it further in North Africa as a unique, flexible, secure means of directing movement in mobile war. No better model exists than Rommel for the study of modern maneuver war. Ground forces staff colleges today would do well to cite him and his battles for study and dedicate a block of instruction on Rommel and maneuver war in the desert.

With their divisions, the Germans characteristically fought in *Kampfgruppen* (battle groups), or combined arms teams, that they continually reorganized. The Germans found that the active stages of mobile war demanded ad hoc formations to meet fluid conditions involving rapidly shifting dangers and vanishing opportunity. The Germans almost always built the *Kampfgruppen* around either a tank or a motorized rifle unit (e.g., infantry, motorcycle, or reconnaissance troops) and almost always added *Flak*, *Pak*, engineers and artillery. German commanders worked continuously through the night in the battles in North Africa directing the formation of new *Kampfgruppen*, physically concentrating the new ad hoc units, and then marching them through remaining darkness for continued maneuver or combat engagement timed for "break of day." German division commanders led from among leading elements of their divisions and their subordinate commanders also led from among the advanced units. The German tactical superiority in North Africa was based largely on this style of constantly reforming Kampfgruppen, moving 24 hours a day, and leading from the front.

The Germans were preoccupied with tanks, *Pak*, and *Flak* in the permissive terrain for fire and maneuver in North Africa. The desert terrain favored maneuver by motorized divisions and direct fire by relatively long-range weapons such as antitank guns and antiaircraft guns used in the anti-armor role. In Panzer Army Africa, Rommel paced the operations he conducted to the numbers and technical qualities of the 5th and 8th Panzer Regiments and the battle fighting skills of their commanders and tank troops. The "striking power" of Panzer Army Africa could be equated with the numbers of tanks ready for insertion in combat at any moment in an operation. When Rommel practiced operational art in Libya the possibilities of success depended on the following numbers of tanks available for insertion in combat from the two panzer regiments. With 260 tanks at the beginning of a battle, Rommel had the operational possibility to destroy the opposing field army. With 80 tanks remaining after heavy fighting, he had the possibility to hold the battlefield but little chance of exploiting the situation into destruction of the opposing field army. After continued heavy fighting and with only 40 tanks remaining, Rommel faced impending disaster with survival dependent on flight. The numbers shown, of course, are relative to the war fighting situation in North Africa in 1941-July 1942 that involved two strong field armies. The numbers, as they show that the operational possibilities in desert warfare are based upon tanks available for battle, represent a lesson of the 1941-July 1942 operations that is applicable to combat in similar areas today.

The Germans used *Pak* and *Flak* to advance with the panzer regiments and enhance their effectiveness. The Germans attached *Pak* units to panzer units and, with impressive tactical flexibility, used the *Pak* cannons in and among the tanks in tank versus tank battles. Faced with two models of British infantry support tanks with armor impervious to the German tank and *Pak* cannons, the Germans employed the bulky 88mm *Flak* cannons to knock them out. Faced with large numbers of lightly armored British reconnaissance vehicles, the Germans employed the light 20mm automatic Flak cannon to fend them off and knock out the older British cruiser tanks from side and rear. The Germans exploited the technical capabilities of the *Pak* and *Flak* weapons with imaginative tactics. Given the British numerical superiority in tanks, the Germans counterbalanced it with a bold selection of unlikely anti-armor weapons and superior antitank gun tactics.

But how are these observations on tanks and anti-armor weapons in the desert useful to U.S. ground forces and particularly the Marine Corps today that continue to be faced with the dilemma of trying to have both strategic air-and-sea-lift credibility and battlefield mobility? Recent wars in the Mideast and South Asia show that tanks continue to be the central weapon in desert war that they were in North Africa. The Marine Corps continues to be a strategic expeditionary force, infantry-styled and with a unique air arm, that may nevertheless have to intervene along a desert coast and conduct mobile operations in depth ashore. The German performance in North Africa suggests the following salvation: The Panzer Army needed more tanks, antitank guns and *Panzerbegleit Flak* (tank escort antiaircraft guns) but it had "enough" to fight successfully. The question for the Marine Corps may be almost identical to that for the Panzer Army: how much is enough for a desert situation?

The German panzer division in Libya fought effectively with a strength of approximately 140 tanks at the beginning of an operation against considerably larger British tank forces. This study shows that the individual panzer division retained significant striking power with a tank force of about 40 tanks, albeit against a shaken enemy after several days of combat. This study supports a view that a well handled tank force of about 100 tanks has some special qualities—perhaps a kind of "critical operational mass"—that give it the capability to perform effectively against much larger mobile forces.

German logistics in the desert centered around the truck columns of the service support battalions of the panzer divisions. The Germans called these truck columns the division trains and used them to move fuel, lubricants, ammunition and rations from *DAK* dumps to the divisions. The truck columns were small military units with their own tables of organization and equipment. In *15.Pz.D.*, the service support battalion had 13 numbered columns each with 30-ton freight or fuel capacity and approximately ten trucks. Rommel depended on these division truck columns and the Army-level truck columns farther to the rear for resupply during battle in big operations. They were his logistics system.

With the absence of fronts in the field conditions of the mobile battles, German and British forces intermingled and each side commonly overran the supply columns of the other. The Germans left the supply columns to their own devices rarely providing combat elements for convoy-style delivery of supplies. Rommel did not order specific protection for the columns until the resupply crisis in the Venezia operation. At that time the Panzer Army began to head for but did not reach an intriguing situation in mobile war in which the service support organization of a division would become a self-defensible "combat" element in its own right. The German experience in North Africa suggests that it would be a worthwhile project for present ground forces to examine the desirability of a service support *Kampfstaffel*, or combat echelon, to provide adequate defense for the service support element of appropriate divisions. Any study should take account of the necessities for defense of the entire service support element concentrated in laager and defense of the ground supply columns in the act of resupply, vehicle retrieval, repair, etc.

Even though the Germans operated "overseas" in North Africa, they employed staffs with fewer officers and lower ranks than other ground forces. Extreme differences exist between the U.S. ground forces staffs of today and the German staffs of World War II. Proportionately greater differences exist between the regimental staffs, but the most exaggerated disparity is at the battalion level. U.S. Army and Marine battalion staffs are so large that the planning function seems to have taken over almost to the exclusion of combat when the staff is compared with that of a German infantry battalion. Obviously the U.S. battalion could fight and the German battalion could plan, but the qualification still holds. The Marine Corps, in particular, accepts a large battalion staff based on the technical complexities of embarking on naval shipping and moving to a target area. Neither embarkation nor debarkation, however, is combat, and, as the fighting begins, U.S. ground forces battalion commanders enter it with staffs justified significantly on the basis of organizing administrative movement to the combat area.[59] In effect, once in combat, battalion commanders find themselves supported by staffs justified significantly by premises irrelevant to combat. In mobile war, both Army and Marine battalion commanders would be slowed in command reaction by such staffs.

Notes for Part Two:

0 Gordon A. Craig, Stanford University, in various conversations with the author between 1965 and the present.

1 Bruce I. Gudmundsson, *Stormtroop Tactics: Innovation in the German Army 1914-1918* (New York, 1989), is a recent account of the tactics that were the forerunner of the blitz style of advance in World War I.

2 Colonel Trevor N. Dupuy, USA (Ret.), *Numbers, Predictions and War* (London, 1979), pp. 99-103.

3 See these data in Dupuy, *Numbers, Predictions and War* (1979), pp. 108, 109.

4 Oberkommando der Wehrmacht or OKW.

5 *Deutsches Afrika Korps* or *DAK*.

6 15th Panzer Division in process of formation February 1941 largely from 33rd Infantry Division. 21st Panzer Division formed on basis of 5th Light Division and transformed into the Panzer Division on 1 August 1941 in Africa. A motorized division was in process of formation early in 1941 out of a melange of German units in Europe and Africa. In November 1941, the Germans designated this "Africa Division" as 90th Light Africa Division.

7 German rank equivalent to U.S. lieutenant general.

8 The projectile fired by these guns weighed approximately two pounds.

9 As quoted in David Irving, *The Trail of the Fox* (London, 1978), p. 51.

10 The German Empire of the day comprised 25 states and one Imperial *Land*. The four most important based on tradition and the strength of regional particularism, maintained their own armies—those of Prussia, Bavaria, Saxony, and Wuerttemberg. The Armies of the latter states, of course, were synchronized in command style and technology with the Prussian.

11 Gazala is a small town located close to the Mediterranean Sea, 65 km west of Tobruk. See Maps 1 and 2 for all such place names.

12 German Africa Corps or *Deutsches Afrika Korps* or *DAK*.

13 *21.Pz.D., Ia, Anlage zum KTB Nr. 5, Gefechtsbericht III. /Schuetz. Rgt. 104 (mot), 2.6.42*, U.S., Archives, German Records, Divisions, T-313, Roll 768, Fr. 000866.

14 *15.Pz.D., Ia, Anlage zum KTB Nr. 2, Gefechtsberichte des Maschinengewehrbataillons vom 22.1. bis 26.1.42*, U.S. Archives, German Records, Divisions, T-313, Roll 666, Fr. 000593.

15 *Pz.AOK Afrika, Ia, Anlage 14 zum KTB Nr. 3, DAK, Aufstellung einer Beute-Panzer-Abteilung, 12.2.42*, U.S. Archives, German Records, Panzer Armies, T-313, Roll 426, Fr. 8719207.

16 *Pz. AOK Afrika, OQu., Umgliederunqen und Neuaufstellunqen, Aufstellung der Kampfstaffel des O.B., 12.2.42*, U.S. Archives, German Records, Panzer Armies, T-313, Roll 437, Fr. 8730292.

17 For these personnel figures, see *Pz.AOK Afrika, Kampfstaffel, OB, Kasta Tagesmeldung, 13.6.42*, U.S. Archives, German Records, Panzer Armies, T-313, Roll 666, Fn. 8776055.

18 *Pz, AOK Afrika, OB, Anlage zum KTB, Kampfstaffel, OB, Kasta Gefechtsbericht, 27.5.42*, U.S. Archives, German Records, Panzer Armies, T-313, Roll 477, Fr. 8775919.

19 *Pz. AOK Africa, OB, Anlage zum KTB, Kampfstaffel, Gefechtsbericht, 3./Flak 43, 28.5.42*, U.S. Archives, German Records, Panzer Armies, T-313, Roll 477, Fr. 8775296.

20 *15.Pz.D., Ia, KTB Nr.2, Seite10, noch 21.11.41*, U.S. Archives, German Records, Divisions, T-313, Roll 664, Fr. 000411

21 *21.P2.D., Ia, Anlage zum KTB Nr. 2, Gefechtsbericht, Pz.R.5,17.11.-31.12.42*, U.S. Archives, German Records, Divisions, T313, Roll 767, Fr 000213.

22 *21.P2.D., Ia, Anlage zum KTB Nr. 2, Gefechtsbericht, Pz.R.5,17.11.-31.12.42*, U.S. Archives, German Records, Divisions, T313, Roll 767, Fr 000214.

23 *Generalmajor* Johannes von Ravenstein had been captured by the British on 29 Nov 41 in the fluid, mobile combat of the Crusader battles.

24 *21.Pz.D., Ia, Anlage zum KTB Nr. 3, Abt. Ia Nr. 98/42 Geh., Unternehmen Bismarck, 13.3.42*, U.S. Archives, German Records, Divisions, T-313, Roll 768, Fr. 000234.

25 *15.Pz.D., Ia, KTB Nr. 2, 27.11, 41*, U.S. Archives, German Records, Divisions, T-313, Roll 664, Fr. 000445.

26 Actually German Africa Corps (1941), Panzer Group Africa (August 1941-January 1942), then Panzer Army Africa for the remainder of the period of this study.

27 Note, for example, *Pz. AOK Afrika, KTB, 15.8/-18.11.41*, U.S. Archives, German Records, Panzer Armies, T-313, Roll 423, Fr. 8715788-89.

28 Sunset that day was at approximately 1715.

29 *15.Pz.D., Ia, KTB Nr. 2, Seite 4, 22.11.41*, U.S. Archives, German Records, Divisions, T-313, Roll 664, Fr. 000417.

30 *15.Pz.D., Ia, Anlage zum Taetigkeitsbericht, Kommando, 15.Pz.D., Anhaeltspunkte fuer die Motorisierte Gefechtsausbildung*, U.S. Archives, German Records, Divisions, T-313, Roll 664, Fr. 000250.

31 *21.Pz.D., Ia, Anlage zum KTB Nr. 5, Division Befehl fuer den Vormarsch am 1./2.5.41 nach Bir Hacheim., 13.3.42*, U.S. Archives, German Records, Divisions, T-313, Roll 768, Fr. 000813.

32 *15.Pz.D., Ia, KTB Nr. 2, Seite 10, 23.11.41*, U.S. Archives, German Records, Divisions, T-313, Roll 664, Fr. 000428.

33 An observation of then *Generalmajor* Fritz Erich von Manstein during the Polish Campaign (!). Manstein seems to be saying that lesser minds and characters see only danger in danger, react accordingly and attempt to remove danger in advance by adherence to rule or principle.

34 *Pz. AOK Africa, Ia, Schlachtberjcht der Panzerarmee Afrika, den 20.11.41*, U.S., Archives, German Records, Panzer Armies, T- 313, Roll 430, Fr. 8723063.

35 *21.Pz.D., Ia, Anlage zum KTB Nr. 2, Gefechtsbericht, Pz,R.5, 17.11-31.12.41, Seite 1.*, U.S. Archives, German Records, Divisions, T-313, Roll 767, Fr. 000213.

36 *15.Pz.D., Ia, KTB Nr. 2, 7.12.41*, U.S. Archives, German Records, Divisions, T-313, Roll 767, Fr. 000229.

37 British 40mm L/52 Tank: 56mm at 500m; German 50mm L/42 Tank: 63mm at 500m; German 75mm L/24 tank: 54mm at 500m. See in F.M. von Senger und Etterlin, *Die Kampfpanzer von 1916 -1066* (Muenchen, 1971), pp. 515, 516.

38 Official name for German forces in North Africa from 9 February - 15 August 1941. On 15 August 1941, the force was designated Panzer Group Africa and then on 30 January 1942 it became Panzer Army Africa

39 *15.Pz.D., Ia, KTB Nr.3, Anlagen C, Deutsches Afrika Korps, Ia/Flak, Richtlinien fuer den Einsatz von Flak - Batterien, 22.5.1942*, U.S. Archives, German Records, Divisions, T-313, Roll 666, Fr. 001446,47.

40 Ibid., Fr. 001447.

41 Bristol-Blenheim: Three-seat, two-engine, ground attack style aircraft with 1,000-pound internal bomb load, and three machine guns able to be directed in strafing.

42 Ibid., Fr. 000321,22.

43 *l5.Pz.D., Ia, KTB Nr. 2, Gefechtsbericht der 3./Flak 33, 19.11.15.12.41*, U.S. Archives, German Records, Divisions, T-313, Roll 666, Fr. 000341, 42.

44 *Pz. AOK Afrika, Ia, Anlage zum KTB, Panzergruppe Panzerabwehrwaffen, 16.11.41*, U.S. Archives, German Records, Panzer Armies, T-313, Roll 423, Fr. 8716049, 50.

45 *Pz. AOK Africa, OQu., Vesorgungssachgebiet, Bestand um Pak, 25.5.42*, U.S. Archives, German Record, Panzere Armies, T-313, Roll 439, Fr. 873031.

46 *Pz. AOK Africa, OQu., Versorgungssachgebiet, Funkspruch vom 21.5.42, 13.20 Uhr, OKH/Gen St d H, Org. Abt. (III) an Pz AOK*, U.S. Archives, German Records, Panzer Armies, T-313, Roll 439, Fr. 8732968.

47 *l5.Pz.D., Ia, KTB Nr. 2, Gefechtsbericht, 3./Pz.J9.33, 15.12.42*, U.S. Archives, German Records, Divisions, T-313, Roll 666, Fr. 000521.

48 Ibid., Fr. 000522.

49 *15.Pz.D, Ia, Anlaqe zum KTB Nr. 2, Pz Jg. 33, Gefechtsbericht ueber die Abwehr feindlicher Panzerangriffe gegen die Suedflanke der 15.Pz. - Div. am 22.11.1941*, U.S. Archives, German Records, Divisions, T-313, Roll 666, Fr. 000378.79.

50 Ibid., Fr. 000379.

51 *15.Pz.D., Ia, Anlage zum KTB Nr. 2, Gefechtsbericht ... des Panzer-Regiments 5 vom 17.11.bis 31.12.41*, U.S. Archives, German Records, Divisions, T-313, Roll 767, Fr. 000234.

52 The German term, supply, included all the supporting services associated today with the more fashionable term, logistics. The researcher will use the term, service, for the rest of the chapter to

include the provision of rations, fuel, ammunition, the maintenance and repair of weapons and equipment, the preparation of food, the providing of medical treatment, etc.

53 Capacities of different columns varied from division to division; for example, 21st Panzer Division at approximately the same time (6 Feb 42), had only one fuel column but with a capacity of about 150 tons.

54 *Pz. AOK Africa, OQu., Versorgungssachgebiet, OKH, Gen St d H, Nr.: I1984/41 g. Kdos., 28.2.41*, U.S. Archives, German Records, Panzer Armies, T-313, Roll 439, Fr. 8732892.

55 For these developments see *Pz.AOK Africa, Ia, Anlage zum KTB Nr. 3, Pz-AOK Abt. Ia/Ic Nr. 1210/42 g., Ueberfaelle, 28.2.42*, U.S. Archives, German Records, Panzer Armies, T-313, Roll 426, Fr. 8719301, 02.

56 *Pz. AOK Afrika, Ia, Anlage zum KTB, Panzerarmee Afrika Ia, Gef. St., den 31.5.42. Takt.zeit. 2235*, U.S. Archives, German Records, Panzer Armies, T-313, Roll 469, Fr. 8766866.

57 *Pz.AOK Afrika, Ia, KTB. Kriegsrangliste, Saemtlicher Offiziere und Beamten im Offizierrang des Oberkommando der Panzerarimee Afrika*, c.Feb.42, U.S. Archives, German Records, Panzer Armies, T-313, Roll 426, Fr. 8719060-62.

58 *90.1.Afr.D., IIa, KTB Nr. 1, Taetigkeltsbericht, Offizierstellenbesetzung nach dem Stande vom 31.101.41*, U. S. Archives, German Records, Divisions, T-313, Roll 768, Fr. 000808.

59 For the Navy, movement to the landing area is combat, involving, for example, antisubmarine war, anti-air war, etc. For the Army and Marine Corps, it is a special form of movement not involving combat by the embarked force.

PART THREE:
Panzer Maneuver War in the Forest and Lakes of the Baltic 1941

14

Introduction

Through the accumulated effects of military victories on the European continent from 1939 to the spring of 1941, Germany stood poised to win the war in Europe in the early summer. As its Armed Forces attacked Soviet Russia on 22 June 1941, Germany reached the single juncture in World War II at which it had the realistic opportunity to win the war in the East, a victory that could also be equated with German victory in the European war. This heady thesis is supported by the decisive effect that must be associated with the defeat of Soviet Russia and its timing in late summer 1941.

To accomplish this vast political result, Germany required its Armed Forces to defeat the main concentration of the Red Army that the German General Staff calculated would be positioned to defend Moscow—the communications, industrial, political, and psychological hub of Soviet Russia. The General Staff conceptualized a plan to drive Army Group center directly at Moscow, force the Soviets to fight for it, and win the campaign in about 10 weeks based on the effects of the destruction of the opposing armed force and seizure of the mobilization space around Moscow. Contrary to the elegantly simple Army plan, Adolf Hitler stood mesmerized by concern over the wings of the advance, specifically St. Petersburg, the Ukraine, and the Crimea. The Army plan virtually guaranteed the defeat of Soviet Russia in World War II through its concentric advance on a single compact spatial objective and the armies defending it. The Hitler plan virtually assured Soviet survival through its eccentric diffusion of the German army against widely separated spatial objectives away from the mass of the Red Army.

Because the Army plan largely guaranteed Soviet defeat, the main factors for consideration of the possibility of German victory in World War II are those that affected the advance of Army Group Center in the summer of 1941. Three factors dominated the issue of victory, namely, Army Group Center's capability to destroy the main concentration of the entire Red Army providentially placed between it and Moscow by the Soviet High Command, Hitler's misplaced will to prevent that victory by diffusing the offensive in eccentric advances on St. Petersburg and the Ukraine, and the capabilities of Army Groups North and South to ensure the success of Army Group Center. In its advance into Soviet Russia, the German Army fought a great double battle in summer 1941, against an unlikely combination of Hitler and the Red Army. The pivotal Army Group Center proved capable of winning the battle against the Red Army from the first days of the advance and faced greater crisis in the other less tangible but equally important battle to overcome Hitler's fear for the immediate, assured seizure of indecisive spatial objectives.

In the first several days of the war, Army Group Center began the rapid destruction of the powerful Soviet field armies deployed in White Russia (Belarus), Adolf Hitler immediately attempted to prevent it from getting loose toward Moscow, and Army Group South pinned down the Soviet armies in the Ukraine preventing them from interfering with the drive against Moscow. In the context of these high points, the question arises for purposes of this story: What was the strategic connection between the breakthrough of Army Group North at Duenaburg and the advance of Army Group Center? The main connection was Hitler's concern for the taking of Leningrad at the expense of the advance of Army Group Center. Hitler stated in his Directive 21 (Case Barbarossa) that only after Army Group North occupied Leningrad would he allow Army Group Center to continue its attack out of White Russia toward Moscow. He noted specifically that "only a surprisingly rapid collapse of Russian resistance could justify the simultaneous pursuit of both objectives."[1] The strategic connection is decisive. German success at Duenaburg can be interpreted as the single catalyst outside the battle in White Russia itself that would have given the German Army victory in its great double battle with Hitler and the Red Army.

The following congruence of events highlights this interpretation of quick victory over the Soviet Union. Army Groups Center and North had to be concretely successful enough against the Red Army that Hitler would be swayed to give the green light for the armor of Army Group Center to drive uninterruptedly toward Moscow. The Germans required the congruence within approximately three weeks of the campaign's opening to successfully paralyze further Soviet mobilization and possible recovery. In the event itself, Army Groups North and Center achieved battle successes so resounding in the opening four days that the Germans seemed assured of victory In that brief time, 8th Panzer Division in the north had seized the Duenaburg bridges opening the way to Leningrad, and 7th Panzer Division in the center had cut communications between the capital of White Russia and Moscow. These events can be extrapolated into Leningrad's fall by mid-July 1941, the associated psychological effect of Hitler ordering uninterrupted continuation of the attack toward Moscow, and Army Group Center continuing its demonstrated prowess into destruction of the mass of the Red Army defending it. Within such a context, the German breakthrough at Duenaburg takes on a special significance. Unlike numerous other military coups de main, which were simply junctures in a seemingly endless series of campaigns gradually accumulating in the defeat of Germany, we witness a single coup whose potential consequence included German victory over the Soviet Union and probably victory in the European War.

Photo 7. The 8th Panzer Division tanks and crews in East Prussia shortly before the drive into Soviet-held Lithuania. In foreground a light Panzer II reconnaissance tank. In background a Czech-built TNHP-38(t) battle tank, the most numerous tank in the division at the beginning of *Barbarossa*. Although these tanks were marginally effective for tank versus tank combat, they were admirably suited for moving through the narrow country lanes and boggy, forest terrain of the Baltic (Bundesarchiv Bestand).

15

8th Panzer Division Advances 92 Kilometers into Lithuania on the First Day of the War (22-23 June '41)

The 8th Panzer Division (*8.Pz.D*)—the hero of this piece—was one of ten German panzer divisions formed by the time of the advance against France in May 1940. The Germans built the new division around the German *Panzer II* and *Panzer IV* tanks and the Czech-manufactured, German-designated *Panzer 38(t)*. The latter Czech vehicle was the most numerous tank but a modest 10-ton vehicle armed with a long barreled 3.7 cm cannon.[2] The Germans also equipped the division with 12 *Panzer III* command tanks, powerful 20-ton vehicles with the main armament removed from the turrets and resultant extremely advanced command tanks, e.g., vehicles with the armor protection and cross-country mobility of a main battle tank with space for commander and staff. The *Panzer III* command tank demonstrates technically the emphasis placed by the Germans on command and control in panzer divisions. With it, the Germans provided the division commander and his tank regiment and battalion commanders with a technical instrument that permitted them to advance in the lead of their units. In the lead, with effective personal protection, German tank force commanders were in touch with battlefield reality in mobile divisions assigned deep strategic targets in major offensives culminating in the attack against Soviet Russia in June 41.

The division advanced within a chain of command that included the next higher 56th Motorized Army Corps (*LVI.A.K.[mot]*), 4th Panzer Group (*Pz.Gr.4*), and Army Group North (*A.Gr.N*). The German Army High Command (*OKH*) set the city of Leningrad (Saint Petersburg) as the strategic target for its Baltic army group, and *8.Pz.D.* found itself caught up in that strategic situation on the eve of the surprise offensive out of peace and into war against the Soviet Union. The single operational success that would result in the quick seizure of Leningrad would be the immediate crossing of the middle reaches of the Great Western Duena (Daugava) River and the resultant breaking up of the strongest natural defensive line between East Prussia and Leningrad. As the only panzer division in

LVI.A.K.(mot), whose zone of operations led through Duenaburg, *8.Pz.D.* was selected as the operational instrument to seize the rail and highway bridges there on the main route to Leningrad. The tanks of the division and other motor vehicles and weapons built around them, and the robust, fluid German command style gave *8.Pz.D.* the capability to advance quickly through Duenaburg to Leningrad.

The Baltic region presented special difficulties for the movement of *8.Pz.D.* and the accompanying 3rd Motorized Infantry Division (*3.I.D. [mot]*), that tended to reduce the impact of tanks and increase the importance of motorized infantry. The Baltic area was characterized by innumerable water courses, lakes, and associated swampy areas and forests. Agriculture dominated the economy of the inland areas and was reflected in a road system of unsurfaced and unpaved roads generally without foundations or drainage ditches. Such roads were largely country lanes suitable for light horse drawn traffic and pedestrians but not passable for heavy motor vehicle traffic, especially in swampy areas or during rainfall. Many "roads" on the German maps proved to be lanes without foundations or ditching approximately eight feet wide. The "main highways" were few in number connecting the larger cities. They were adequate for two way traffic for motor vehicles but unpaved and consisting of graded rock foundations with crushed rock surfaces reasonably effective for water runoff and load bearing. Along this communications system with soft swampy terrain bordering roads, *8.Pz.D.* faced "about 7 medium (*25m to 50m river width)*, 14 smaller (with names on 1:300,000 scale maps), and 16 smaller water courses to cross" from the border to Duenaburg.[3] The division faced 38 significant streams to be crossed by its 5,000 motor vehicles during movement along sandy lanes and unpaved roads.

The Baltic terrain reduced the importance of tanks in the panzer divisions by presenting few areas for the sweeping employment of tanks cross-country. The same terrain presented numerous possibilities for the tanks of the division to be immobilized waiting for bridges to be constructed across water courses too deep for fording. Under these conditions, the motorized infantry of *8.Pz.D.* played a relatively more important role in offensive movement. Motorized infantry could deploy out of its vehicles and continue to advance on foot using the rubber boats organic to the motorized rifle regiments to cross unfordable streams and set up bridgeheads. In contrast, the tanks of the division would be completely "immobilized" in terms of advancing. In the actual historical event, the picture is more complex because in come cases on over-loaded, soft, unpaved roads, tanks and other tracked vehicles would be the only ones able to advance while the predominantly wheeled vehicles of the motorized infantry would be immobilized. The end result for understanding the movement of *8.Pz.D.* is that the motorized infantry tended to be more important in the advance than previously in the West and elsewhere on the Russian front in the summer of 1941.

Because *OKH* equated panzer divisions with offensive operations and deep strategic targets, it held back the panzer divisions from the Soviet border as long as possible in order to achieve surprise. The *OKH*, for example, stationed *8.Pz.D.* in the area around Prague in the Protectorate of Bohemia (present Czech Republic), where it would have been difficult for the Soviets to believe that it would be shortly before an attack against the Soviet Union. With impressive nerves, *OKH* did not begin to move the division to the vicinity of the Lithuanian border until "1357 on 16.6 according to plan."[4] The division transport commandant moved the entire force from Prague into a new billeting area (*Unterkunftsraum*) immediately south of the Memel (Neman) River on the Lithuanian border in only 51 hours. The

Germans, accordingly, placed this panzer division close to the enemy border less than three days before the planned attack. At 2000, 18 June, the division began to move into its battle concentration area (*Aufmarschraum*) on the south bank of the Neman River. Then, during the brief hours of darkness on the evenings of 19 and 20 June, the division moved forces across the river into the attack assembly areas (*Bereitstellungsraum*) in an extremely restricted space north of the Neman and against the Lithuanian border.

For the assault at 0305, 22 June 41, into Soviet-occupied Lithuania, the division commander, *Generalmajor* (one star) Erich Brandenberger, organized the division into four battle groups. Characteristically for the German style of fighting, Brandenberger set up the following ad hoc (i.e., for a particular purpose) units for battle:

1. Advanced Detachment under Commander, 1st Battalion, 28th Motorized Rifle Regiment.
2. Battle Group Crisolli under Commander, 8th Motorized Rifle Regiment (LtCol Crisolli).
3. Battle Group Scheller under Commander, 8th Motorized Rifle Brigade (Col Scheller).
4. Battle Group Bodenhausen under Commander, 28th Motorized Rifle Regiment (Lt Col Bodenhausen).

The division commander and his operations officer[5] organized these battle forces as combined arms teams with each having attached artillery, antitank gun (*Pak*), and pioneer units. Each battle group held one panzer battalion of the division's 10th Panzer Regiment (*Pz.R.10*), a situation reflecting the necessity to break through border defenses and lingering concern about Brandenberger's decision to place the *Schwerpunkt* (point of main effort) of the attack in the north. The two strongest battle groups, Scheller and Crisolli, also included anti-aircraft (Flak) units that the Germans intended especially to defend bridge crossing sites.

The division commander planned to launch the attack across the border using 503rd Infantry Regiment (*I.R.503*) of his northern neighbor, 290th Infantry Division (*290.I.D.*), employing the German infantry to make the first move against anticipated field fortifications. The foot marching infantry regiment would occupy the entire front of the division for the initial attack and be followed by Battle Group Crisolli in the southern sector along the north bank of the Neman River. The division Advanced Detachment lay north of Crisolli where the division expected most success. Battle Group Scheller, the strongest of the battle forces also lay in the north immediately behind the Advanced Detachment, showing that Brandenberger sensed the breakthrough would be there followed by an advance northeast to the first day's target, the big bridge over the gorge of the Dubysa River near the city of Ariogala (See Maps 8 and 9). Battle Group Bodenhausen and the Division Trains (59th Panzer Supply Battalion arranged in various truck columns) and parts of the medical battalion lay rearward.

Almost immediately the Division Commander confronted a picture different from that developed during the weeks of planning for the attack. In the division command post at 0355, the operations officer (Ia) received a message from Battle Group Crisolli in the anticipated difficult sector: "advancing easily in continuous attack; hardly any resistance"[6] along the road to the Mituva River. The river was the most important obstacle to the advance toward Ariogala and lay 12 km from the border. By 0540, the tanks of Battle Group

Crisolli had arrived close to Jurbarkas and the two bridges across the Mituva but neither division nor next higher headquarters knew the bridge situation. The river was 30m wide at Jurbarkas and would be almost impossible to ford. In the event that the structures were not seized intact, the German advance would be halted for several hours, a devastating blow to the division with its sights set on Ariogala approximately 80 km distant and the first day's target. At 0600, however, Battle Group Crisolli signaled by radio that it had taken both bridges intact. By 0650, the group had broken Soviet resistance on the east bank in the city and was ready to move on. Only four hours into the war, the division commander faced the situation that the planned breakthrough in the north was unrealistic in the face of Crisolli's success in the south.

During the same period of time farther north, the Advanced Detachment of the division had moved through *I.R.503* and come up against tough (*zaeh*) resistance from Russians fighting in field fortifications in difficult terrain with a less well developed road system than farther south. Battle Group Scheller advancing behind the Advanced Detachment would run into the same difficult conditions and by 1100 the two battle forces would report combat against Russians in concrete bunkers. In his analysis of the situation as it had developed by 1430, the Ia made the candid point in the division war diary that the command estimate of the enemy had been false (*Unzutreffend*).[7] *Generalmajor* Brandenberger reacted vigorously to the new reality. Originally moving with the Advanced Detachment of the division for the first several hours of the attack, he informed the Ia at 0734, 22 June that he was changing position to ride with Battle Group Crisolli. The Ia noted further in the war diary that the Russians had not placed a single obstacle along the southern route through Jurbarkas, but had created a 100m-wide barrier of felled, intertwined trees across the northern sector.

Brandenberger and Crisolli pressed forward along the new *Schwerpunkt* achieving an astounding leap forward that included entering Seredzius at the confluence of the Dubysa and Neman Rivers at 1220, and crossing the big ford on the Dubysa River at the southwest edge of Ariogala at 1515, 22 June. In these advances, Battle Group Crisolli covered 54 and 80 km by road respectively and reached the optimistic first day's target for the advance by mid-afternoon. To comprehend the high-tempo command style of the Germans in this success, note what happened to the original main force. After the division commander's almost immediate shift away from the faulty main attack, the former *Schwerpunkt* force did not break through Soviet bunker line near Girdziai, still only 13 km from the border, until 1600 on the same day.

At 1620, 22 June, *General der Infanterie* (three stars) Erich von Manstein, Commander, *LVI.A.K.(mot)*, appeared in the division command post. German command style stood sharply etched there. Manstein did not expect to find the division commander in the command post but rather the Ia of the division in touch with the operational scene and in communication with everybody. The division commander rode at that moment with the forward elements of the new *Schwerpunkt* battle group under Crisolli near Ariogala. Brandenberger personally directed the battle at the point selected by him as crucial for the advance. As the outcome of his visit to the division command post, Manstein gave the order to the Ia face-to-face for *8.Pz.D.* still on 22 June to reach the east bank of the Dubysa River at Ariogala with all its combat units. He also ordered the division to throw advanced elements toward Kedainiai and keep the Seredzius crossings at the mouth of the Dubysa open (See Maps 8 and 9).

The division commander located with the mass of Battle Group Crisolli at the ford over the Dubysa near Ariogala at approximately 1530, 22 June, ordered the tank battalion with Crisolli and one motorized infantry company in armored, three-quarter-tracked vehicles across the ford immediately to seize the eastern heights above the river and the city. With this attack accomplished, the division commander ordered an immediate push to take the highway bridge over the Dubysa Gorge lying 2.5 km northwest of Ariogala. Elements of Battle Group Crisolli seized intact the big bridge on the unpaved but well constructed *Autobahn* (main highway) running through the city. Shortly after this successful coup de main, at approximately 1800, the corps commander, now 80 road kilometers forward of the German border, stood in Ariogala discussing continuation of the attack with the division commander. Manstein directed Brandenberger still on 22 June, to advance toward Kedainiai, the next big city on the road to Duenaburg and location of a large military airfield. The division commander, in turn, directed LtCol Crisolli to move out with the available elements of his battle group. Twelve kilometers east of Ariogala in the vicinity of two bridges over large streams crossing the highway, the battle group met strong resistance—almost always presented by the Germans as a sizeable infantry force supported by tanks and artillery—and was ordered to halt. At this moment, 2300, 22 June, *8.Pz.D.* stood 92 km by road from where it began the attack earlier at 0305 on the same day.

This initial drive of 20 hours into Soviet-occupied Lithuania is a convenient one for presenting the anatomy of the advance of a motorized force in offensive maneuver war. Because the action was an historical event, the anatomy or structural makeup of the advance consists of historical data that answer the questions: what makes an advancing force go, and what makes it stop? The author suspects that the answers to those questions for *8.Pz.D.* apply through historical analogy to all forces advancing in all times and all places. The following pages, however, can claim to answer those questions only for *8.Pz.D.* in June-July 41 in Soviet Russia. And, to begin to show what made *8.Pz.D.* function so effectively in terms of maneuver war, the following pages address those questions from the division's perspective on the first day of advance, 22 June 41, out of East Prussia and into Lithuania.

The context of the initial hours of the advance of *8.Pz.D.* was vast and unique. Adolf Hitler as head of state in Germany and leader of the national socialist movement had determined to launch a surprise attack against Soviet Russia with the purpose to seize quickly three areas that he considered crucial for the permanent, long term establishment of Germany as a great power. Hitler's expressed targets were Leningrad, the Ukraine, and the Crimea followed by occupation of European Russia to roughly the west bank of the Volga River. Within this grand political and ideological framework, *OKH* took the lead in planning the campaign and concentrating the German Armed Forces, especially the Army but dictating also to the tactically oriented *Luftwaffe*. On the first day of the war, *8.Pz.D.* moved according to the political logic of Hitler and the ideology of national socialism. It also moved on 22 June 41, and thereafter almost exclusively, to the military grammar of the advance of *LVI.A.K.(mot)* through the Baltic toward Leningrad.

Headquarters *LVI.A.K.(mot)* controlling *8.Pz.D.* set the city of Duenaburg, Latvia, and the highway and railway bridges there as the operational target for the corps. Manstein selected his strongest and most mobile division, *8.Pz.D.* to lead an advance directly at

Duenaburg. The city and its bridges represented a distant target—295 km straight-line increments along the road system—classically suited for panzer divisions. Quick seizure of the city would dismantle Soviet defenses along the greatest single obstacle to the German advance on Leningrad. If such a coup could be pulled off by *8.Pz.D.*, the Soviets would be forced into delaying actions for a vast distance back to the only other and last, distinct barrier line between the Germans and Leningrad, the Mshaga and Luga River system. The middle reaches of this system lie only 120 km from the big city on the Gulf of Finland.

How does this discussion of the assignment of Duenaburg as the first great operational target for the advance of German Army Group North *(H.Gr.Nord)* contribute to an understanding of what made *8.Pz.D.* move in the Baltic Area? The division had a mission to perform with all the psychological urgency suggested by the word. Other divisions in *H.Gr.Nord* also had missions to perform that drove them to extraordinary exertion in the early stages of Barbarossa when the defeat of the Soviet Union and victory in World War II beckoned. No German division in *H.Gr.Nord*, however, had a mission with the heroic quality of the immediate seizure of a big, distant, foreign city. During planning Manstein was asked about the chances of taking Duenaburg in a way that would seal the destruction of the Soviet defenses between the border and Leningrad. He remarked that if it could not be done within four days, *LVI.A.K.(mot)* could hardly count on taking the bridges intact with catastrophic consequences for the continuation of the campaign because of the necessity to mount an attack across a huge river barrier.[8] Brandenberger and his officers and men not only had a distant target but one in which every hour counted for the taking. The division moved with a sense of urgency that must be understood to comprehend why it stayed in motion so effectively and several times accelerated so dramatically towards its target in Latvia.

Brandenberger put *8.Pz.D.* in motion toward Duenaburg on the morning of 22 June with enormous respect for the intervening obstacles several of which could doom the whole enterprise by forcing halts. These halts along with accumulating frictions would prove fatal to a successful breakthrough. The German drive east toward Duenaburg and then north northeast to Leningrad could be characterized as a string of stream crossings and bridge seizures. Operational level maps for the Baltic area show 18 watercourses crossing the route of Battle Group Crisolli from the border at Smalininkia to Ariogala that between 0305 and 1515, 22 June had been negotiated by the mass of the group.[9] The division put together special detachments ahead of time to seize the border bridge near Smalininkia and the two bridges over the Mituva River at Jurbarkas enroute to Ariogala (See Map 8). The division had to assume, however, that it might not be successful in the coup de main planned for Jurbarkas and in the later seizure of the bridge near Ariogala. Corps headquarters, therefore, attached two large pontoon bridge columns (B-Columns) to the division to begin pioneer bridge construction quickly in the event of the failure of intact bridge seizures over the Mituva and Dubysa. On 22 June, along the route of advance of Battle Group Crisolli, *8.Pz.D.* captured intact every bridge along the route of advance to Ariogala by mid afternoon. One answer to the question: What kept *8.Pz.D.* advancing, therefore, is that the division seized undamaged every significant bridge along the *Schwerpunkt* line of advance. This answer, although accurate and important for understanding what happened on 22 June 41, does not tell the reader how the Germans overcame poor, crowded roads, tough Soviet resistance, deep space and short time factors to move 92 km by mid afternoon of the first day of the war.

Command style significantly accounts for German success on the first day of the war. Witness the following events involving the German leaders. *Generalmajor* Brandenberger assigned the *Schwerpunkt* of the advance to the northern sector of the division front and personally moved with the Advanced Detachment of the division followed by the *Schwerpunkt* Battle Group Scheller in the first hours of the attack. The Ia dominated the division command post, issued orders in the name of the commander to keep things moving, and was the point of contact for higher headquarters to pinpoint the division and give it new speed and direction as appropriate to corps and panzer group perspectives. When the division commander personally observed the resistance of the Soviets fighting in field fortifications and was informed by the Ia of the "fluid" forward motion of Battle Group Crisolli he moved to the leading elements of the battle group, redirected the *Schwerpunkt* of the operation, and kept the division in motion effectively enough to reach the distant first day's target. Along the route of advance of Battle Group Crisolli, both the corps (Manstein) and panzer group (Hoepner) commanders physically showed up at the division command post to find out what was going on and to keep the division moving through instructions to the Ia. At the crucial moment on the first day of the war when the mass of Battle Group Crisolli, at that moment 80 km by road into Lithuania attacked north to seize the great highway bridge over the Dubysa, the division commander was physically present personally to accompany the attack at approximately 1730 on 22 June 41.

At the tactical level the leaders and troops of Battle Group Crisolli inspired by the physical presence of the division commander showed similar energy and decisiveness in seizing intact every bridge along the route of advance. The battle group forded water courses alongside of bridges seized intact but not capable structurally of taking the military loads and volume of traffic or having the width to sustain two-way traffic. The energy and boldness of the division commander and the tactical effectiveness of the troops of Battle Group Crisolli is illustrated by the fact that Battle Group Scheller would be able to disengage from the fortified positions on the border only at 1650, 22 June 41, still lying 77 km by road west of Crisolli in Ariogala (See Map 8 and note Scheller's location at 1645). In summary, Brandenberger lay with the advanced battle group of the division in the day's target of Ariogala far ahead of schedule at 1650 while the second strongest of the three battle groups of the division lay 77 km to the west.

The command style of Brandenberger as division commander in accompanying the leading elements of the *Schwerpunkt* battle force was largely responsible for accelerating the division forward. Riding with a staff assistant, communications personnel, and a small bodyguard element (*Kampfstaffel*), Brandenberger made the quickest moves possible on the spot. By 0740 he had redesignated Battle Group Crisolli as the *Schwerpunkt* battle force driven over to it to take advantage of the weaker Soviet resistance in the south and begun to accelerate the division forward. Looking at the same situation from a different perspective, one could also say that what made the division advance more rapidly, was that it had found a weak spot in the Soviet defenses and advanced more successfully through it. It is not effective from the viewpoint of what makes a force go, however, to say that it discovered a "weak spot" in enemy defenses. Such spots had to be exploited by quick action on the part of the division and this action should be the focus of what made the division move. The road to military hell is paved with instances of weak, weakening, or weakened enemy resistance—all representing gates of opportunity—not being exploited by forces with the necessary technical capabilities in weapons and transport but without the command and combat soldier style to advance to a distant target. The point for understanding what made *8.Pz.D.* accelerate is that the division had an urgent style of operations. That style was characterized by a division commander leading from the front and a dominating operations officer effecting supporting action. They did so in an atmosphere of the dangerous uncertainty and exaggerated opportunity of a great mobile offensive.

Because of the road system over which the division passed and the numerous intersecting water courses, *8.Pz.D.* needed immense efforts to press forward one moderately strong battle group. An alert Soviet engineer detachment with only a handful of men could easily have spotted the Germans advancing bolding in daylight and blown up the two bridges at Jurbarkas 10 km from the German border with already prepared charges.[10] Even with small forces not capable of effective combat along the southern route of the German advance, the Soviets could have slowed the motorized Germans by a few successful road, bridge, culvert, and ford demolitions. The successful destruction of the two bridges at Jurbarkas and the cratering of potential fords would have made it virtually impossible for *8.Pz.D.* to have reached Ariogala on 22 June because of the time lost establishing bridgeheads and constructing bridges.

Battle Group Crisolli was little delayed by the Soviets, cross country terrain, river, road, or other similar factors on 22 June. In contrast, the other half of *8.Pz.D.* in terms of the deployment for the advance over the border—the Advanced Detachment and Battle Group Scheller—was slowed and then blocked by Soviet resistance in a system of obstacles, field fortifications, and concrete bunkers. Battle Group Scheller did not subdue the

8TH PANZER DIVISION (8.Pz.D.)

Div Hq (Bgen Brandenberger)
10th Panzer Regiment (*Pz.R.10)* (LtCol Fronhoefer)
Hq. 8th Motorized Rifle Brigade (*S.B.8)* (Col Scheller)
8th Motorized Rifle Regiment (*S.R.8)* (LtCol Crisolli)
28th Motorized Rifle Regiment *(S.R.28)* (LtCol Bodenhausen)
8th Motorcycle Battalion *(K.8)* (LtCol Kuett)
80th Panzer Artillery Regiment (*A.R.80)*
59th Panzer Reconnaissance Battalion *(Pz.A.A.59)* (Capt Wolff)
43rd Antitank Detachment *(Pz.Jg.43)*
92nd Light Flak Battalion *(1.Flak 92* or *le.Flak 92)*
59th Panzer Supply Battalion *(Pz.D.59)*

Note the names of the commanders of the major headquarters and maneuver elements. Those names predominate in the designations of the battle groups *(Kampfgruppen*, or *K-Gr)* into which the division reorganized itself daily to meet the latest tactical changes on the battlefield.

Figure 8. Units Comprising 8th Panzer Division.

Soviets in these defenses until after a difficult battle lasting 13 hours. At that moment, it lay approximately half a day behind Battle Group Crisolli, which was now reinforced by most of the tanks of the division and had become the strongest battle force. Scheller would not effectively come abreast of the new *Schwerpunkt* force led by Crisolli until 23 June in the Ariogala bridgehead. Scheller would advance behind and then north of Crisolli and parallel to his route of advance, backing him up and then developing a second axis of advance (See Maps 9 and 10). By approximately 0740, 22 June, Battle Group Crisolli had become, in effect, *8.Pz.D.* being simultaneously the leading and the *Schwerpunkt* force for the advance on Duenaburg.

The division commander continued to place the operational fortunes of *8.Pz.D.* on the broadened shoulders of Battle Group Crisolli by 2300, 22 June. At that time for the first moment on the first day of the war the division stopped. Brandenberger had placed Battle Group Crisolli reinforced now by most of the tanks of *8.Pz.D* near Ariogala, and the division needed time for reorganization during darkness on the evening of 22 June for advance in the best new configuration toward Kedainiai and Ukmerge (See Maps 9 and 10). The leading elements of *8.Pz.D.* halted, therefore, at 2300 on orders of the division commander to prepare for the continuation of the advance a few hours later, early on the morning of 23 June.

Past research on the empirical historical factors that have determined rates of advance in ground combat has produced no factors that have proven successful in powerful multivariate statistical equations used to generalize about and predict rates of advance. The hypothesis that advance rates are governed primarily by chance is probably the most realistic given the present state of deterministic equations and models of ground combat. Studies have presented, however, the following quantitatively styled factors as those that influence military advances:

1. Force Ratios
2. Attacker's Casualties
3. Defender's Posture
4. Terrain
5. Road Net
6. Weather
7. Nightfall
8. Duration of Operation

The experience of *8.Pz.D.* on 22 June supports the following generalizations about the eight mechanistic factors: the division was affected by every one of them in its attack.[11] Since the division moved ahead successfully on 22 June, however, no factor or any combination of factors can be said to have halted it. In advancing, nevertheless, the division had to overcome the challenges presented by those that proved to be adverse. The division overcame adverse factors of poor road net, difficult terrain, and the characteristic toughness of the Russian in every defensive posture to reach the first day's target hours ahead of schedule. While doing so, the division experienced favorable warm, dry weather, brought to bear superior force ratios, took minimal casualties, and used nightfall to its own advantage. These factors favored the Germans in their advance and were important reasons for their success, but they cannot be regarded as the main reasons for the extraordinary gains. Both the adverse and favorable features were important for understanding how far the Germans moved on 22 June, but secondary compared with overriding factor of German war fighting style.

In an extraordinary scene on 23 June, *8.Pz.D.* did not move forward during almost the entire day. This fact makes the accomplishment of the division in reaching Duenaburg 4 days, 3 hours, and 30 minutes into the campaign all the more remarkable because the division was in motion for only 3 days. In terms of average rates of advance the difference is striking: the division reached Duenaburg at an average rate of advance of approximately 74 km/day; the division when actually in motion during the three days of movement would advance at an average rate of almost 100 km/day. Both figures are impressive and the latter extreme figure gives pause for thought about the capabilities of motorized forces in difficult terrain with poorly developed road nets. The questions, finally, of what started and kept *8.Pz.D* in motion on 23 June 41 are non-sequiturs because the division did not move.

Brandenberger realized at midnight on the evening of 22 June, that the division stretched from the German border to the area 12 km east of Ariogala. He knew that it would be necessary to concentrate the division at Ariogala in order to move out with enough strength early on the morning of 23 June. Although both he and the corps commander agreed on the necessity to keep the division moving, they both agreed that some balance had to be struck between concentration of *8.Pz.D.* and the exploitation of the first day's penetration. As Brandenberger and his Ia, *Major i.G.* Friedrich Berendsen, labored to concentrate the division on the east bank of the Dubysa near Ariogala on Monday morning 23 June, they ran into substantial frictions involving the march of *8.Pz.D.* battle groups and supply columns along the main road on the north bank of the Neman. Battle Group Scheller, for example, was ordered off the road for more than two hours by corps traffic regulating officers who were pressing forward units of *3.I.D.(mot)* moving with high priority in their attempt to join in the advance with *8.Pz.D.* Then at 0930, 23 June, corps headquarters informed the division that the Soviets were advancing with strong tank forces from the east toward Ariogala with the aim of retaking the highway bridge there. Corps-level aerial reconnaissance noted the advance of two columns of Soviet vehicles from the east through Kedainiai, and given the existing road network, probably moving toward Ariogala. The aviators estimated that the columns held 300 to 400 tanks. This large Soviet force on the move west with obvious intention to attack something, froze *8.Pz.D.* in place.

The division commander concentrated the motorized infantry on the east bank of the Dubysa in a perimeter around and to the north of Ariogala to include the highway bridge. He massed the division artillery close up against the west bank of the river along with the tanks of the division. Brandenberger intended to use the artillery on the west bank and the motorized infantry and the division antitank guns on the east bank to "break up" the enemy attack and then launch a counterattack with all of the division tanks. At 1130, however, reconnaissance aircraft signaled that the big Soviet tank force seemed to be moving northwest toward Raseinia. This reevaluation was confirmed when the division received a message at 1315, 23 June, that *6.Pz.D.*, lying northwest around Raseinia, stood in combat with a strong motorized enemy (See Map 1).

At this point in the advance, the German officer commanding *Pz.Gr.4, Generaloberst* Erich Hoepner, had to make one of the more important operational decisions in the war on the eastern front. Hoepner had to decide whether to halt *8.Pz.D.* and turn it to the northwest to assist in the battle around Raseinia or to direct it toward the original deep operational target of Duenaburg. Brandenberger's division would face extremely dangerous conditions with *6.Pz.D.* pinned down far behind it. Hoepner made the bold decision to direct Brandenberger's division and Manstein's corps toward the original blitz goal. Challenged for several hours by the danger surrounding *6.Pz.D.*, Hoepner issued orders for continuation of the drive east that did not allow Brandenberger to push out his Advanced Detachment toward Kedainiai until 1750, 23 June. The mass of Battle Group Crisolli, still in the division lead, did not move until 1900. Brandenberger in his urgent, high tempo command style rode with Crisolli straight through the evening of 23 June. Battle Group Crisolli, however, had been halted for approximately 26 hours (from 1645, 22 June to 1900, 23 June) by the circumstances related above.

In summary the following factors halted *8.Pz.D.* during almost all of 23 June. In order to rest the lead elements and concentrate the following battle groups and supply services at Ariogala, Brandenberger kept the division halted for the early morning hours of 23 June. By approximately 0600, as reconnaissance reports began to come in from different sources that powerful Soviet tank forces were located in the vicinity of Kedainiai and on the move west, Brandenberger continued to concentrate the division while clarifying the size and intention of the approaching Soviet forces. Upon receipt of aerial reconnaissance reports that an enemy force of 300-400 tanks supported by other arms was heading toward Ariogala, *8.Pz.D.* deployed defensively to fight off an anticipated attack by the powerful armored enemy. Brandenberger halted *8.Pz.D.* on 23 June, to counter a perceived threat that never materialized but could not be ignored.

16

Classic Blitzkrieg Breakthrough: 8th Panzer Division Advances 200 Kilometers in 59 Hours to Rupture the Soviet Baltic Front (24-26 June '41)

The division commander set up an Advanced Detachment for the division, organizing it around *Pz.A.A.59*, that began to advance eastward at 1750, 23 June, from the area approximately 12 km east of Ariogala. From the beginning, events moved fast. The Advanced Detachment signaled at 1945 that it was in combat with a company-sized enemy force at Losvainiai (See Map 2 for this large easy to find city just west of Kedainiai).[12] After taking approximately 1.5 hours to subdue this force, it informed division headquarters that it would be in Kedainiai at 0200, 24 June, illustrating the tempo of German operations—the detachment would move straight through the hours of darkness out of touch with any other German forces to flank and rear and into the streets of a large Soviet city still at night. In the actual event, the Advanced Detachment reached the outskirts of the city at that time. The mass of Battle Group Crisolli following closely behind fought its way through the streets, seized the bridge there intact, and completed the capture of the place by 0340. Continuing to outstrip the units on its flanks, the division seized Kedainiai as the mass of *6.Pz.D.* in the neighboring 41st Army corps (motorized) still lay 45 km west of that city. From this juncture in the advance, *8.Pz.D.* would be exposed to attack on both its northern and southern flanks. Just as the Germans secured Kedainiai, for example, they located a strong Soviet tank force only 8 km north at Dotnuva (See Map 9) with full freedom of maneuver because of the lack of neighboring friendly units advancing with the division.

Personally riding with Crisolli, Brandenberger pushed the leading battle group of his division at a rapid pace under conditions that demanded the strongest nerves on the part of the division commander. The advanced Detachment of the division now attached to Battle Group Crisolli, signaled at 0743, 24 June, that it had just crossed an intact bridge in Seta lying 17 km by road east of Kedainiai (See Map 9). For the next several hours, the division commander required all the sang froid[13] he could muster to keep the division in motion. Witness the following succession of jarring movements and actions on the part of the Soviets: the division discovered through aerial reconnaissance strong Soviet forces advancing west out of Ukmerge toward the division front, came under attack from the south at Seta by a strong Soviet force including tanks at 0900, and came under attack from the north at Kedainiai also by a strong Soviet force with tanks at 1100. Brandenberger faced the above situation with his closest neighbors to the north, 6.Pz.D. and *290.l.D.*, both approximately 45 km to the rear. His immediate southern neighbor, *3.l.D.(mot)*, lay approximately 48 km straight line distance to the rear late in the morning. Brandenberger, nevertheless, pushed Battle Group Crisolli forward to Bukonys by 1110 and its *Spitze* (spearhead or leading elements) to within 3 km of Ukmerge by 1410, 24 June, now 83 km by road from Ariogala (See especially Map 9).

On the morning of 24 June 41, *8.Pz.D.* had moved forward with extraordinary speed. Manstein, as corps commander, became concerned about the success of the division and sent his Ia to the command post who passed on his order at 1300 that *8.Pz.D.* would immediately form a battle group to engage the strong Soviet force located north of Kedainiai and advancing toward it. Fifteen minutes later, the division commander arrived back at the command post and described the tough fighting experienced by Crisolli that involved the destruction of 15 Soviet tanks including a heavy KV-2 armed with 15.2 cm cannon and the ensuing total destruction of the city of Seta by fire. Later in the afternoon, Battle Group Crisolli in a prepared attack that included artillery support moved into Ukmerge. At 1650, Crisolli signaled that his battle group had secured the city of Ukmerge (Wilkomierz), and Brandenberger, who had returned to the leading elements of the division ordered Crisolli "as quickly as possible to advance in the direction of Duenaburg."[14] The division commander, leading from the front, and personally sensing the confusion and disarray of the Soviets, ordered this move notwithstanding the chaotic dispersal of the division that included the location of Battle Group Scheller under command of the next-senior officer of the division at Josvainiai 67 km to the rear of Battle Group Crisolli at 1700, 24 June. Things grew tense when Brandenberger with the advanced elements of the division around Ukmerge informed the Ia at 1905 that a strong enemy force was moving against him from the west (!) i.e., from the direction of the German Border. After a battle lasting until 2130, the division regained freedom of maneuver and began to advance east again. At midnight on 24 June, Battle Group Crisolli, as leading element of *8.Pz.D.* lay 11 km northeast of Ukmerge on the Swentoje River.[15]

At this time in the middle of the hours of darkness the Ia of the division described his commander's intention as "after a short fueling halt and reorganization of the formations to push forward as quickly as possible toward Duenaburg to seize the bridges at the latest by the evening of 26 June 41."[16] Engaged against a confused but hard fighting enemy virtually surrounding them, Brandenberger and the battle group leaders set a fierce tempo to the advance from the viewpoint of sleep and stress among the troops and maintenance and resupply. By midnight, 24 June, Brandenberger had kept the division in continuous movement or combat for 30 hours; but, nevertheless, he ordered the division to advance at 0330, 25 June, with the brief halt punctuated by refueling, remunitioning (tanks and artillery), and reorganization for a new advance along two axes. Brandenberger could no longer ignore the threat to his northern flank and reacted by reorganizing Battle Group Scheller and giving it the mission to advance along the byways north of the main highway and seize Ilukst lying 15 km northwest of Duenaburg (See Maps 9 and 10).

Battle Group Crisolli now advanced from the bridgehead over the Swentoje River 11 km northeast of Ukmerge along the main highway to Duenaburg. The battle group advanced with difficulty slowing from its earlier pace on 24 June. The Germans gave the reasons as weak but skillfully led Soviet detachments repeatedly bringing Battle Group Crisolli to a halt in terrain difficult to deploy off road for combat. After 5.5. hours of attempting to accelerate forward out of the Swentoje bridgehead, the Germans had advanced only 10 km by 0900, 25 June (See Map 9). By 1015, the Germans had evidently worn down the small Soviet delaying detachments and advanced 10 km further to combat with a strong Soviet force supported by artillery just east of the Virinta River (see Map 2). Battle Group Crisolli quickly subdued this force and began to accelerate after 1100, driving the *Spitze* of the group into Antalze at 1415. The battle group was now 55 km northeast of Ukmerge, an advance of 44 km from the Swentoje bridgehead earlier at 0330. Forty-five minutes later, at 1500, the same *Spitze* drove through the big Lithuanian town of Utena (see Map 9) accompanied by Brandenberger. Minutes later immediately east of the town, Brandenberger and the battle group ran into strong Soviet combat forces. The division commander, in touch with reality, immediately ordered the entire, trailing *Pz.R.10* forward with all the tanks of the division to destroy the Soviet force and continue the advance. With this massive attachment, Battle Group Crisolli drove through the Soviets by shortly after 1930, 25 June, and reached Degucaia. At this moment with Brandenberger riding with it, Battle Group Crisolli had advanced 86 km by road from the Swentoje bridgehead earlier in the day in a period of 19 hours, 20 minutes. The officers and men had been on the move continuously by this time for close to 50 hours; the division leaders — the division commander, Ia, Ib, and battle group commanders — faced a nerve wracking situation in which they lay almost completely isolated in Soviet held territory, faced difficult challenges in resupply, maintenance and repair, but were impelled to move even faster to assure taking the Duenaburg bridges intact.

Brandenberger used the hours of darkness to place two of the three panzer battalions of *Pz.R.10* in the lead of Battle Group Crisolli and added motorized infantry, artillery and two special detachments of pioneers and Brandenburg Regiment personnel for the seizure. The lead elements of the division would be the Russian and Baltic speaking personnel of Brandenburg with captured Soviet trucks, uniforms, and weapons. The fierce tempo of the advance and the dependence on elements of both skill and fortune (luck) on the part of the troops, is shown by the fact that the force had to seize the narrows between two lakes to capture the city of Zarasai and cross four streams large enough to be shown on a 1:250,000 scale map before reaching the Duenaburg bridges. The possibilities for disaster were legion. Battle Group Scheller, the other half of the division advancing farther north toward Ilukst, would be halted in front of destroyed or intrafficable bridges for 7.5 hours on 26 June 41 before it arrived near that city at 1655. This astounding figure compared with the uninterrupted motion of Battle Group Crisolli, illustrates the importance of bridge destruction or impassibility for the advance of motorized forces.

At approximately 0600, 26 June, an engineer and Brandenburg combat team[17] approached the road bridge over the Duena (Daugava) River while the tanks of two battalions of *Pz.R.10* lay back approximately 2 km to the west. The division combat team managed to get in and among the Soviet troops on the south entrance to the bridge and shoot them down. One German truck then moved across the bridge to begin to control the north entry to the bridge.

Oberleutnant Knaak, the commander of the Brandenburg personnel, moved across in the front seat of the second German truck on the bridge only to meet death from an antitank projectile fired into the vehicle from a Soviet antitank gun still sited to fire across the bridge. The engineer personnel simultaneously removed charges and cut wires on the bridge. After this action had developed for about 20 minutes, the nearby German tanks led by the commander of the tank regiment himself arrived with one supporting battalion of motorized infantry and pushed across the bridge now under heavy fire from Soviet troops in the houses and streets on the north bank. By 0728, irretrievably for the Soviets, the Germans had "broken into" Duenaburg.[18] Simultaneously, the Germans attempted to seize the rail bridge 2 km to the northwest but were less successful. The combat team assigned to make the seizure was thwarted by the chance presence of five Soviet armored reconnaissance vehicles parked and manned at the south entry and forced to turn off to the south and assist the team at the highway bridge. The Germans, accordingly, sent their remaining one battalion of tanks supported by motorcyclists of *K.8* straight at the bridge. The surprised and unnerved Soviets set off only part of the demolition charges allowing the motorcyclists and motorcycles to get across and contribute to the break-in to Duenaburg but preventing any tanks from traversing the bridge.

For the remainder of the day, Brandenberger labored to safeguard the bridges, clear out the city of Duenaburg immediately adjacent to them, and gain a modest amount of ground farther north. After the division broke into the city early in the morning, it faced a hard battle with numerically strong Soviet units occupying or passing through this big communications center and manufacturing city in Latvia. The division declared itself master of the situation at 1215, 26 June, taking 400 prisoners in the fighting and seizing intact a munitions train. By 1400, at which time the Germans still encountered resistance from the Soviets in "the factory" in town, the division had placed two panzer battalions, two motorized rifle battalions, one pioneer company, one *Pak* company and two batteries of heavy artillery in a bridgehead 7 km deep at that moment. By 1730, it had become apparent to Brandenberger from ground and aerial reconnaissance that the Soviets would soon make a strong attempt to regain the city. He braced the division for an attack and 30 minutes later the Soviets advanced with infantry and tanks supported by artillery. The Soviets broke through the east sector of the division's defensive positions and with a force of seven medium tanks and an infantry company drove into the inner city, moved down *Leningrader Strasse* and nearly reached the highway bridge. Near the south entry to the bridge, Brandenberger personally ordered the heavy *Flak* battery there to move into the city to combat the Soviet tanks. After heavy fighting lasting until 2130, Battle Group Crisolli regained its original lines while the bridge remained untouched by Soviet artillery fire and air attack.

Just what was the anatomy of the extraordinary German offensive maneuver war of the preceding several days? Between 1315 and 1900, 23 June 41, the following chain of events put *8.Pz.D.* in motion again toward Duenaburg. At 1315, division headquarters was informed that *6.Pz.D.* was heavily engaged with the forces originally thought to be heading for *8.Pz.D.* Later in the afternoon, the commander of *Pz.Gr.4* made the decision to continue the drive with *LVI.A.K.(mot)* and *8.Pz.D.* toward Duenaburg. The division commander noting virtually no contact with Soviet forces, set off the reconnaissance battalion of the division on the road to Kedainiai at 1750 followed by the mass of Battle Group Crisolli at 1900. Based on the bold plan to drive *8.Pz.D.* straight at Duenaburg notwithstanding the extreme dangers to its flanks, Hoepner, Manstein, and Brandenberger, or what might be referred to as the three Es (each had the first name Erich), pushed off the division with that same mission. As a result for *8.Pz.D.*, Brandenberger moved out the division with the electrifying sense of a distant mission and the associated urgency and imperatives. Brandenberger moved it out early in the evening of 23 June because of the new reality that his division was no longer in danger of attack by Soviet tanks and, indeed, had virtually no contact with any Soviet forces near the German positions around Ariogala.

The main factors cited in the literature as affecting rates of advance in land combat all came into play but, since they are fundamentally secondary factors, they fail to correlate usefully with the actual performance of the division in war. Take, for example, the factors of terrain, road net, weather, and nightfall. These are substantial elements that must be considered in any analysis of what made *8.Pz.D.* move or halt but the factors allow the following mixed comment. The Lithuanian lakes, streams, swamps, and forests decisively favored the defending Soviets. The Lithuanian road net was primitive by West European standards of the day having no paved roads (bituminous or concrete), few surfaced roads (graded rock), but almost entirely unimproved roads and country lanes with low capacity bridges and culverts crossing innumerable water courses. Brandenberger's division nevertheless averaged approximately 100 km/day across such countryside and roads. Nightfall, or the hours of darkness, on the evenings of 23, 24, and 25 June 41 should also have contributed to slow movement or halt on the part of *8.Pz.D.* Brandenberger's division, however, used the hours of darkness for operational and logistical movement associated with the constant German reorganization into new battle groups, and thus used night to continue the advance.

Overall on the Baltic Front, the Germans were outnumbered in men and most weapons. The overall front ratio, therefore, fails to correlate with or explain the success of either *A.Gr.N.* or *8.Pz.D.* Force ratios in the individual battles, nevertheless, are useful in explaining *8.Pz.D.* success because the division advanced against or fought off seemingly endless Soviet combat units against each of which it managed to achieve roughly parity in numbers of men and weapons or superiority. *8.Pz.D.* fought a series of engagements along the line of advance in which it was consistently successful and in which success was significantly explained by sufficient German numbers combined with superior German tactics.

In consideration of rates of advance, the factors of the attacker's casualties and defender's posture are theoretically important. If an attacker suffers 100 percent casualties, for example, he must of logical and practical necessity be brought to a halt. In the empirical world of historical experience, the factor of attacker's casualties is less useful because of its dependence on defender's posture. It is not clear thinking to claim that an attacker attempting to move against a strong defender is slowed due to heavy casualties because the casualties are clearly dependent upon the more fundamental factor of defender's posture. In the case of the fluid, distant advance of *8.Pz.D.*, the factor of defender's posture becomes relatively more important. A statement, for example, to the effect that *8.Pz.D.* stayed in motion so effectively toward Duenaburg on 24-26 June 41, because it suffered few casualties is neither credible nor useful for purposes of understanding rates of advance. Battle Group Crisolli was slowed because of the defensive posture adopted by the Soviets numerous times but not because of casualties.

The following factors identified earlier in the study under the general headings of command style and battle style along with technology and numbers combine to explain the rapid advance of 24-26 June 41. The primary factors of command and battle style were clearly the most important. The intermediate factors of technology, e.g., especially weapons and their performance characteristics, and numbers of men and weapons were also important but tended to be similarly matched between the opposing sides in the Baltic. The division had enough weapons with requisite performance characteristics and enough men to advance in the face of the secondary factors of terrain, road net, weather, and nightfall, and the factors of force ratios, attacker's casualties, and defender's posture. The reader must sense from the description of the advance that everyone of these factors was important for understanding that *8.Pz.D.* had the capability to advance against an opposing force of approximately equal size in its zone of operations. All of the factors taken together, however, do not even begin to explain why the Germans advanced at so astounding a rate during the period 24-24 June 41.

The factors of command and battle style among the Germans were primary and most decisive for explaining the speed of advance. *Generalmajor* Brandenberger, his Ia., *Major i.G.* Friedrich Berendsen, and the battle group commanders *Oberst* Scheller, *Oberstleutnants* Fronhoefer, Crisolli, and Bodenhausen pulled along tank crews and motorized riflemen of consummate tactical skill organized into continuously changing battle groups. Similarly to the situation of 22 June 41, *8.Pz.D.* command and battle style was exemplified by descriptive adjectives such as fluid, agile, nimble, vigorous—words showing the Germans dedicated to perpetual action in battle. One sees little concern with rule and formula, for example, for the protection of open flanks. On the offensive against distant targets, they rejected phase lines and other restrictive mechanisms that proliferated among their opponents. This style of bold, uninhibited advance contrasted with their adversaries' rigid formalism, long staff conferences and lengthy written orders rather than quick decisions and short orders.

The division commander and all other commanders led from the front because the Germans affected a style in war that the leader must see for himself. The division commander was in touch with reality at the main point in the battle and in a position to issue orders for movement either by brief radio message or face to face to subordinate commanders with the least friction and greatest speed. The division Ia and every staff subordinate in the streamlined general staff of *8.Pz.D.* made decisions and took action that contributed to keeping the division in motion. The author found not one example of a restrictive order or tone of expression in the war diary or in any of the approximately 700 "operational" messages sent or received by the command post of the division in the period 1750, 23 June - 0728, 26 June.

The division commander moved the division 24 hours a day either in terms of advance forward or the challenging reorganizations and associated movements to pull together new battle groups for changing situations. The division commander maneuvered the division in ad hoc, constantly changing battle groups designated in a psychological tour de force by the names of their leaders. Each fresh battle group demanded special movements usually at night to get itself organized and positioned for the next advance. Each fresh battle group had an urgent new mission in the mobile drive. This combination of continuous reorganizational motion and purposeful advance gave the division an advantage in the chance, meeting engagements that characterized the drive. Notwithstanding the fact that the battle groups often drove into expectant Soviet rear guard forces, the German battle groups always seemed more alert, less surprised and quicker acting than the Soviet formations. The result: quick division success in the tactical engagement and continuation of the strategically fateful advance into the Soviet Union.

1941	Distance (km)	Comments
June 22	92	Crisolli*
23	0	Half of approximately 26 hrs.**
24	100	Crisolli
25	100	Crisolli
26	7	Crisolli over Duena bridges, 0635, 26 June

1941	Location Advanced Elms 8.Pz.D End of Day***
June 22	Vicinity of Ariogala (13 km east)
23	Vicinity of Ariogala (13 km east)
24	Vicinity of Seta
25	East of Zarasai near Duenaburg
26	Duenaburg (7 km north)

* Name of battle group that achieved maximum advance.
** Specifically 1645, 22 June through 1900, 23 June 41.
*** Each of these cities is shown on one or more maps in the map section and underlined or overlined in red.

Figure 9. Daily Advances and End of Day Locations of 8th Panzer Division in Drive through Lithuania into Latvia, 22-26 June '41.

17

Operational Paralysis at Duenaburg, Latvia 27 June - 1 July '41

When *8.Pz.D.* seized the bridges at Duenaburg intact at approximately 0630, 26 June 41, it presented a concrete opportunity for *Pz.Gr.4* to advance immediately through Pskov to Leningrad, the strategic goal of Army Group North in the war against the Soviet Union. Adolf Hitler, who for reasons that have remained obscure until the recent publication of a revisionistic account of World War II,[19] described Leningrad as the single most important target of the war that he willed politically against the Soviet Union. Capture of the city early in the campaign would have collapsed the Soviet war effort on the Baltic and Northwestern Fronts. Most importantly, though, quick seizure of Leningrad would probably have relaxed Hitler enough as concerns his preoccupation with Leningrad and the Ukraine to give the green light to German Army Group Center for an immediate advance to Moscow and the Central Volga area and resultant victory in the war against the Soviet Union.

German *Pz.Gr.4* was the operational instrument capable of quickly seizing the Duenaburg bridges. The bridges in turn were the single most significant means for the immediate continued advance to the strategic target for the entire campaign—Leningrad. Brandenberger (*8.Pz.D.*), Manstein (*LVI.A.K.(mot)*), and Hoepner (*Pz.Gr.4*) knew that Leningrad was the strategic goal; each knew from his particular perspective the necessity to press on immediately. Yet Brandenberger would not advance on the main road out of Duenaburg to Leningrad on his own initiative on 27 June 41. Manstein would not only hold him in place, but with monumental disregard for his historical reputation as the number one operational brain of World War II, would state in his memoirs that "the Panzer Group Commander (Hoepner), who flew over to see us in a *Fieseler Storch* on 27th June, could tell us nothing."[20] With the unmistakable strategic target of Leningrad clearly established, Manstein failed to have already ordered *8.Pz.D.*, *3.I.D.(mot)* arriving alongside of it to the east, and S. S. Division Totenkopf (*S.S."T"*) now assigned to his corps and moving in behind it to continue the advance along the main road through Pskov to Leningrad. Once aware that Hoepner was not prepared to make a decision—to take action in the war—Manstein failed to offer argument to Hoepner in favor of an immediate advance north.

There are no villains in this piece but rather an unlikely set of German army officers in *H.Gr.Nord*, who, for reasons that would be difficult to unravel, temporarily lost the capacity to make independent decisions. Hoepner commanded the operational instrument with the command and battle style and the weapons in *H.Gr.Nord* to reach Duenaburg and Leningrad (and a lot of intermediate targets) at a campaign-winning pace. Hoepner failed to order *LVI.A.K.(mot)* to advance immediately along the road to Pskov and failed to redirect *XXXXXI.A.K.(mot)* to advance in the most effective way to exploit the fleeting opportunity offered for quick victory in the Baltic by the success of Brandenberger's *8.Pz.D.* When every hour counted in the war, Hoepner could not convince his commander at *H.Gr.Nord, Generalfeldmarschall* Wilhelm *Ritter* von Leeb, to order the mobile divisions to continue the advance without a pause. Leeb was a very senior officer in his mid-60s, a cool, reserved man out of another era who had retired from the army in early 1938 after 43 years of service.[21] Leeb had experienced war between1914-18 in the bruising battles of attrition on the Western Front as a general staff officer and artillery specialist. He published a book, *Die Abwehr* (Defense) (Berlin, 1938), revealing a predilection for a conservative, controlled style of operations and was ordered back on active duty in August 1939 to command German Army Group C on the Franco-German border. He was assigned the mission of holding up any French or allied offensive that might develop as a result of the German advance into Poland on 1 September 39. This brief sketch suggests that the *Ritter* (Knight) was not the man to lead a deep strategic advance dependent upon the qualities and capabilities of the mobile divisions in *Pz.Gr.4* to produce the required quick victory.

Manstein notes almost petulantly in his memoirs that Hoepner should have been in the picture about future objectives and goes on to say that his orders from Hoepner were to widen the bridgehead while waiting for *XXXXI.A.K.(mot)* and the Sixteenth Army, a foot marching, horse drawn infantry army (!) to catch up. Hoepner, of course, was in the picture but could not influence Leeb to move out the armor in a bolder immediate advance toward Leningrad. Leeb, a strong willed man with one foot planted in an era of the more relaxed pace of operations of World War I, did not have the operational style or nerves to set the armor loose. Hoepner, finally on 1 July 41, would order *LVI.A.D.(mot)* with *8.Pz.D.* to advance in the direction of Pskov for "the breakthrough to Leningrad." In correspondence to the commanding generals of his two panzer corps penned on 1 July 41, Hoepner would elaborate that "the Commander in Chief of the Army Group is strongly influenced by the idea that given the existing situation, the Panzer Group alone cannot break enemy resistance between the Duena and Leningrad and is taking measures to bring up the infantry armies closer yet to the panzer group."[22] Based on such evidence, it can be said almost unequivocally that what halted *8.Pz.D.* on 27 June 41 and kept it halted for five days through and including 1 July, was the timorous concern of the commander in chief for the safety and control of his operations at the expense of boldness, daring, and quick victory.

Although heavy fighting had taken place in the Duenaburg bridgehead until late evening 26 June 41, *8.Pz.D.* had broken Soviet resistance in the north of the city by midnight. Battle Group Crisolli had inflicted casualties on the Soviets so severe that for the first time in the war diary of the campaign the entry appeared that "enemy losses in dead were extremely high."[23] At daylight on the morning of 27 June 41, in the immediate area of the counterattack near *9./Pz.R.10* (9th Company, *Pz.R.10*), the Germans found abandoned or destroyed 20 tanks, 20 artillery pieces and infantry guns, and 17 antitank guns. On the west bank of the river in the area near Ilukst, the other half of the division—Battle Group Scheller—also successfully fought off strong Soviet attacks that unlike the situation in the bridgehead, continued into the morning of 27 June 41 (See Map 10 for the general area of the fighting northwest of Duenaburg). By noon on 27 June, however, the division was no longer in serious contact with Soviet forces. The continued confusion and disruption among the Soviets caused by the deep penetration is illustrated by the following incident: at 1345, three Soviet reconnaissance aircraft landed on the big airfield (Duenaburg Northeast) occupied by Germans. Surprised but quickly reacting Germans of a nearby pioneer platoon, rushed the aircraft and captured them intact. One would have thought that reconnaissance pilots and observers would have been in closer touch with the realities of the battle. Most importantly the incidents show that an enormous fleeting opportunity was beginning to be missed by *8.Pz.D.* in not exploiting the surprise and confusion on the part of a hard fighting but brittle enemy.

Paralyzed by the conservative anxiety of the German army group commander, *8.Pz.D.* pushed out the bridgehead to the north in cooperation with *3.I.D.(mot)*, now in the eastern sector of the German holdings. The Ia of the division stated that on 28 June 41, *8.Pz.D.* had no contact with the enemy, even when pushing its lines a short distance forward. The situation was an outlandish one. The division, an elite panzer formation, had just broken open the main barrier to a rapid advance to Leningrad yet spent the entire day "advancing' approximately 3 km with no contact with the enemy. The only thing that can be said in mitigation is that its right-hand neighbor in the bridgehead, *3.I.D. (mot)*, experienced violent fighting during which it suffered heavy casualties of 63 KIA and 195 WIA. The overall picture is therefore a mixed one. Brandenberger's division should have been advancing against the distant operational target of Rezekne but would have had to have taken account of strong Soviet forces still lingering on its right flank. Alternatively, of course, it can be stated that both *8.Pz.D.* and *3.I.D.(mot)* by 28 June 41 at latest should have been advancing rapidly northward in which case they would have run over and destroyed the Soviet forces now instead attacking the eastern sector of the bridgehead at 1600, 28 June 41. Instead of advancing, *8.Pz.D.* and its neighbor were attracting Soviet formations and presenting them with a situation in which they could attack immobilized German mobile divisions while building up fronts immediately to the north to reduce the rates of advance of the German divisions once they attempted to move north. By the end of 28 June, more than three days after *8.Pz.D.* had seized the Duenaburg bridges, the division lay only 13 km to the north. For all practical purposes, 8.Pz.D. had been frozen into an operational halt punctuated by a modest amount of tactical movement.

On 29 June 41, in accordance with continuing corps directives to enlarge the bridgehead, Brandenberger moved the division a substantial distance forward (See Map 11). Corps headquarters had shifted the boundary between *8.Pz.D.* and *3.I.D.(mot)* several kilometers eastward giving Brandenberger's division the main highway from Duenaburg through Rezekne to Pskov and Leningrad as its main route of advance. The division commander organized Battle Group Fronhoefer around the tanks of *Pz.R.10*, designated it as the Schwerpunkt force, and ordered it forward along the main highway toward the narrows between two lakes at Spogi (See Map 4). Brandenberger organized three additional Battle

Groups, namely Scheller to advance left of Fronhoefer, Bodenhausen to advance behind Scheller, and Crisolli to screen the left flank of the division. The division began its advance at 1130, 29 June 41. Battle Groups Fronhoefer and Scheller in the lead of the division made little or no contact with the Soviets. At 1255 Battle Group Scheller entered Dubna now 25 km north of the highway bridge in Duenaburg and experienced only light contact with a weak enemy by that time. Shortly afterward, Scheller informed the division command post that he had taken the important road junction of Bramani (noted as "Peleci?" on Map 11). Now only an hour later, Scheller had advanced to a location 34 km north of the Duenaburg highway bridge still with no significant contact with the Soviets. Shortly after this advance, however, Scheller would be halted at Bramani for the remainder of the day and Fronhoefer stopped to the southeast along the main highway in the course of a battle that developed to get through the Spogi narrows on 29 June 41 (See Map 11 and the maximum advance achieved by Fronhoefer's motorcyclists in K.8).

After having widened the Duenaburg bridgehead about as much as it could under the spiritless and restrictive orders to that effect, and in the absence of any further directives for movement *8.Pz.D.* advanced not at all on 30 June and 1 July 1941. The observer is treated to a scene of a German panzer division on the high road to Leningrad sitting motionless for two days while the Army Group commander assured himself that the horse drawn infantry divisions of Sixteenth Army drew closer. The total of five days of operational-level halt doomed any reasonable chance of the Germans seizing Leningrad in the month of July 41. The German command and battle style in the corps and divisions of *Pz.Gr.4* was so superior, however, that even this wise generalization about the possibilities of a German advance to Leningrad must be handled with care. Between 2-14 July 41, in a mixed picture of acceleration and deceleration, *8.Pz.D.* would advance to the Mshaga River near Lake Ilmen approximately 380 km (straight line road increments) from the highway bridge at Duenaburg.

The questions of what started and kept *8.Pz.D.* advancing and accelerated or decelerated it during this period do not apply. Although the division moved north 34km during the period from 0600, 26 June - midnight, 1 July 41, the motion represented tactical adjustment of the bridgehead outward from Duenaburg and no movement in any direction toward an operational target. The question of what halted the division can be summarized from earlier discussion as follows: one man, the Commanding General, *H.Gr.Nord*, halted *8.Pz.D.* during the period based on his expressed concern to bring forward his infantry divisions to operate at a closer, safer distance to the motorized infantry and panzer divisions of *Pz.Gr.4*. Leeb's concern was based on his perception that Soviet resistance between Duenaburg and Leningrad would be too strong for *Pz.Gr.4* to break by itself. Leeb's perception of the quality (and quantity) of Soviet resistance brings into play the factors of Attacker's Casualties, Defender's Posture, and Force Ratios which must be assumed to have played on Leeb's mind in some significant but unknown degree. The noteworthy point is that *8.Pz.D.* was not halted around Duenaburg by actual adverse Attacker's Casualties, Defender's Posture, or Force Ratios. It was halted by the Commander in Chief's perception that *Pz.Gr.4* and *8.Pz.D.* as part of it, would not be able to break Soviet resistance alone an impression based on Leeb's anticipation of future adverse Casualties, Defender's Posture, and Force Ratios.

It would be instructive, nevertheless, to look through the eight factors associated with rates of advance and briefly check their importance during the monumental halt. Some of the factors may have accumulated between 22-26 June and afterward in the period 27 June

- 1 July 41 to cause the halt. What about Attacker's Casualties, for example, so easy to quantify and relate with the combat capabilities of the division? The figures for personnel casualties are the following:

8.Pz.D. Casualties 22-30 June 41 (Personnel)

	22	**23**	**24**	**25**	**26**	**27**	**28**	**29**	**30**
KIA	20	0	8	4	11	17	1	21	1
WIA	65	6	10	12	41	33	4	54	9
MIA	0	0	0	0	0	17	0	4	0

The numbers show that *8.Pz.D.* was not decelerated or halted operationally by the factor of casualties. The casualties, indirectly, as they are related with Defender's Posture, show that this factor also did not seriously slow the advance of the division on the way to Duenaburg or halt it operationally in the bridgehead, i.e., an organization with a strength of approximately 15,500 men cannot be said to have been halted operationally by Defender's Postures which resulted in the casualties shown above. This generalization must be handled carefully because the division might have suffered another type of casualty, namely tank losses, which could have slowed or halted the advance. The division, however, suffered extremely light tank losses to Soviet action and only moderate losses due to cross country hazards and mechanical breakdown on the primitive and challenging road system. Neither accumulated casualties and tank losses in the period 22-26 June 41, nor the same factors from 27-30 June 41, can be said to have been significant in the halt of *8.Pz.D.* in the Duenaburg bridgehead.

The factors of terrain, road net, and weather although fundamental for consideration in land combat do not explain the halt. The main road exiting to the north out of Duenaburg was the biggest and best road in the Baltic for a direct advance from East Prussia to Leningrad, and farther north at Ostrov it fed into an even bigger road. The bigger road had not been constructed to link Leningrad with East Prussia, but more importantly for the original builders, to connect it with the rest of Russia lying to the south of the former capital. By Baltic and Russian standards, the roads were excellent ones for the advance of *8.Pz.D.* The warm, dry weather continued to favor the Germans and the terrain remained the same difficult but surmountable countryside for the advance of a panzer division.

Force Ratios favored the Germans in the Duenaburg bridgehead and therefore cannot be given as explanation for why the Germans halted. The division faced a difficult combat situation on the morning of 26 June 41 as the advanced elements of Battle Group Crisolli, which in turn was the advanced group of the division, pushed the Soviets out of Duenaburg. Then, strongly reinforced by everything that Brandenberger could spare, the battle group fought off Soviet counterattacks successfully for the remainder of 26 June and on 27 June 41. The situation in Force Ratios continues to be intriguing though because the Soviets attacked the division for two days in the bridgehead and continued to attack the adjacent *3.I.D.(mot)* on the third day of the river crossing. The logic seems to hold that the Soviets felt that they had favorable enough ratios to attack and probably superior enough ratios to bring the German advance to a halt. The Soviets, however, had no such illusions. Faced with the equilibrium destroying appearance of the Germans already 295 km from the border, they simply gathered up every man and weapon that they could muster and threw them against the Germans in the city. The Soviets without regard for force ratios that they scarcely could have calculated under the conditions of the surprise German appearance, were forced to attempt to regain the bridges. By midafternoon of 26 June 41, the Germans had roughly the same number of men and weapons as the Soviets around the bridgehead and the Germans were reinforcing more rapidly. As concerns the battle fighting itself, the Germans seized the bridges, crossed them, seized the city, held it, and enlarged the bridgehead, and must be considered to have been tactically superior to the Soviets. The observed operational situation in which the Germans remained halted, must, therefore, be explained by some other factors than force ratios and tactical skill that favored the stalled Germans.

The Germans fought with command and battle Styles superior to those of the Soviets. Since the Germans were halted operationally in the bridgehead for five days, however, the five factors developed from that style by the researcher specifically to explain the German superiority — commanders forward, streamlined decision making staffs, 24-hour movement, battle group organization, hyper reconnaissance — do not explain the halt at least at the levels of command in *8.Pz.D.* The superior command and battle style on the other hand illustrates the great possibilities in rates of advance that went unrealized in the German attack toward Leningrad. Five days after the seizure of the Duenaburg bridges, this panzer division would accelerate forward again and outstrip the infantry divisions to get to the Mshaga River 335 km distant by 14 July 41. The situation suggests that the division would have been there sooner with greater result if it had moved out five days earlier. In the closely run, finely tuned conditions of the blitz in the Baltic, greater result would probably have been the fall of Leningrad in July 41.

In the actual event, however, as the campaign developed from 22 June – 1 July 41, the Commander in Chief, *H.Gr.Nord*, made the cautious misjudgment to halt *8.Pz.D.* and *LVI.A.D.(mot).* What generalizations can be made about this historic misjudgment that helped in the understanding of rates of advance in land war and especially the qualities that foster effective offensive maneuver war? Leeb's cautious decision in the ultra blitz that the German advance through the Baltic demanded for success, can be characterized as part of German command style and not, for example, Road Net, Force Ratios, Defender's Posture, and similar factors. Faced with same uncertainty and chance but still standing with one foot in a world with fewer internal combustion engines, Leeb attempted to master chaos by slowing German movement and pacing it to the safer and more certain advance of the horse drawn infantry.

Then as *XXXXI.A.K.(mot)* and Sixteenth Army finally approached the Daugava River and established new bridgeheads, Leeb gave the green light to Hoepner to direct Manstein and Brandenberger out of the aging bridgehead at Duenaburg. Leeb had dealt a severe blow to hope of quick German victory in the Baltic and Northwestern Soviet Russia by his paralysis of the armor and motorized infantry at Duenaburg. From the beginning, the attack against the Soviet Union was a race by the Germans to seize deep strategic targets, e.g., Leningrad, while simultaneously defeating the Soviet armies initially in place defending them. On the part of the Soviets, the campaign was a race to regain their equilibrium, and, as the Germans smashed to pieces the Red armies on the frontiers, to mobilize reserves and "advance" them forward to defend the strategic areas. To win, the Germans had to advance fast, take chances, be bold. To survive, the Soviets had to slow the Germans enough to prevent them from seizing the strategic areas and paralyzing Soviet mobilization.

Brandenberger's *8.Pz.D.* had just lost five irretrievable days of forward motion and the Soviets had been given the same days to throw forces into defenses north of Duenaburg. Ordered at last to advance out of the tactically widened bridgehead toward Leningrad on 2 July 41, Brandenberger faced almost insurmountable obstacles to an advance fast enough to qualify as a blitz. The commanders above Brandenberger had placed him in an operationally disastrous situation. Leeb had done this through misjudgment in facing high level challenges of uncertainty and chance in war. Hoepner and Manstein had placed Brandenberger and, indeed, the entire Panzer Group in an unenviable position through their failure to continue the attack out of Duenaburg on their own initiative on 27 June and unwittingly force the hand of their braking commander. Brandenberger now faced an opposing Soviet command recovering its equilibrium, knowing now where the division was located, and having precious days to mass forces along the obvious path of advance. Based on the evidence of the earlier advance, it is apparent that the Soviet High Command in the Special Baltic Military District had lost an entire German panzer division on its operational maps. The division remained lost from shortly after the opening of hostilities until its appearance four days and 295 km later at Duenaburg. This surmise helps to explain the success of the division on the morning of 26 June in placing two panzer battalions and one motorized rifle battalion 2 km away from the south entrances to the rail and highway bridges without even the local Soviets having an inkling that this strong force was located there and an entire panzer division about to arrive.

18

The Blitz Renewed but Misdirected: 8th Panzer Division Advance Toward Leningrad 2-9 July '41

By 1 July 41, *8.Pz.D.* had been in the Duenaburg bridgehead for almost six days from approximately 0630, 26 June when the German tanks clattered over the highway bridge in support of Special Unit Knaak. Then, mid-afternoon at 1400, *LVI.A.K.(mot)* ordered the division to attack north on the morning of 2 July out of its present positions with the *target for the day* the city of Karsava 85 km distant. For consideration of rates of advance of armored units in modern war, this order is instructive. Apparently without missing a heart-beat, Manstein ordered *8.Pz.D.* to seize a city 85 km away against a prepared, tough, well armed opponent defending in difficult terrain. Manstein passed down the order at 1400 giving the division little time to organize itself for an attack that would have to begin at roughly first light the next morning. The corps commander obviously considered it within the capabilities of a panzer division in combat against a stabilized defender to attack on short notice and gain 85 km in approximately 19 hours of moving and fighting.[24] These data give pause for thought about rates of advance because Manstein must have believed that the same panzer division moving out five days earlier against an opponent pushed to the brink of disintegration could have been given a deeper target.

Brandenberger placed the *Schwerpunkt* of the attack with Battle Group Scheller, that included the tanks of *Oberstleutnant* Fronhoefer's *Pz.R.10.* Brandenberger gave Scheller the mission to advance along the main road from Duenaburg to Rezekne directly through the latter city lying 32 km south of the day's target of Karsava. Because of the short notice given by corps for the advance, Fronhoefer's *Pz.R.10* was forced to leave behind 24 tanks in the regiment's tracked vehicle workshop company for continuing repairs. It moved out, nevertheless, with approximately 80 percent of the original number of tanks that crossed the border or approximately 145 tanks. Brandenberger assigned Battle Group Bodenhausen, consisting largely of motorized infantry, the mission to advance along the more difficult road system to the left of Battle Group Scheller and enter Rezekne from the west (See Map 4). At 0400, 2 July, the division commander personally rode with Battle Group Scheller along the main highway and left adjacent rail line to Rezekne and Karsava. The *Schwerpunkt* battle group and the division commander began the advance from just south of the city of Ardava.

After approximately one hour of rain-slowed movement northward, Battle Group Scheller ran into Soviet resistance. The tanks of I./*Pz.R.10* (1st Battalion, *Pz.R.10*) ran into strong enemy defenses at 0515 around Ardava that signaled a tough battle for the *Schwerpunkt* force during the remainder of 2 July. After heavy fighting, at 0935 the forward elements of the battle group reached Stacija Aglona (Aglona Station). In the heights northeast of the train station fighting intensified in a battle that went on until 1620 in the afternoon. At that time, Battle Group Scheller signaled division headquarters that it had forced the Soviets out of their positions and back to the bridge near Seksti (See Map 4) at the end of the lake narrows that the Soviets had chosen to defend so strongly. Shortly afterward, at 1700, the division commander boldly shifted the division reconnaissance battalion (*Pz.A.A.59)*, from Battle Group Bodenhausen and drove it from the west into the rear of the Soviet forces around the bridge forcing them completely out of the narrows. At the end of the day, 2 July, the division *Schwerpunkt* force lay north of Sekste having advanced a modest 19 km. Farther west, Battle Group Bodenhausen met weaker resistance but extremely difficult road and bridge conditions. The end result: Bodenhausen managed to get the mass of his Battle Group to the road junction shown on Map 4 near Silajani by 1720 after a day's advance of approximately 22 km. His advanced elements, moving more nimbly through the light Soviet resistance and difficult roads lay 22 km farther north near Rezekne representing the maximum advance of the division of 44 km. The division experienced disappointing results on 2 July that were clearly the result of Defender's Posture and Road Net factors.

The next day, 3 July, Brandenberger continued the attack with Battle Group Scheller as the *Schwerpunkt* along the main highway and rail line toward Rezekne and Battle Group Bodenhausen along the primitive road net farther west. The division commander faced a confused, fluid situation. By 1215, the mass of Battle Group Bodenhausen was only 5 km from the southwest outskirts of Rezekne but locked in combat with strong Soviet forces that stopped it there for the remainder of the day (See Map 4). The division commander with Battle Group Scheller and the tanks began the day at 0700 far to the south of Rezekne and had advanced only to Malta (See Map 4 and be advised that the German operational maps identified this city as Baraviai) through extremely strong Soviet resistance by 1515. The Ia noted in the division war diary that the division committed the bulk of the tank regiment, one motorized rifle regiment, and the artillery regiment to the battle but nonetheless was almost halted. The war diary summed up the situation: "the enemy was apparently stronger than the division assumed."[25] The Soviets had tolerances to the battering, however, and broke under the pressure at 1510 when Battle Group Scheller reported them "fleeing" north. At this point Brandenberger moved personally with the leading tanks of Battle Group Scheller to a point 5 km south of the outskirts of Rezekne where Soviet resistance stiffened again. After several further hours of fighting, Battle Groups Bodenhausen and Scheller moved into and occupied Rezekne by 2150 in the evening. The division commander, aggressive and as far forward as ever, ordered advanced elements north but stopped them at full darkness 5 km north of the city.

The division had met strong Soviet resistance again on 3 July. The *Schwerpunkt* Battle Group Scheller, nevertheless, advanced 41 km and shared with Battle Group Bodenhausen in the taking of Rezekne. Bodenhausen's group, whose advanced elements *(Spitze)* had already lain only 5 km outside of Rezekne at 0415, 3 July, advanced only 16 km. The picture of the attack of *8.Pz.D.* during the two difficult days, 2, 3 July, can be summarized as follows: taking the starting point of the attack as the front lines of *Schwerpunkt* Battle Group Scheller, the division advanced 19 km on 2 July and a further 44 km on 3 July for total movement of 63 km along Scheller's path. The advance would be from a point 2 km south of Ardava to the point shown on Map 4 as the forward elements of Scheller at darkness on 3 July 41. The division had been ordered to move 85 km to seize Karsava in one day. The division advanced, however, only 63 km in two days well short of the original objective. The factors that slowed the advance were firstly, Defender's Posture, secondly, poor Road Net, and thirdly, the factor of rainy weather on the morning of 2 July 41. The factor of Force Ratios also comes into the picture because the Soviets were stronger in numbers of men and weapons than the Germans expected. The numerically strong Soviet forces made the factor of a determined defense having the mission to halt the Germans, i.e., Defender's Posture, more effective than delaying rear guards.

With the operational advance begun again on 2 July, Headquarters, *Pz.Gr.4* had ordered *LVI.A.K.(mot)* to move northeast toward Porkhov, Dno, and the mouth of the Mshaga River on Lake Ilmen, the latter only 193 km straight line distance south of Leningrad. Brandenberger's *8.Pz.D.* advanced on the left of the army corps with *3.I.D.(mot)* in the center farther east and *S.S."T"* on the right. Manstein directed *8.Pz.D.* when it reached Karsava to turn off to the northeast in conformance with the general outlook and what an examination of the map would seem to make reasonable (See Map 5). Brandenberger ordered Battle Group Scheller to move north from its forward positions at 0600 and to advance along the main highway to Karsava. He organized a new Battle Group Crisolli and ordered it to move along the more difficult road system to the east of the main highway in anticipation of the turn to the northeast at Karsava. Battle Group Scheller accelerated forward moving 28 km in 2.5 hours to reach Karsava at 0830, 4 July 41. During the night the Soviets, who had put up so much resistance during the last two days, had slipped away to the north, and the group advanced against almost no resistance. Moving across a poor road network, Battle Group Crisolli would move more slowly for the remainder of the day toward its goal of Goliseva 15 km by road east of Karsava on the Latvian frontier with Russia.

As Battle Group Scheller arrived at the big road intersection at the east edge of Karsava, it came under artillery fire and spotted Soviet tanks close by just east of Malnava (See Map 5). Now, around 0830, 4 July, the division began to move east toward Goliseva, Krasnoye, and Pushkinskyegory in accordance with the new operational order and northeast toward the Mshaga River and Novgorod (See Map 5 for the first three towns along the line of advance). At this time, Scheller bumped into strong rear guards of an immense Soviet force attempting to escape east along the new route of advance of *8.Pz.D.* German reconnaissance aircraft reported Soviet motorized columns largely halted, crowding the roads from 3 km east of Karsava all the way to Krasnoye (Krasnogorodskoye on Map 5)—36 km of road jammed with Soviet vehicles.[26] The advance guard of Scheller reported being slowed by masses of abandoned, halted vehicles blocking the road. Battle Group Scheller moved slowly eastward out of Karsava encountering weaker rear guards but a poor road bordered by soft ground, and blocked by abandoned enemy trucks. At 1445, as he approached Goliseva on the significant barrier of the Ludza River 15 km from Karsava, Scheller signaled that the road had now become partly blocked by burning motor vehicles. To get through Goliseva to the bridge on the Ludza, Scheller had to employ a platoon of *Panzer 38 (t)* tanks to clear the road of about 50 Soviet trucks. Enemy resistance stiffened at the river and in a tactical disaster for the Germans, at 1705, the Soviets destroyed the bridge. At this point, Scheller was forced to organize a deliberate attack across the river which succeeded in creating a bridgehead by 2000. Shortly before, at 1900, Battle Group Crisolli arrived from the southwest after an arduous march through virtually no Soviet resistance but slowed by poor roads dotted with impassable bridges requiring repairs. By 2000, 4 July, Brandenberger had concentrated the division on the Ludza River after an advance of approximately 42 km for the day.

During the day, Battle Group Scheller had advanced 28 km from north of Rezekne to Karsava in only 2.5 hours. The division moved that rapidly because it met no Soviet resistance and advanced over a well constructed highway. Scheller then spent the remainder of 4 July 41, moving only 14 km to the Ludza River slowed by factors of moderate Soviet resistance combined with a poor road flanked by soft, impassable terrain and blocked by abandoned often burning Soviet motor vehicles. Battle Group Crisolli would move approximately the same total distance of 42 km against almost no Soviet resistance but slowed by poor roads and flimsy bridges.

For 5 July, Brandenberger intended to advance the distance between Ludza and the Sinyaya River at Krasnoye (See Map 5) and at least establish a bridgehead there for further advance to the northeast. The division moved out at 0800 led by Battle Group Crisolli but was halted at 0930 by extraordinarily difficult road and terrain conditions that immobilized the wheeled vehicles of the Group and demanded a reorganization to continue the advance. Then, as Battle Group Crisolli moved out, it observed the amazing spectacle of hundreds of motor vehicles and weapons of the Soviet 163rd Motorized Rifle Division stuck and abandoned in the swampy terrain alongside of the road. The battle group advanced over a poor road and was unable to deploy off it because of the same conditions that had finished off the retreating Soviet division. At 0930, the Germans ran into a stretch of road that division headquarters estimated would take a construction column (*Arbeiterkolonne*) of 1,500 - 2,000 men and an entire pioneer battalion two days to make passable for the wheeled vehicles of the division. The division commander aggressively ordered tanks and *Pak* towed by three-quarter tracked vehicles to move through the 1.0 to 1.5 km long stretch of road and continue all the way to Krasnoye to answer the question of how seriously the Soviets were prepared to defend the place. Simultaneously, Hoepner and Manstein wrestled with the question of the further direction and speed of advance of *8.Pz.D* At that time, Brandenberger requested that the division be assigned a new route of advance back through Karsava and then north behind *6.Pz.D.* leaving some dismounted forces to contain the Soviets on the Ludza River.

Manstein concurred with this bold suggestion, but then at 1100, 5 July he ordered the division to advance east through the swamp. Although opposed to this route, Manstein issued the order under the direction of Hoepner. This fateful decision would force *8.Pz.D.* to continue eastward in an ineffective direction from 5-10 July. Reacting quickly to the disastrous decision, Brandenberger observed that only 400m of the road in the worst part were utterly impassable to wheeled vehicles and ordered complete concentration on that part of the road with corduroying materials to get through enough motorized riflemen and artillery to seize Krasnoye and break up any new front that the Soviets might be setting up. Through this tactic, Brandenberger pushed through all the tanks of the division, two battalions of motorized infantry and one artillery battalion to Krasnoye and seized it at 1800. By 2000, the forward elements of the division had established a bridgehead across the Sinyaya River and advanced 27 km during the entire day. Brandenberger halted the division in the bridgehead because the road to the rear that had supported the passage of the combat elements was incapable of being used as a supply road for further movement.

On 5 July, therefore, at the operational level, Hoepner slowed the division and almost halted it over the next four days by his decision to continue eastward in the teeth of paralyzing road and terrain conditions. Hoepner made an inflexible and questionable decision in the face of action taken by Brandenberger with the concurrence of Manstein to shift the advance of *8.Pz.D.* north. In violation of the German principle that in war, the leader must see for himself, neither Hoepner nor his chief of staff nor Ia moved to the front of the division to see for himself the conditions that drove Brandenberger to suggest a change in direction of advance. At the immediate, tactical level of consideration, *8.Pz.D.* was slowed by a combination of poor roads, impassible surrounding terrain for motor vehicles, and substantial resistance of Soviet units in a posture calculated to slow the Germans as much as possible—factors described in past studies as Road Net, Terrain, and Defender's Posture.

On 6 July, *8.Pz.D.* spent the entire day constructing a new road through an impassable stretch of the former road approximately 1 km long near the east bank of the Ludza River. This short length of road combined with the swamp on both sides and other difficult stretches of road had conspired to hold back *8.Pz.D.* on 5 July. Now on 6 July, Brandenberger halted the division and concentrated six battalions of troops to construct a road capable of taking the full traffic of a panzer division. Corps headquarters provided one pioneer battalion and two construction battalions from corps troops and the division contributed its pioneer battalion (*Pz.Pi.59*) and two motorized rifle battalions. Division headquarters directed this force in the construction of a corduroy road based on approximately 4,000 tree trunks felled out of neighboring forests. The pioneer troops directing the construction opened the road for traffic at 2200, 6 July, in conjunction with two bridges completed nearby over the Ludza River. During the evening of 6 July, the division pushed forward strong forces to Krasnoye to get the advance going again. Earlier, during the afternoon, Hoepner had called Brandenberger to a brief meeting at Malnava and encouraged him to move out as fast as possible in what continued to be a questionable direction of movement now northeast from Krasnoye through Pushkinskyegory (See Map 5). The division was finally poised on the morning of 7 July, to begin an operational advance.

At midnight, 6 July the division began to move *I./S.R.8* and the wheeled elements of the panzer regiment across the newly constructed corduroy road toward Krasnoye. The division moved units from the west bank of the Ludza River hoping to concentrate its entire strength near that city for the continuation of the push northeast. At 0500, however, the corduroy portion of the road so painfully constructed collapsed under the strain of the heavy traffic. The engineer and construction troops returned almost immediately to effect repairs and labored from 0500-1200 to make the corduroy road passable once and for all. At 1200, the wheeled elements of Battle Group Scheller began moving forward to concentrate in Krasnoye as the *Schwerpunkt* force for the advance out of the bridgehead northeast toward

Pushkinskyegory. Battle Group Scheller advanced out of the bridgehead at 1800, 7 July. Scheller and Battle Group Bodenhausen behind him made slow progress over a difficult road system with narrow, foundationless lanes flanked by difficult terrain for cross country movement. By 1930, Scheller passed through Vel'ye (immediately northeast of Lake Vel'ye on Map 5) but not much beyond for an advance of approximately 22 km for 7 July.

The division moved only a disappointingly short distance for the day. The reasons for the slow movement were the frictions along the corduroy road just east of the Ludza, the generally impassable cross country terrain and difficult roads and terrain northeast of Krasnoye on the road to Pushkinskyegory. The division met weak Soviet resistance, suffered almost no casualties, was favored in movement by warm, dry weather, yet the division moved slowly because of the dominating poor roads and swampy off road conditions. In turn, the presence of (extremely) poor roads and difficult off-road conditions was a function of the command style of Hoepner, who made the operational-level decision to direct *8.Pz.D.* through the difficult terrain.

Still being misdirected eastward by Hoepner, *8.Pz.D.* drove the advanced elements of Battle Group Scheller to the Velikaya River 6 km from the western outskirts of Pushkinskyegory at 0500, 8 July. The advanced elements were not able to seize the bridge there intact and forced to wait for the mass of Battle Scheller to mount a prepared attack against growing Soviet forces. Because of severely bad road conditions, Brandenberger was able to get the mass of Battle Group Scheller and the following Battle Group Bodenhausen into position only by 1700 for an attack. The division attacked with these battle groups at 1800 but ran into Soviet resistance that included strong artillery fires and KV-2 heavy tanks able to be knocked out only by the 8.8 cm *Flak* cannons pushed forward that day by the Ia of the division in anticipation of such a fight. After tough fighting for 3.5 hours, *1./S.R.8* (1st Company, 1st Battalion, *S.R.8*) would successfully get across the river at 2130, 8 July. This dismounted motorized infantry company was the first German unit into a bridgehead that would be about 1.5 km deep by 2300 but not much larger through the rest of the hours of darkness. During the entire day, *8.Pz.D.* had advanced 28 km by road, scarcely a successful distance for a target as far away as Leningrad. Hoepner's operational decision of 4 July, to move *8.Pz.D.* east kept it imbedded in primitive Russian countryside. Luckily for the division, the Soviets had been hurt so badly during the fighting of the last two weeks that they were not able to offer strong resistance. At 1800, 8 July 41, however, as the division attacked at the Velikaya River it ran into strong opposition intended to halt it and the promise of more hard fighting along its direction of attack eastward. Battle Group Crisolli, which had moved out from Krasnoye early in the morning of 8 July to support the attack on the Velikaya, ran into strong Soviet resistance just east of Krasnoye at Platischino (See Map 5) that held it up for the entire day and prevented it from supporting the attack.

Bad roads, cross country terrain not trafficable for motorized forces, and determined Soviet defenders accumulated by 9 July 41, to paralyze operational movement by *8.Pz.D.* during that day. Brandenberger intended to advance on one axis 28 km east to Novorzhev and then continue the advance on two axes into the area around Ashevo 39 km farther east by road (these two cities lie just off Map 6 to the east). The division would never reach these optimistic objectives. At 0300, the Soviets launched a heavy infantry attack against the bridgehead with artillery and tank support that resulted in sustained combat through 0630. One "super heavy" KV-2 tank supporting the attack could not be destroyed by the 8.8 cm

Flak cannons which still lay on the west bank of the Velikaya River at ranges now too long to penetrate the tank's armor. As the fighting subsided at 1130, 9 July, pioneer troops began to construct a satisfactory bridge for further advance east. Battle Group Scheller simultaneously but only slowly advanced towards Pushkinskyegory to within 600m of the western outskirts. The pioneers took until 2300 to complete the bridge that would allow further operational level advance. As a result of the Soviet attack that delayed both bridge construction and further advance, and the tough defense by strong Soviet forces for the rest of the day, the division advanced only 5 km. Challenges of river crossing and bridge construction combined with Defender's Posture to present *8.Pz.D.* with the operational disaster of no effective forward movement for a panzer division with deep strategic targets. The German foot marching, horse drawn, 126th Infantry Division (*126.I.D.*), for example, had even caught up with *8.Pz.D.*, arriving at Krasnoye this same day.

When *8.Pz.D.* had begun to advance again operationally on 2 July 41, it moved toward the distant operational target of the Mshaga River and the strategic goal of the campaign itself — the city of Leningrad. During the entire period, 2-9 July, the division would cover in 8 days a total of 186 km and decelerate ominously at the end nowhere near its target. Compared with the first four days of the campaign in which the division moved 295 km along its route of advance, including a one-day halt to defend against a threat that did not materialize, the division had moved slowly. Manstein had set the city of Karsava 85 km distant as the first day's target for the advance. The division did not achieve such distance any single day of its drive and it averaged only 23 km/ day during the period. On the other hand, *8.Pz.D.* fought its way through enemies both foreign (the Soviets) and domestic (its own high command) that make its performance operationally creditable and provides instructive data on the factors that make a force stop or go.

The division faced three quantitatively oriented factors that significantly slowed it. On several days it faced the Soviets in a Defender's Posture intended to stop the Germans with numerically strong forces skillfully led at the tactical level (2, 3, 8, 9 July). The division faced challenging roads and terrain during the whole period. These factors slowed the division and on one day virtually by themselves brought it to a halt (6 July). The division also faced the more important qualitative factor of a failure in the Command Style of Hoepner that projected the division through avoidable tough defenders and restrictive roads and terrain. Hoepner ordered *8.Pz.D.* against the advice of Manstein and Brandenberger to advance in a direction eastward calculated by him to be safe and sure by providing nerve-relaxing certainty in the protection of the east flank of the panzer group. Instead of having the operational nerve to vector *8.Pz.D.*, lying on the left flank of Manstein's corps, as directly as possible toward the mouth of the Mshaga River, Hoepner deflected it east into impossible conditions for operational movement. In an inane situation for a panzer division with a deep operational target, Hoepner vectored *8.Pz.D.* into tough Soviet forces defending themselves in a local tactical context completely removed from the defense of the Mshaga River.

Brandenberger, nevertheless, led the division with remarkable success through Hoepner's operational misdirection, along impassable roads, across difficult terrain, and in the face of accumulating and eventually strong Soviet resistance. After all, the division advanced 186 km during this period of eight days. How is it possible that Brandenberger was able to manage such a performance? The answer lies in a tactical battle style of the division that overrode the momentarily faulty operational command style of Hoepner and the factors of Road Net, Terrain, and Defender's Posture. The Germans continued to exert this superior tactical command and battle style especially through the actions of their commanders leading from the front and a predator-like curiosity about the location and strength of the opposing Soviet formations. After eight days of confrontation between the accelerative factors of German tactical superiority and the decelerative factors of Hoepner's operational misdirection, the division ground almost to a halt on 9 July.

19

Accelerated Advance of the 8th Panzer Division to the Mshaga River 10-14 July '41

Close to first light, at approximately 0400, 10 July 41, Brandenberger sent Battle Group Fronhoefer in the advance east through Pushkinskyegory. Headquarters of both corps and panzer group pressed the division commander and the Ia to move the division fast enough to reach the area around Porkhov by no later than the morning of 11 July 41. The Soviets, however, attacked the battle group from the south with infantry supported by tanks and artillery forcing it to deploy and fight off the Soviet attack. By approximately 0600, Fronhoefer moved forward again only to be stopped 2 km east of Pushkinskyegory by massive demolition charges that had cratered the road severely enough to halt all movement. In a short time, the pioneers of the battle group repaired the road. By about 0730, however, just as the leading *Panzer 38(t)* tanks began to advance again, the Soviets attacked this time with a force of 24 tanks including four of the unnerving heavy vehicles. The 7th Battery, 23rd *Flak* Regiment (Corps troops) was close to the front of the column supporting the advance and deployed its 8.8 cm *Flak* cannons in direct fire against the heavy tanks destroying three of the 52-ton vehicles. In the meantime, the Ia of the division received a phone call from Corps headquarters informing Brandenberger that Manstein required an immediate assessment of the possibilities of the advance east and anticipated eventual turn north toward Porkhov. Brandenberger informed Manstein that *8.Pz.D.* would successfully fight its way through the Soviet forces but would not be in Porkhov by the next morning (11 July) as required by Panzer Group headquarters. This assessment would be pregnant with consequence for the division.

As morning continued on 10 July and Brandenberger continued to press his division farther east, the following rush of events exploded in the division command post. In the laconic, streamlined style of the Germans, Manstein sent the following six-word message to the division commander received at 0900: "Halt attack immediately. March through Ostrov."[27] Brandenberger reacted with an immediate oral order directing *Pz.R.10*, the main element in Battle Group Fronhoefer, to cross back over to the west bank of the Velikaya River to lead the movement north. He set up a reinforced *K.8* simultaneously as rear guard of the division. Corps headquarters passed on a short written order which elaborated that *LVI.A.K.(mot)*, still on 10 July 41, would concentrate around Porkhov. When Brandenberger received this order at about 0930, *8.Pz.D.* lay massed between the Velikaya and Pushkinskyegory, 143 km by road south of the city. The corps order elaborated that *8.Pz.D.* would move out from Porkhov the next morning in an advance on "Petersburg" (Leningrad). Here one sees a no-nonsense, streamlined Command Style in action. Hoepner had been convinced to try another avenue to get *LVI.A.K.(mot)* in motion northward. Manstein passed on the new operational direction of advance in six words to the division. The new decision came with little warning to Brandenburger and the Ia, who reacted with consummate tactical dexterity[28] to turn the division around 180 degrees, disengage from a strong enemy, and then turn another 90 degrees north (See Map12). The division would begin assembling by 1130 in the area near the great north road to Ostrov (See Map 12) and move off in four battle groups arranged in a division march column led by the tanks of Battle Group Fronhoefer at 1600, 10 July.

By the end of the day, 10 July, Brandenberger had placed advanced tank elements of Battle Group Fronhoefer near Shmoylovo on the main road connecting Ostrov and Porkhov. These tanks were headed north 105 km distant from where the same vehicles had stood headed east earlier at 0900, 10 July.[29] The mass of Battle Group Fronhoefer stood close behind its advanced elements. The remainder of the division lay strung out over 95 km of now mostly good road by Soviet standards all the way to the Velikaya River where the screening and rear guard forces continued to disengage. The logistics officer of the division, the Ib, *Major i.G.* Jobst Brand, quietly kept the division supplied with fuel and ammunition for both the tough fighting on the eastern axis of advance and the turn about and acceleration north. The move north would be over roads largely cleared of Soviet forces by the neighboring *XXXXI.A.K.(mot)*, but the achievement of the division was extraordinary in light of the following facts. It had fought two tough engagements between 0400-0900, 10 July, and then with an active enemy at its back reversed itself and moved in a dramatic advance toward Leningrad. The division did not just make a lateral move behind German lines; it moved most of the distance during the day closer to Leningrad.

Battle Group Fronhoefer as *Schwerpunkt* force of the division moved remarkably far on 10 July. If one adds the 6 km the group advanced through and beyond Pushkinskyegory during early morning against stiff resistance and physical obstacles, the total distance was 111 km during the day. The group moved the following distances and directions:

Battle Group Fronhoefer, 10 July 41

Distance	**Direction**	**Comment (See also Maps 12 and 13)**
6 km	East	Advance vs Tough Resistance
26 km	West	Turn About and Reorganization
79 km	North	Advance Late Afternoon and Evening
111 km	Mostly North	Impressive Tactical Dexterity

With movement as impressive as this, the question naturally arises: what accelerated the division largely forward on 10 July? The most important reason for the sudden acceleration compared with the average movement of 26 km/day for the previous eight days was the factor of Command Style. After stubbornly persisting in directing *8.Pz.D.* east through difficult terrain, Hoepner flexibly made the decision to retract it westward and send it north toward its operational objective through the zone of advance of the neighboring corps. Driven by the strategical mission to get to Leningrad fast, Hoepner finally projected *8.Pz.D.* and *LVI.A.K.(mot)* forward with speed and daring. Several days earlier, Hoepner had shifted the *Schwerpunkt* of the advance of the Panzer Group to the same neighboring *XXXXI.A.K.(mot)*, that had now advanced farther north than *LVI.A.K.(mot)* and *8.Pz.D.* and required security on its right flank that would be provided by the advance of *8.Pz.D.* to the Mshaga River. Hoepner, then, for operational reasons associated with his bold handling of *XXXXI.A.K.(mot)*, finally accelerated *8.Pz.D.* northward to keep pace with the Panzer Group *Schwerpunkt*, provide security to its eastern flank, and move toward Leningrad on a second major axis of advance.

Hoepner's decision, which was more than agreeable with Manstein, set *8.Pz.D.* in decisive advance toward the Mshaga River. The command and battle style of Brandenberger and his division was the main reason for the successful movement on 10 July. When Manstein ordered the halt and redirection of *8.Pz.D.* at 0800, Brandenberger was personally accompanying the leading elements in the attack east. With little friction or lost motion, he turned the leading elements of the division around and directed them 30 km west to the area near the road junction with the big highway to Ostrov where they could lead the move north as Battle Group Fronhoefer, i.e., tanks still in the lead. Brandenberger immediately directed the Ia and streamlined division staff to begin moving forces north. The Ib, for example, began to anticipate and take measures to get the division refueled unit by unit as it passed through Ostrov. The tactical units in Battle Group Scheller, which would be the rear guard and screening force to south and east, skillfully covered the new movement. The battle groups quickly reorganized and eventually advanced throughout the hours of darkness on the road to Porkhov. The division also began to receive aerial and ground reconnaissance reports from *3.I.D.(mot)* that lay closer to the objective area about bridge conditions for an advance through and north of Porkhov.

The more conventional quantitative rate of advance factors all favored the Germans. After the modest advance of 6 km east on the early morning of 10 July, during which the Germans met factors of road net, terrain, and defender's posture that slowed their advance, they accelerated forward partly on the basis of improvement in every one of the quantitatively oriented factors. Road net and terrain favored a more rapid advance. Weather favored a German advance; the war diary of the Ib noted that it was very warm and sunny on both 10 and 11 July. The Germans moved with confidence and skill in their night marches using the hours of darkness to help to achieve the distances demanded in a blitz offensive. The factors of force ratios, attacker's casualties, and defender's posture did not come into play significantly because the division would be advancing through an area largely cleared by other German forces now farther ahead. The duration of operation, of course, was brief and tended to be a factor that kept the division advancing.

On the early morning of 11 July, Battle Group Fronhoefer in the lead of the division and Bodenhausen next behind it, lay along the big road running northeast out of Ostrov. Although the two battle groups were spread out along 44 km of road from Ostrov to Shmoylovo, Brandenberger intended to advance with them through Porkhov and Sol'tsy to the Mshaga River on the same day. He put *K.8*, the motorcycle battalion of the division, in the lead, moving it out at 1200 from the area near Shmoylovo toward Porkhov The motorcycle battalion reached the bridge over the Uza River near Pustoy on a road crowded with units of *3.I.D.(mot)* that were advancing in front of *8.Pz.D.* to move through Porkhov and redeploy on the left flank of the panzer division. Due to the heavy traffic of the day, the bridge remained passable only for passenger cars and motorcycles, allowing the wheeled elements of *K.8* to advance to Porkhov by 1300. In the meantime, at 1230, Brandenberger ordered the mass of Battle Group Fronhoefer to begin its advance from around Shmoylovo to Porkhov. At 1635, before Fronhoefer reached the bridge near Pustoy on the Uza River that was impassable for his tanks and trucks, the corps commander ordered *8.Pz.D.* to rest in the positions it had reached at that time, put out security elements to the south, and wait for the bridge to be reconstructed. Manstein also halted *8.Pz.D.* to allow *3.I.D.(mot)* to move across its front on 11 and 12 July and advance on the left flank of the division toward the Mshaga. The final result: the pioneers finished the big bridge during the evening and added an additional 4-ton capacity bridge that allowed *8.Pz.D.* to concentrate Battle Group Fronhoefer around Vereteni and advance northeast from there at 1330, 12 July (See Map 13).

Events moved swiftly but unevenly on 12 July. The advanced detachment of the division out in front of Fronhoefer reached Borovichi at 0830, 42 km northeast of the starting point at Vereteni and built up a small bridgehead there. By mid morning, Battle Group Bodenhausen, that should have been following close behind Fronhoefer, lagged badly. Bodenhausen reported difficult road conditions and noted that at 0900, the head of his battle group was located at Malyye Peti still 18 km southwest of Vereteni and 60 km from the lead elements of the division at Borovichi. In contrast, the leading Battle Group Fronhoefer pushed through Sukhlovo at 1255 slowed though in its advance by small packs of Soviet tanks that appeared on several occasions and demanded serious efforts to repel. By 1430, for example, the advanced elements of Fronhoefer had destroyed 12 Soviet tanks in these running engagements. By 1530, the advanced elements, consisting of reinforced K.8, reached the Sitnya River near the city of Sitnya and seemed on the verge of pushing on to the Mshaga River later in the day. By 1600, the advanced elements of Battle Group Bodenhausen finally established physical contact with the rear elements of Fronhoefer near Borovichi and were ordered to continue in column behind the lead battle group.[30]

As fighting developed on the Sitnya River, *K.8* was unable to seize the bridge over the river intact and attempted to establish a bridgehead with motorcyclists on foot moving across the 25m-wide river at a ford suitable for tracked vehicles. By 1900, however, the mass of Battle Group Fronhoefer had arrived with tanks, motorized infantry, and artillery and pushed across into a bridgehead 2 km deep destroying eight Soviet medium tanks in the advance. At 1915, the Soviets attacked the bridgehead with a force of 20 tanks, but Fronhoefer immediately launched a counterattack with tanks of *Pz.R.10* that quickly broke up this last Soviet attempt to smash the German bridgehead. Brandenberger ordered construction of a new bridge and continuation of the advance early the next morning at 0300, 13 July. The terrain obstacle of the river, the associated necessity to reconstruct the destroyed bridge, and determined Soviet resistance conspired to halt the division momentarily. The Germans, however, were only 38 km from the Mshaga; and, the mass of Battle Group Bodenhausen, that included a large part of one motorized rifle regiment with artillery, *Pak*, and pioneer support, had reached the area around Opoka by 2000 only 24 km from the Sitnya Bridgehead (See Map 14).

Brandenberger and 8.Pz.D. encountered the frictions of war in numerous ways as 13 July dawned on a "very warm and sunny"[31] day. As directed by corps, but in accordance with his own predilection, Brandenberger attempted to move out Battle Group Fronhoefer at 0300. The Battle Group depended significantly, however, on a deep ford next to the pioneer bridge to advance and met terrain difficulties of soft ground and steep slopes that slowed forces moving through and delayed the attack against the Soviets 4 km farther east until 0500. At that time, however, as II./*Pz.R.10* (2d Battalion, *Pz.R.10*) was about to attack, it was hit by advancing Soviet forces including 52-ton, KV-2 tanks.[32] As the battle developed 4 km east of the Sitnya crossing, the Ia remarked that the strong Soviet tank force seemed to be covering the retreat of large Soviet infantry forces eastward. The division commander held the opinion, however, that the Soviets under cover of the attacking tanks were reinforcing their infantry with the intention of making a major attack. Heavy fighting continued until early afternoon by which time, Brandenberger had committed three panzer battalions (i.e., the entire *Pz.R.10)*, two motorized rifle battalions, two heavy and one light artillery battalions and other supporting forces in an attempt to advance again to the Mshaga. At 1500, 13 July, the division finally broke up the attacking Soviet forces having destroyed 3 Soviet KV-2 and 19 medium tanks in the fighting and overrun positions holding 10 artillery pieces. Brandenberger pressed his forward elements to Raytsy for the final advance of the day. Delayed by bridge and ford conditions and the Soviet defenses, *8.Pz.D.* gained only 8 km on 13 July, although it defeated and scattered strong Soviet forces in front of it.

Brandenberger continued to meet difficulties in concentrating all of the division battle groups forward. During early evening of the previous day, 12 July, for example, Bodenhausen pushed forward the main concentration of his battle group only to Opoka still 20 km by road from the Sitnya crossing. Battle Group Scheller should have been close behind Bodenhausen but lay far away to the southwest. The next day at 0300, 13 July, as the forward elements of Battle Group Scheller began to move through Porkhov, corps headquarters ordered it off the road to make way for higher priority combat forces of *3.I.D.(mot)* advancing over the same road across the front of *8.Pz.D.* to move up on its left flank. Corps headquarters initially ordered Scheller to halt and make way for other traffic until 0930 (6.5 hours!) and extended the halt until 1430 (11.5 hours!) to allow higher priority supply forces to move along the main road north out of Porkhov. Fixed in position for half a day, Battle Group Scheller finally got started at 1430 and advanced the *Spitze* of the battle group column to the area east of Sukhlovo to link up with Battle Group Bodenhausen by 1750. The limited road net for the advance of both a panzer and motorized rifle division, combined with firm German traffic control, had halted Battle Group Scheller for an exorbitant period and weakened the division in its fight through the tough Soviet resistance around Sitnya.

On 14 July, Brandenberger led *8.Pz.D.* to within 3 km of the Mshaga River bridges on the road to Novgorod and Leningrad. The division commander and the battle group commanders displayed great energy in intervening personally at various critical points in the action. The troops displayed great tactical skill and self-confidence in the battle that day in advancing against forces that proved a day later to be superior in numbers. In spite of strong Soviet fighter and bomber forces over the battlefield, Brandenberger continued to receive aerial reconnaissance reports that made him aware that a strong enemy was close at hand

and moving against the division. The picture of effective command and self-assured tactical skill was mixed, however, with ominous events and continuing frictions.

At 0300, Battle Group Scheller, west of Sukhlovo began to advance again in order finally to link up with Fronhoefer in the lead of the division. Almost immediately, the battle group was slowed this time by ill disciplined traffic of corps staff, corps troops, and *Luftwaffe* elements. The battle group also came under fire from Soviet units in this area far behind the lead elements of *8.Pz.D.* At approximately 0400, 14 July, corps headquarters located near the battle group column came under attack by Soviet ground forces and ordered units of *S.R.8*, roughly half the strength of Scheller, to intervene in the fighting. Scheller aggressively moved the rest of the battle group forward but only slowly on the overcrowded road and with half of his force separated from him now and defending corps headquarters. As Scheller reached the Sitnya River at 0600 with his forward elements, he faced disastrous traffic, bridge, ford and off road trafficability problems. These problems prevented him from getting the last elements of his battle group through the crossing until 1600, 14 July 41. The division war diary commented that his personal intervention at the crossing for two hours was primarily responsible for "freeing up" the route.[33]

At the head of the division, Battle Group Fronhoefer continued to advance. At 1000, the *Spitze* of Fronhoefer's group in very slow movement forward, nevertheless, passed through the big town of Sol'tsy and lay 1 km east of it. At the same hour, as a consequence of the continued presence of the KV-2 tanks in front of the division, the corps commander, during a personal visit to the division command post far to the front only 3 km west of Sol'tsy, ordered forward to the division all of the 8.8 cm *Flak* cannon at the disposal of *LVI.A.K.(mot)*. By 1300, the advanced elements of the division had moved 6 km east of Sol'tsy and at 1430 met two Soviet KV-2 tanks simultaneously with the arrival of the 8.8 cm *Flak* cannons ordered forward by Manstein. At this moment, Brandenberger led the division at this point in the battle in and among the leading German tanks. He personally ordered two reinforced tank companies to continue the advance side by side toward the Mshaga now only 12 km away. German air reconnaissance pilots and observers reported extremely strong Soviet forces moving along the roads and through the forests to the north and northwest of the division and heading for it. Brandenberger nevertheless pushed his tanks ahead reaching positions only 3 km from the Mshaga River just west of Shimsk on Lake Ilmen at 1900, 14 July 41. The next morning the Soviets would attack the division from every direction and far to its rear. A day later, the division would be encircled temporarily but with great tactical skill and self confidence remain in positions around and to the west of Sol'tsy.

The Ia of the division specifically noted the slow movement of Battle Group Scheller in its attempt to get to the front of the division and into the battle. In the war diary, he analyzed the situation as follows. The road conditions were wretched but the road conditions in general were bad in the Baltic. Battle Group Scheller, therefore, experienced conditions that were not exceptional for the campaign. He then goes on to say that on 14 July 41, over and above the sandy stretches of road cut to pieces by traffic, another factor of a different nature came into play and was unsatisfactory. The Ia described the chaotic streaming into Scheller's combat march column of numerous units from rest positions and side roads. He used the term, "partly undisciplined conditions," to describe the situation and noted that corps troops were the worst offenders. The Ia's analysis of the situation shows

Battle Group Scheller slowed in its advance by problems of traffic control exacerbated by poor road conditions. The point that stands out is that the Germans, early in the campaign, could do little about reconstructing the Baltic roads, but they might have been able on some occasions to move more effectively with better, or more ruthless, traffic control.

The Ia also elaborated on factors that had contributed by this time in the campaign to the rapid advance. Based on a captured Soviet document, he describes the great breach made in the Soviet defenses through the capture of the Duenaburg bridge and associated destruction and demoralization of defending Soviet troop units and the throwing off balance of the Soviet leadership in the Baltic. The division had achieved these effects for the Germans in the Baltic in significant degree by the advance to Duenaburg. It would owe much of its further success in the advance toward the Mshaga River to the continued effects. In spite of the exorbitant delay of *8.Pz.D.* and *LVI.A.K.(mot)* at Duenaburg, the Soviets had been hit so hard that the accumulated casualties, equipment losses and demoralization of the troops combined with disequilibrium on the part of command, remained as major factors in the rapid division advance.

Toward the end of the drive to the Mshaga, the Ia commented that the swift movement of the Division led to an extremely dangerous tactical situation. As *3.I.D.(mot)* moved across

Photo 8. Shown here are two of the formidable Soviet KV-2 tanks with armor impervious to the projectiles of any German tank or antitank cannon in 1941. The tanks weighed more than 52 tons and carried a massive 152mm howitzer for fire in support of Soviet motorized infantry. The tanks were produced in the Kirov factory in Leningrad and most were encountered by the Germans in the Baltic. The tanks in the photo were damaged and captured by 6 th Panzer Division on 24 or 25 June 41. The 8 th Panzer Division mastered them with the heavy 88mm Flak pressed toward the front of its battle groups for direct fire (Bundesarchiv Bestand).

the front of *8.Pz.D.* to take up position on its left flank, the motorized infantry division slowed down in its advance and the panzer division moved forward faster leaving 40 km of its left flank without a friendly German unit. By the same time (14 July), *Pz.Gr.4* had made the decision to put *S.S. "T"* into reserve leaving a horse drawn infantry division on the right flank of *8.Pz.D.* and 70 km to the rear. The Ia ended his discussion with a revealing comment about the combat power of a panzer division and the self confident command and battle style of the Germans in such a situation. He stated that with both flanks of the division exposed so severely, the rear area of the division would face heavy danger in the following days. The comment is revealing because he mentioned nothing about danger to the division as a whole. The reader is driven to conclude that he had utter confidence in the forward combat elements through their superior battle style to defeat the Soviets even if encircled.

With Hoepner' s approval, Manstein ordered *8.Pz.D.* at 0900, 10 July 41, to move north immediately, cross the Mshaga River, and advance on Leningrad. Hoepner's decision which was pressed for by Manstein and then implemented, put Brandenberger and his panzer division into rapid motion toward a distant operational target. As *8.Pz.D.* adjusted to the new situation, the war diary begins to give its reader the same sense of urgent mission that characterized the passages in the diary from 22-26 June 41, and which disappeared during most of the period from 27 June - 9 July 41.

Brandenberger moved *8.Pz.D.* the impressive distance of 230 km in the period 10-14 July 41. He moved the division in spite of adverse road conditions that developed past Shmoylovo, overcrowded traffic involving the mutual use of one road by two mobile divisions and significant numbers of corps troops and *Luftwaffe* units, and difficult terrain for the cross country deployment of vehicles. Brandenberger also moved in the face of serious resistance in the area from Borovichi eastward on 12 July and a defender's posture on the part of the Soviets that was intended to halt the Germans on 13 and 14 July. On the other hand, the weather continued to be warm and sunny and favored the Germans as concerns air support and aerial reconnaissance, low river levels, and dry roads. Although casualties in the period 10-14 July would be *relatively* higher than in roughly comparable earlier periods of combat, they would have to be considered as moderate in terms of actual numbers for a panzer division close to full strength.[34] The division continued to use night time for the characteristic reforming of battle groups and tactical movement, and used it more effectively on the offensive than the Soviets on the defensive. As fighting developed in the period 12-14 July, within its zone of advance, the division fought with numbers of men and weapons that consistently favored the division, i.e., superior force ratios. The Germans, however, advanced against Soviet forces that continued to accumulate rather than disperse and retreat during this three-day period, and it is likely that the Soviets had superior numbers overall in the zone of action but not in the individual tactical engagements. As concerns the factor of combat power, the division advanced with only moderate casualties in the face of Soviet resistance during the whole period supporting a conclusion that the division fought with command and battle style superior to the Soviets.

PART THREE:

Map Section

Notes on Abbreviations

AA = *Aufklaerungsabteilung* = Reconnaissance Detachment

Bodenhausen, Crisolli, Fronhoefer, Scheller = Names of the Commanders of Battle Groups of *8.Pz.D.*

Elms = Elements

Fwd Elms = Forward Elements

K-Gr. = *Kampfgruppe*, or Battle Group

Mass = Main Body

Recon = Reconnaissance Detachment

Spitze = Spearhead, or Advanced Elements

3.I.D.(mot) = 3rd Motorized Infantry Division

6.Pz.D. = 6th Panzer Division

30.I.D. = 30th Infantry Division

290.I.D. = 290th Infantry Division

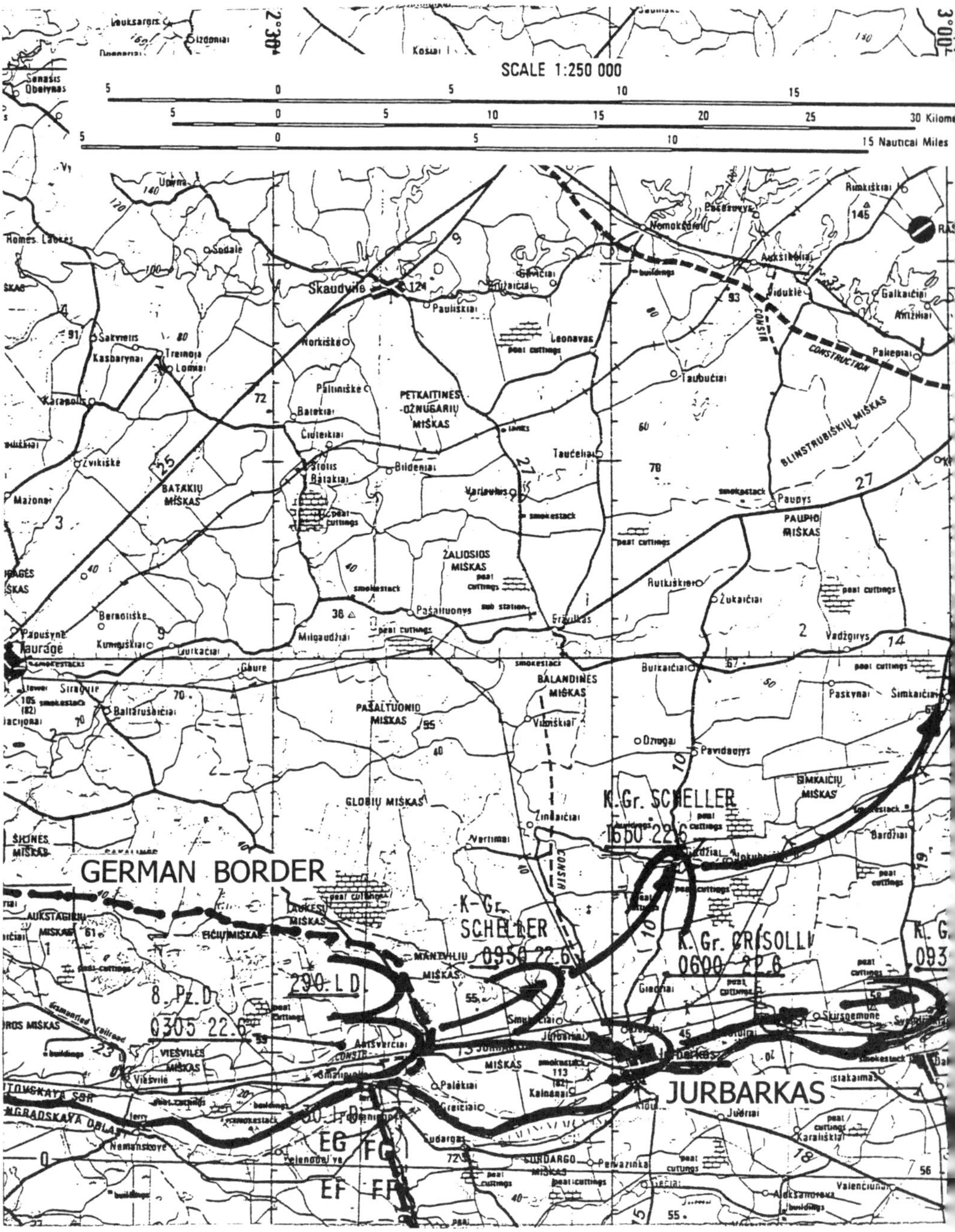
SCALE 1:250 000
15 Nautical Miles
GERMAN BORDER
K.Gr. SCHELLER
1650 22.6
K-Gr. SCHELLER
0950 22.6
K.Gr. CRISOLLI
0600 22.6
290. I.D.
8. Pz.D
0305 22.6
JURBARKAS
Skaudvilė
Tauragė

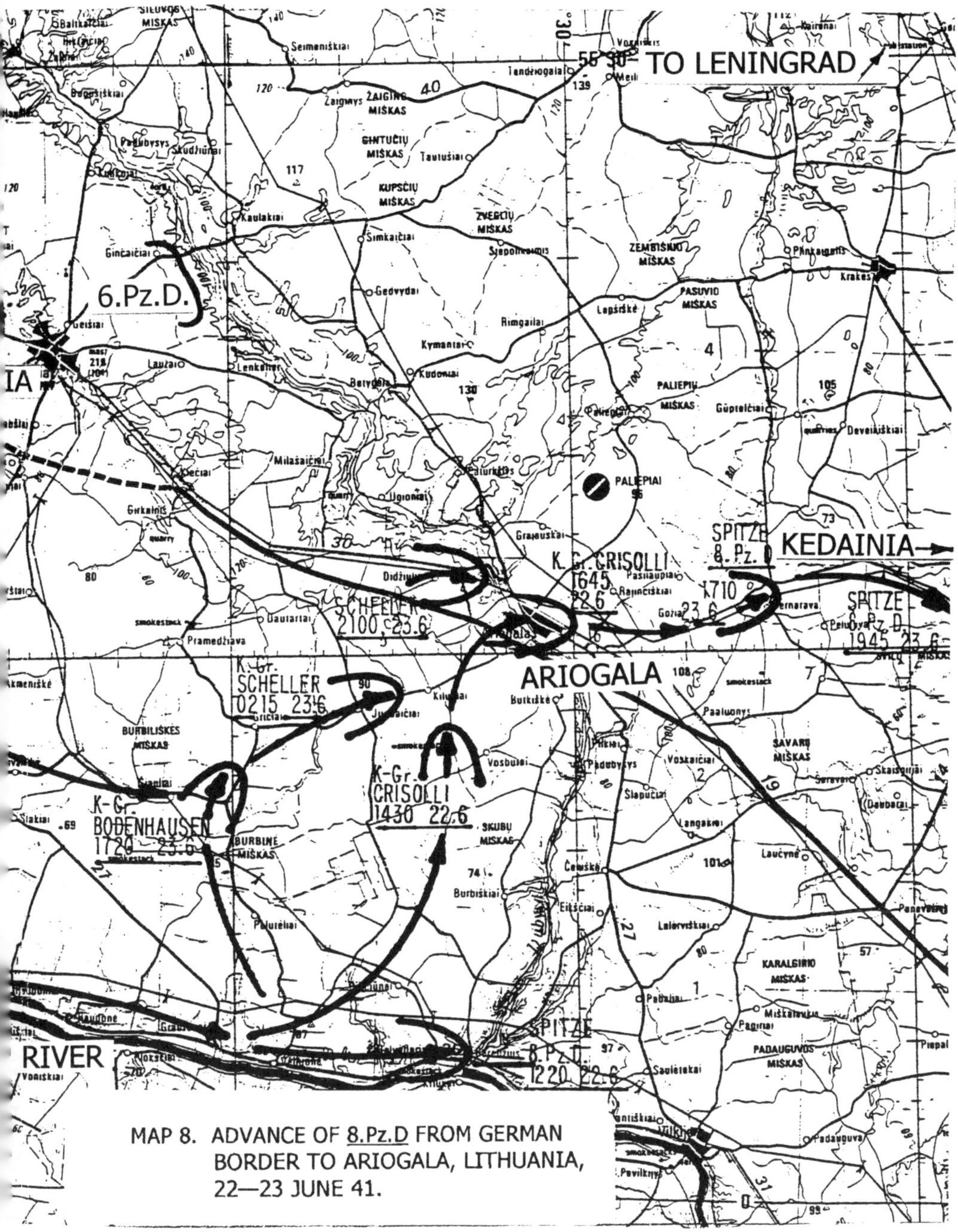

MAP 8. ADVANCE OF 8.Pz.D FROM GERMAN BORDER TO ARIOGALA, LITHUANIA, 22—23 JUNE 41.

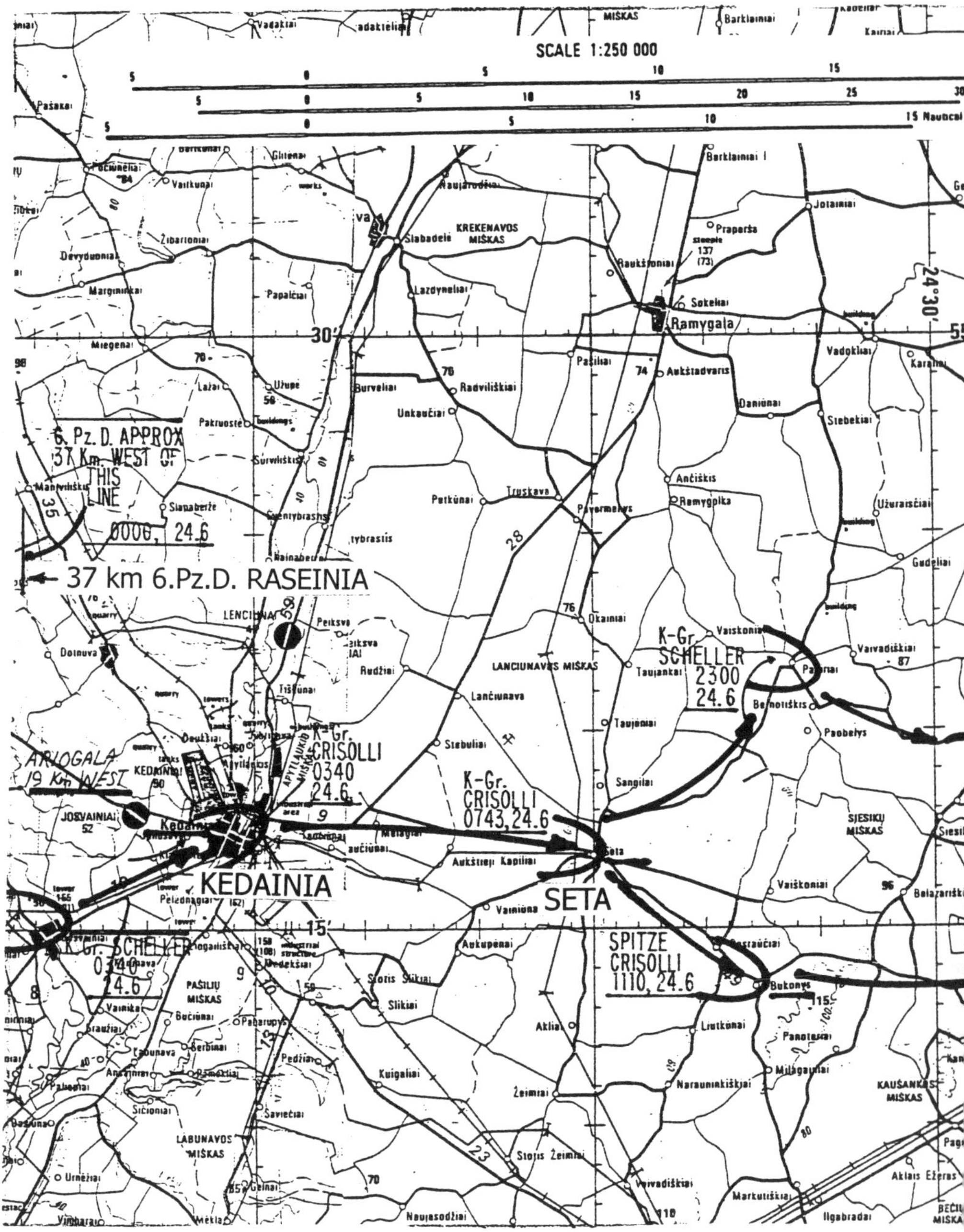
SCALE 1:250 000
6. Pz. D. APPROX
37 Km. WEST OF
THIS
LINE
0000, 24.6
37 km 6.Pz.D. RASEINIA
ARIOGALA
19 Km. WEST
K-Gr.
CRISOLLI
0340
24.6
K-Gr.
CRISOLLI
0743, 24.6
K-Gr.
SCHELLER
2300
24.6
KEDAINIA
SETA
K-Gr. SCHELLER
0340
24.6
SPITZE
CRISOLLI
1110, 24.6
Ramygala
KREKENAVOS
MIŠKAS
LANCIUNAVOS MIŠKAS
SIESIKŲ
MIŠKAS
PAŠILIŲ
MIŠKAS
LABUNAVOS
MIŠKAS
KAUŠANKOS
MIŠKAS
Jotainiai
Dotnuva
Bukonys
Truskava
Lančiunava
Šlabadele
Paberžė
Taujėnai
Sangailai
Žeimiai
Liutkūnai
Vaiskoniai
Gudeliai
Sirutiškis
24°30′
55
30′
15′

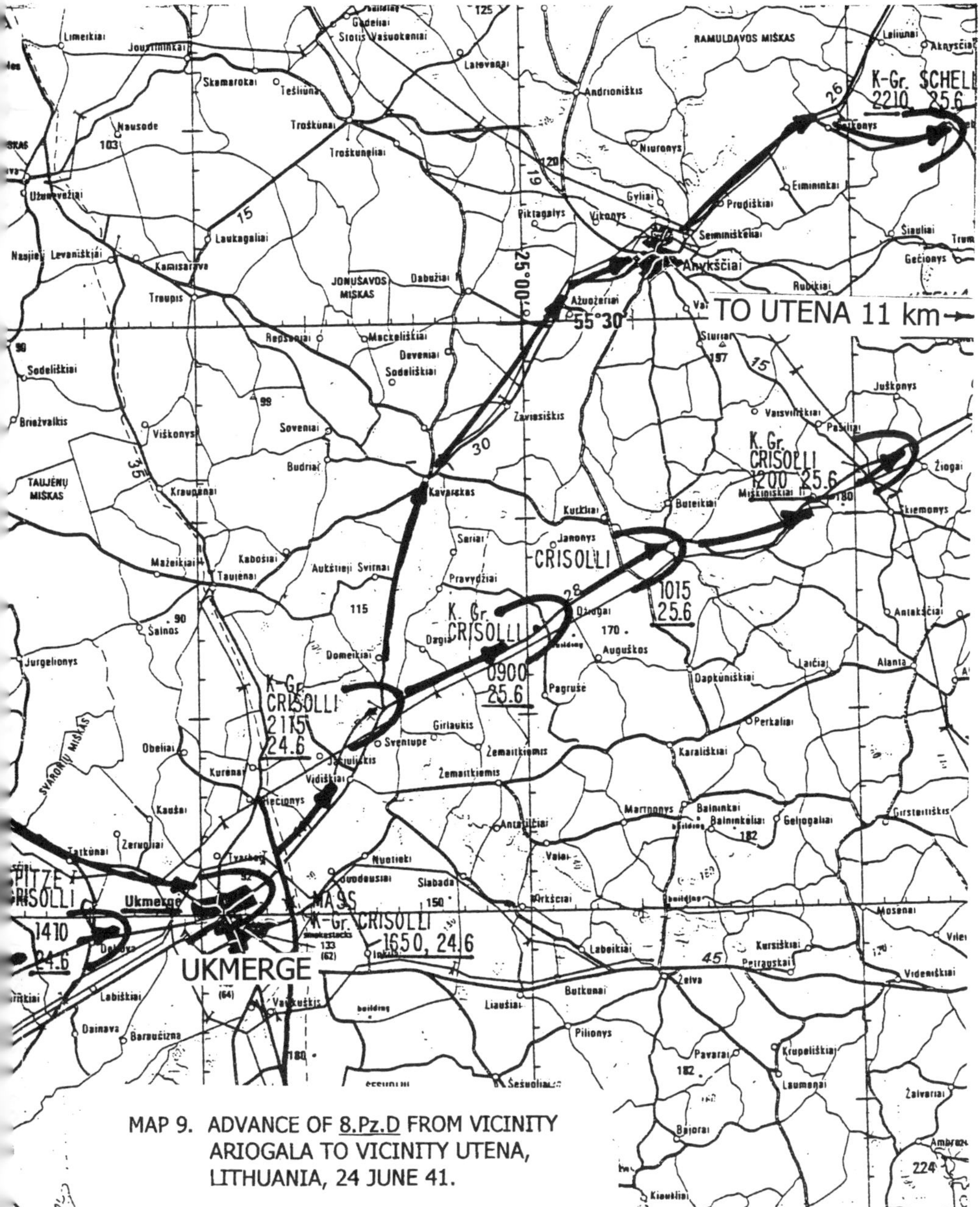

MAP 9. ADVANCE OF 8.Pz.D FROM VICINITY ARIOGALA TO VICINITY UTENA, LITHUANIA, 24 JUNE 41.

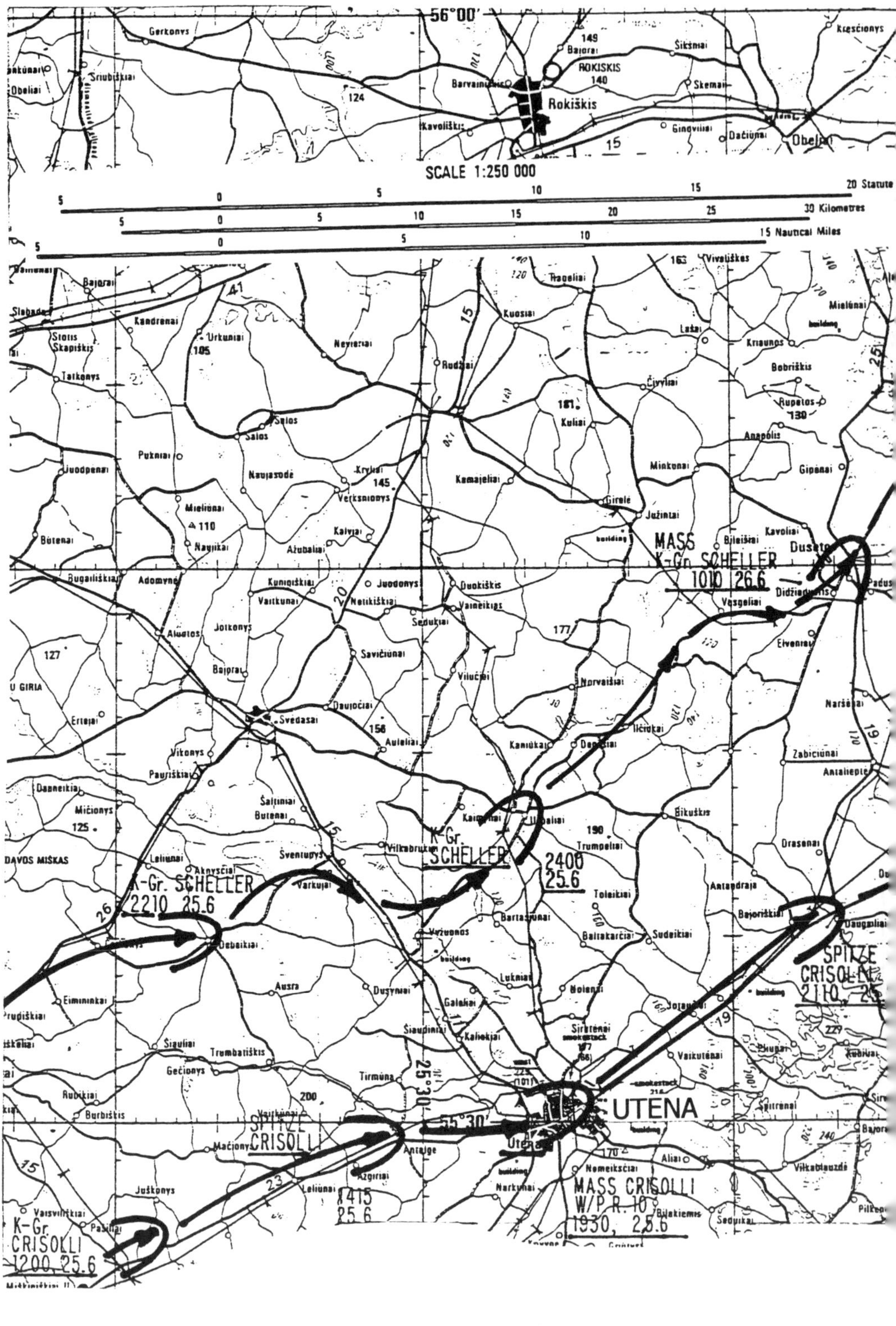
56°00'
Rokiškis
ROKIŠKIS
Obeliai
SCALE 1:250 000
20 Statute
30 Kilometres
15 Nautical Miles
MASS
K-Gr. SCHELLER
1010 26.6
K-Gr.
SCHELLER
2400
25.6
K-Gr. SCHELLER
2210 25.6
SPITZE
CRISOLLI
2110 25
UTENA
55°30'
25°30'
SPITZE
CRISOLLI
1415
25.6
MASS CRISOLLI
W/P.R. 10
1930, 25.6
K-Gr.
CRISOLLI
1200 25.6
Svėdasai
Dusetos

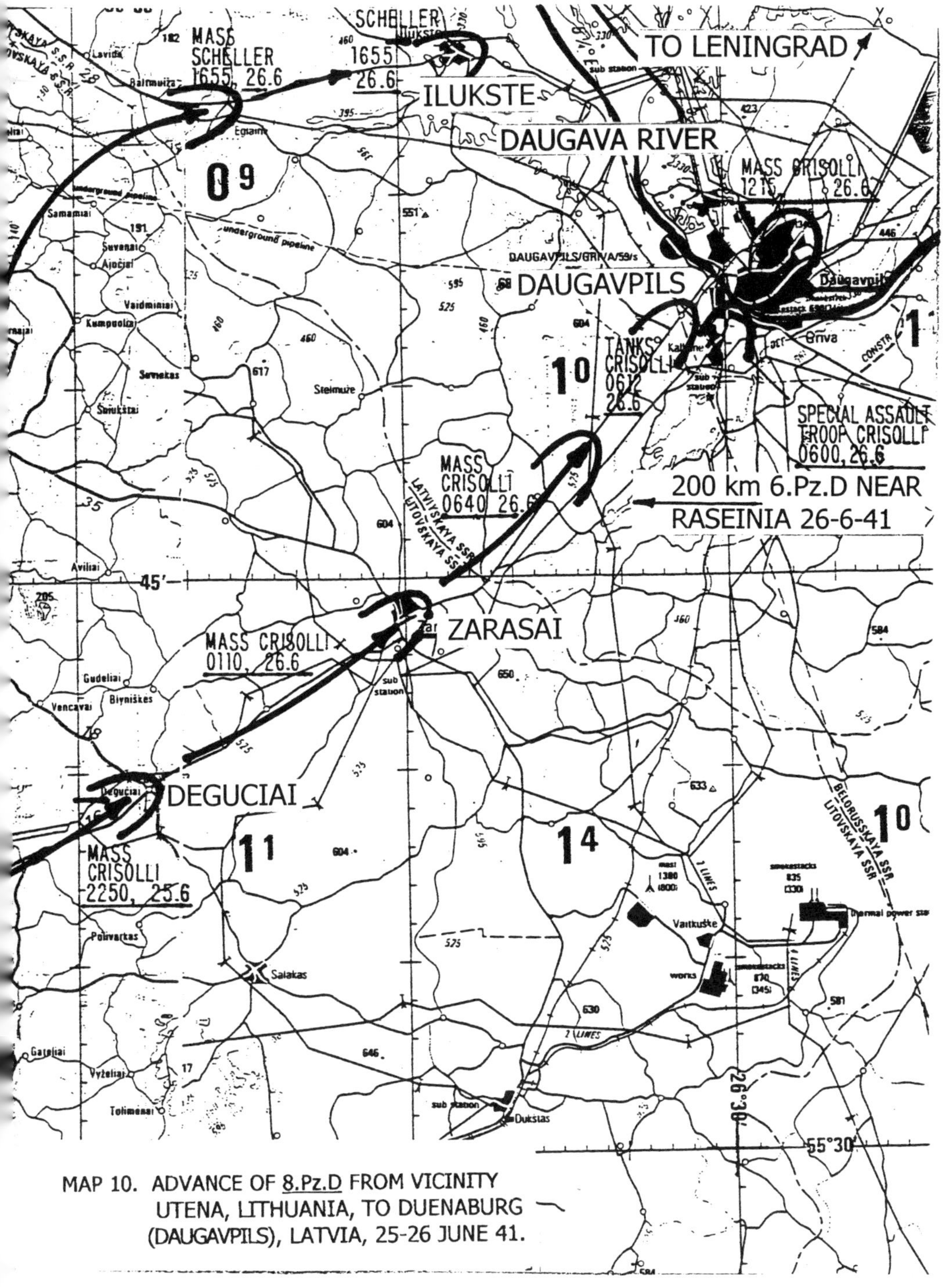

MAP 10. ADVANCE OF 8.Pz.D FROM VICINITY UTENA, LITHUANIA, TO DUENABURG (DAUGAVPILS), LATVIA, 25-26 JUNE 41.

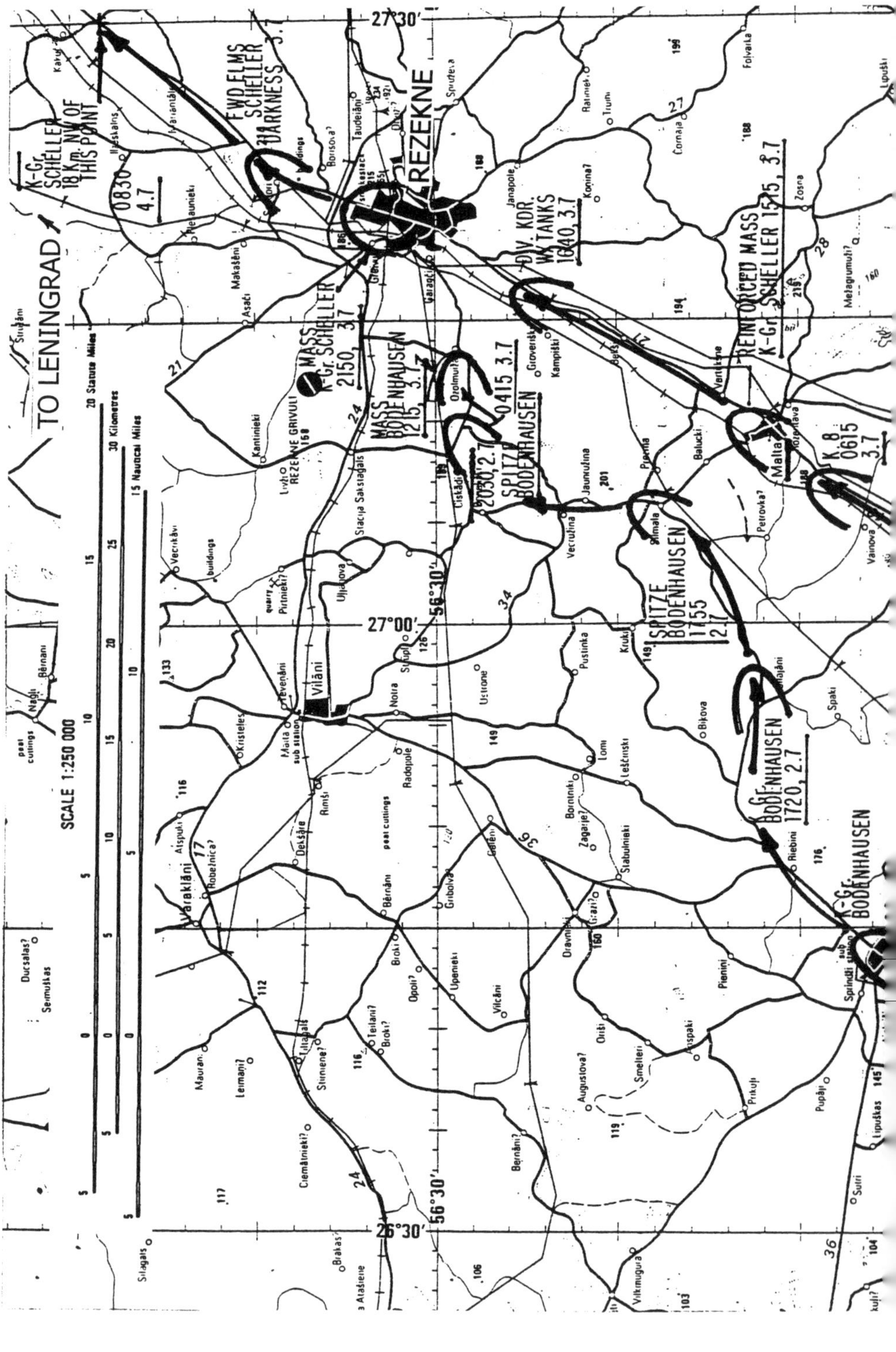
TO LENINGRAD
REZEKNE
K-Gr. SCHELLER 18 Km. NW OF THIS POINT
0830 4.7
FWD ELMS SCHELLER DARKNESS 3.7
DIV. KDR. W/ TANKS 1640 3.7
REINFORCED MASS K-Gr. SCHELLER 1515 3.7
MASS K-Gr. SCHELLER 2150 3.7
MASS BODENHAUSEN 1215 3.7
0415 3.7
SPITZE BODENHAUSEN
2030 2.7
SPITZE BODENHAUSEN 1755 2.7
K-Gr. BODENHAUSEN 1720 2.7
K-Gr. BODENHAUSEN
K. 8 0615 3.7
SCALE 1:250 000
Viläni
27°30'
27°00'
26°30'
56°30'

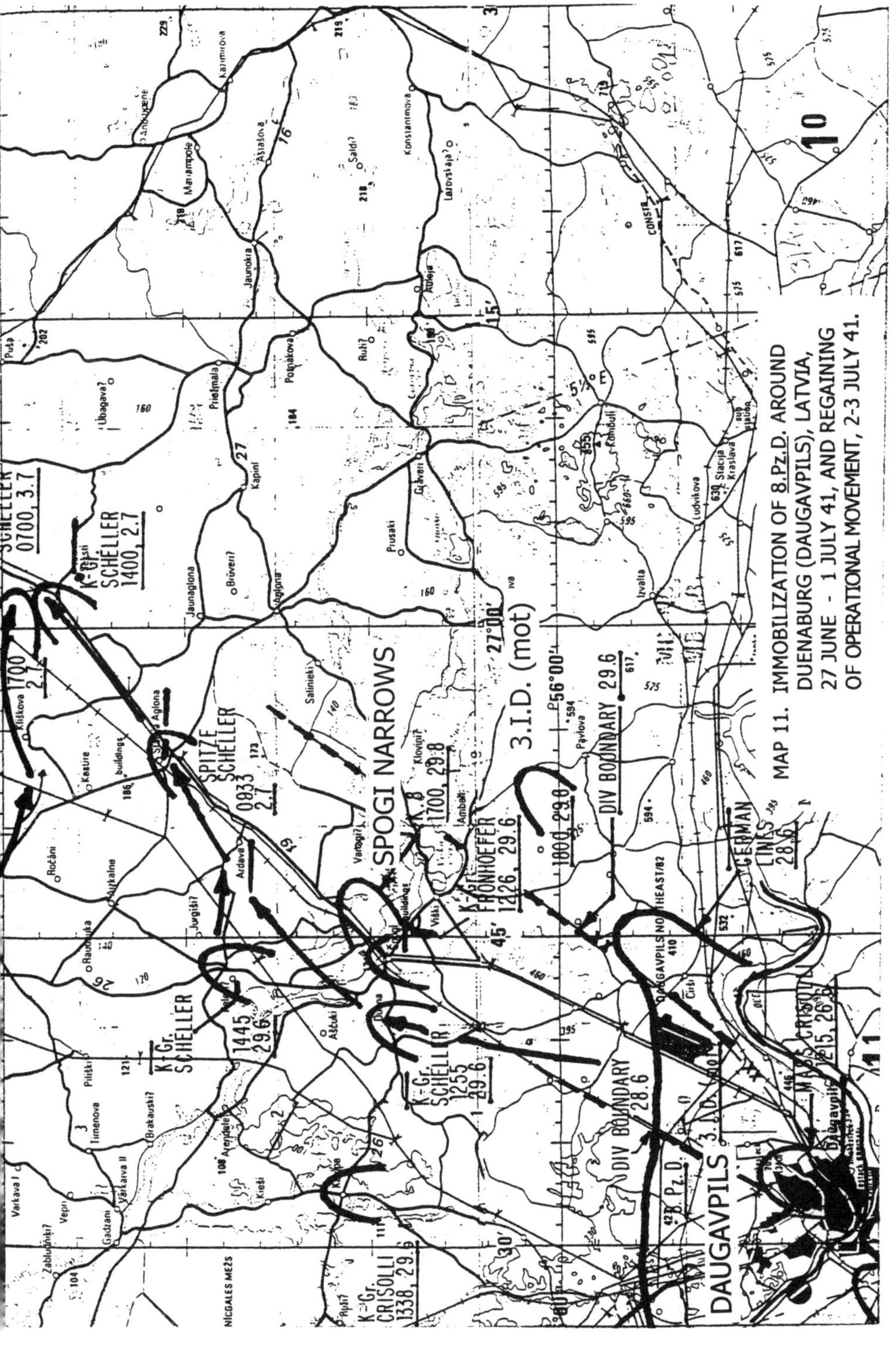

MAP 11. IMMOBILIZATION OF 8.Pz.D. AROUND DUENABURG (DAUGAVPILS), LATVIA, 27 JUNE - 1 JULY 41, AND REGAINING OF OPERATIONAL MOVEMENT, 2-3 JULY 41.

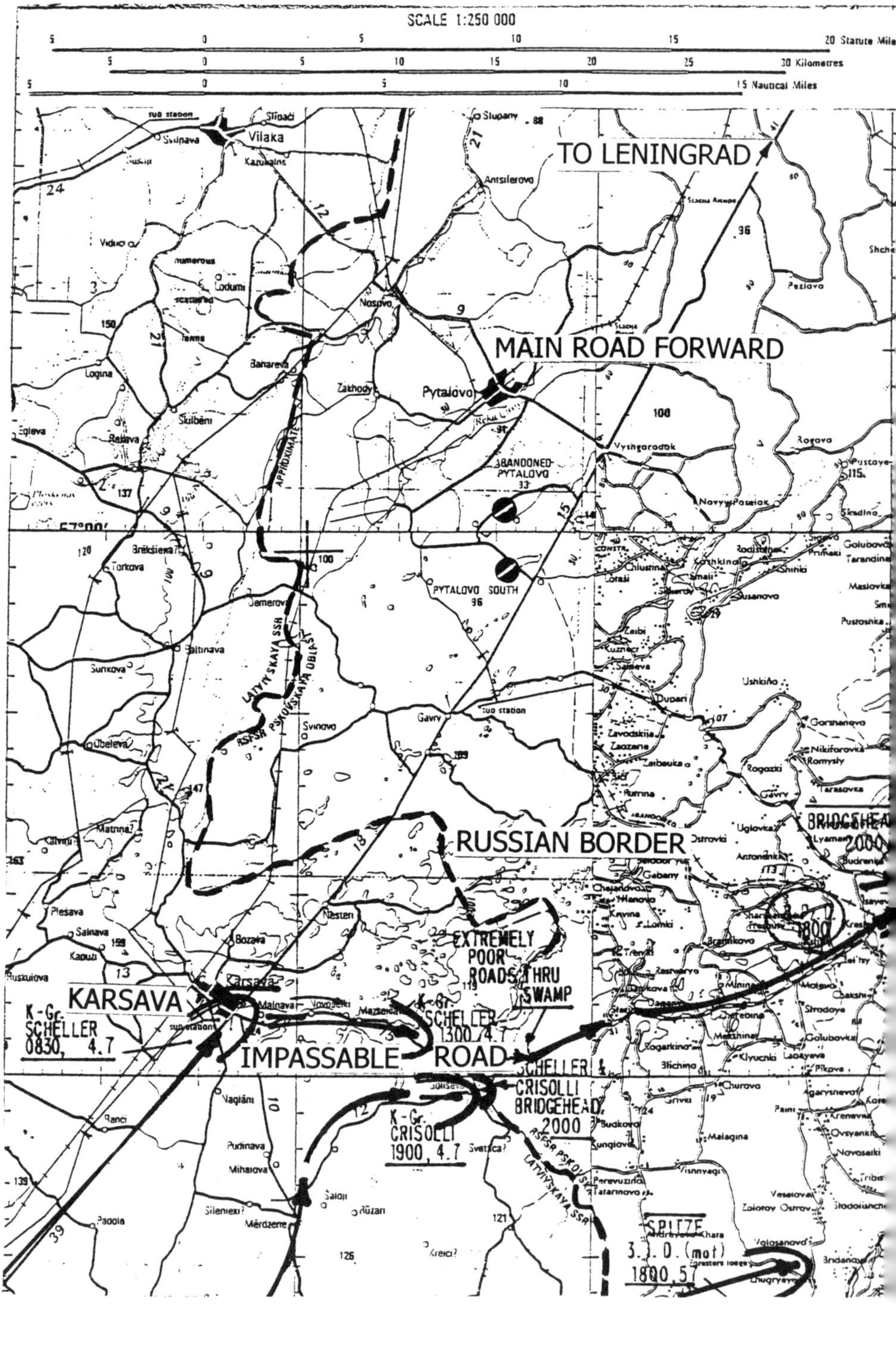
SCALE 1:250 000
Statute Miles
Kilometres
Nautical Miles
TO LENINGRAD
MAIN ROAD FORWARD
ABANDONED PYTALOVO
PYTALOVO SOUTH
RUSSIAN BORDER
EXTREMELY POOR ROADS THRU SWAMP
KARSAVA
K-Gr. SCHELLER 0830, 4.7
K-Gr. SCHELLER 1300/4.7
IMPASSABLE ROAD
SCHELLER
CRISOLLI BRIDGEHEAD 2000
K-Gr. CRISOLLI 1900, 4.7
SPITZE 3. I. D. (mot) 1800, 5.7
Vilaka
Pytalovo
Karsava

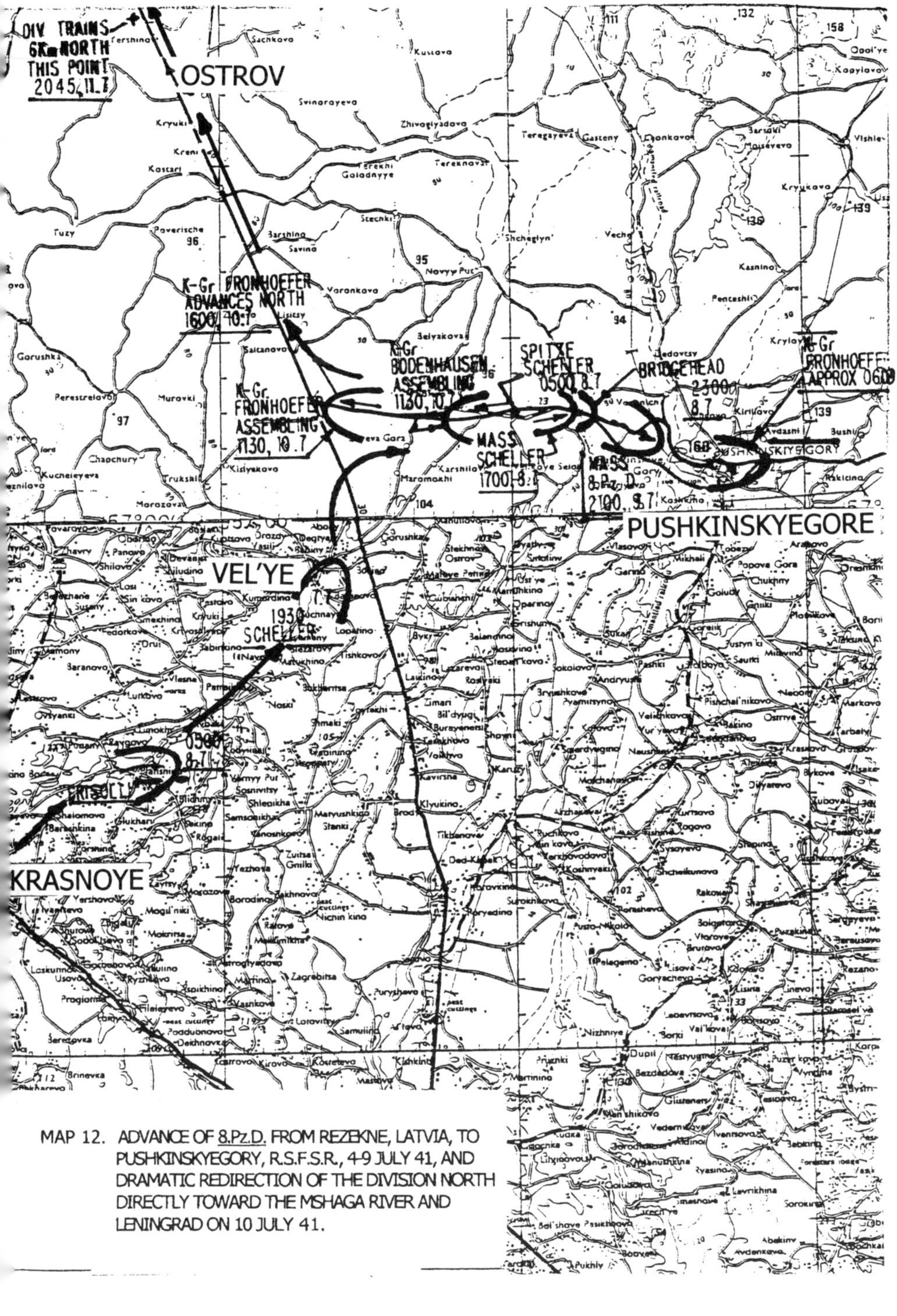

MAP 12. ADVANCE OF 8.Pz.D. FROM REZEKNE, LATVIA, TO PUSHKINSKYEGORY, R.S.F.S.R., 4-9 JULY 41, AND DRAMATIC REDIRECTION OF THE DIVISION NORTH DIRECTLY TOWARD THE MSHAGA RIVER AND LENINGRAD ON 10 JULY 41.

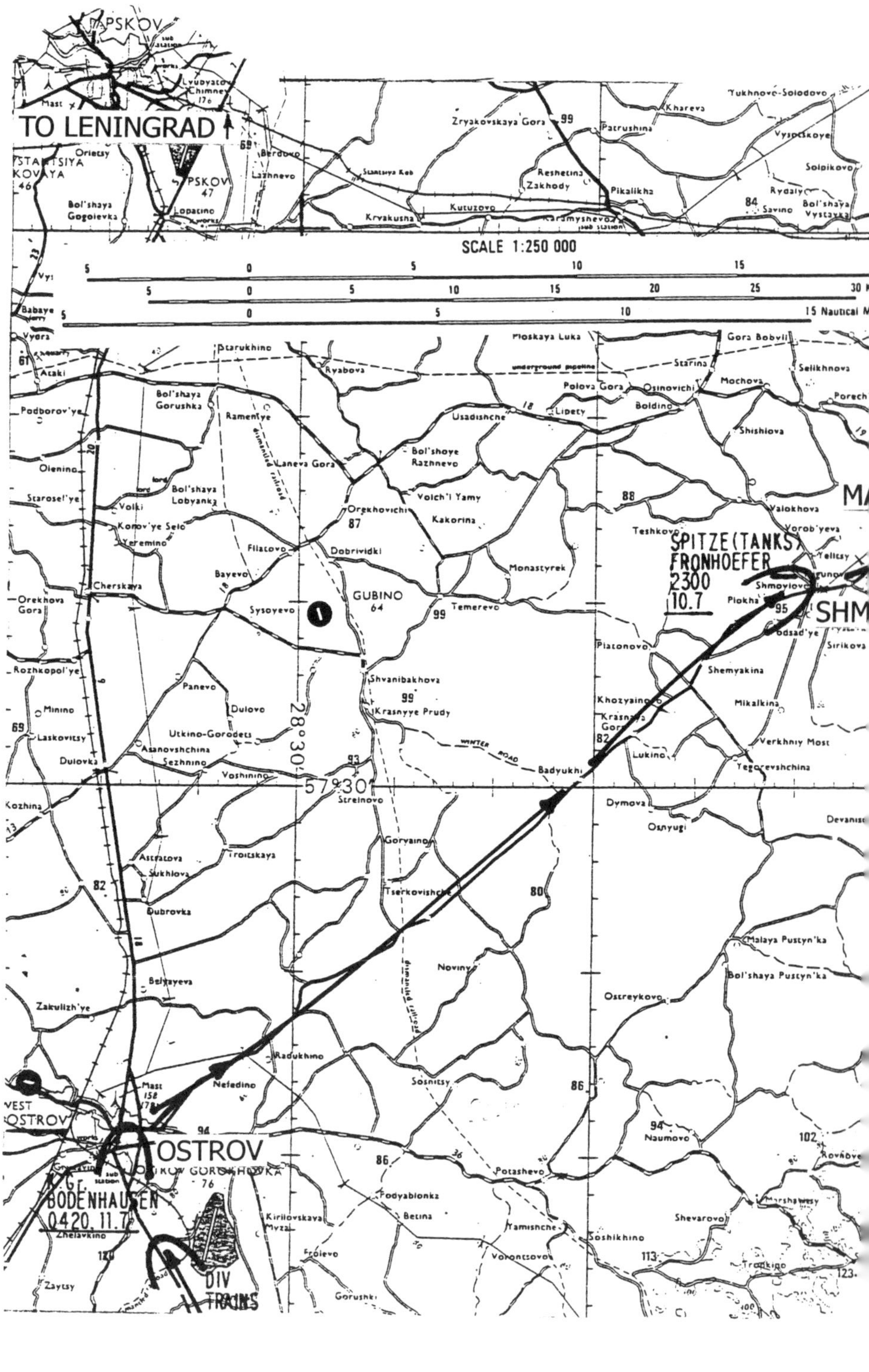
TO LENINGRAD
PSKOV
SCALE 1:250 000
SPITZE (TANKS)
FRONHOEFER
2300
10.7
SHM
GUBINO
28°30'
57°30'
OSTROV
WEST OSTROV
K.GF. BODENHAUSEN
0420 11.7
DIV TRAINS

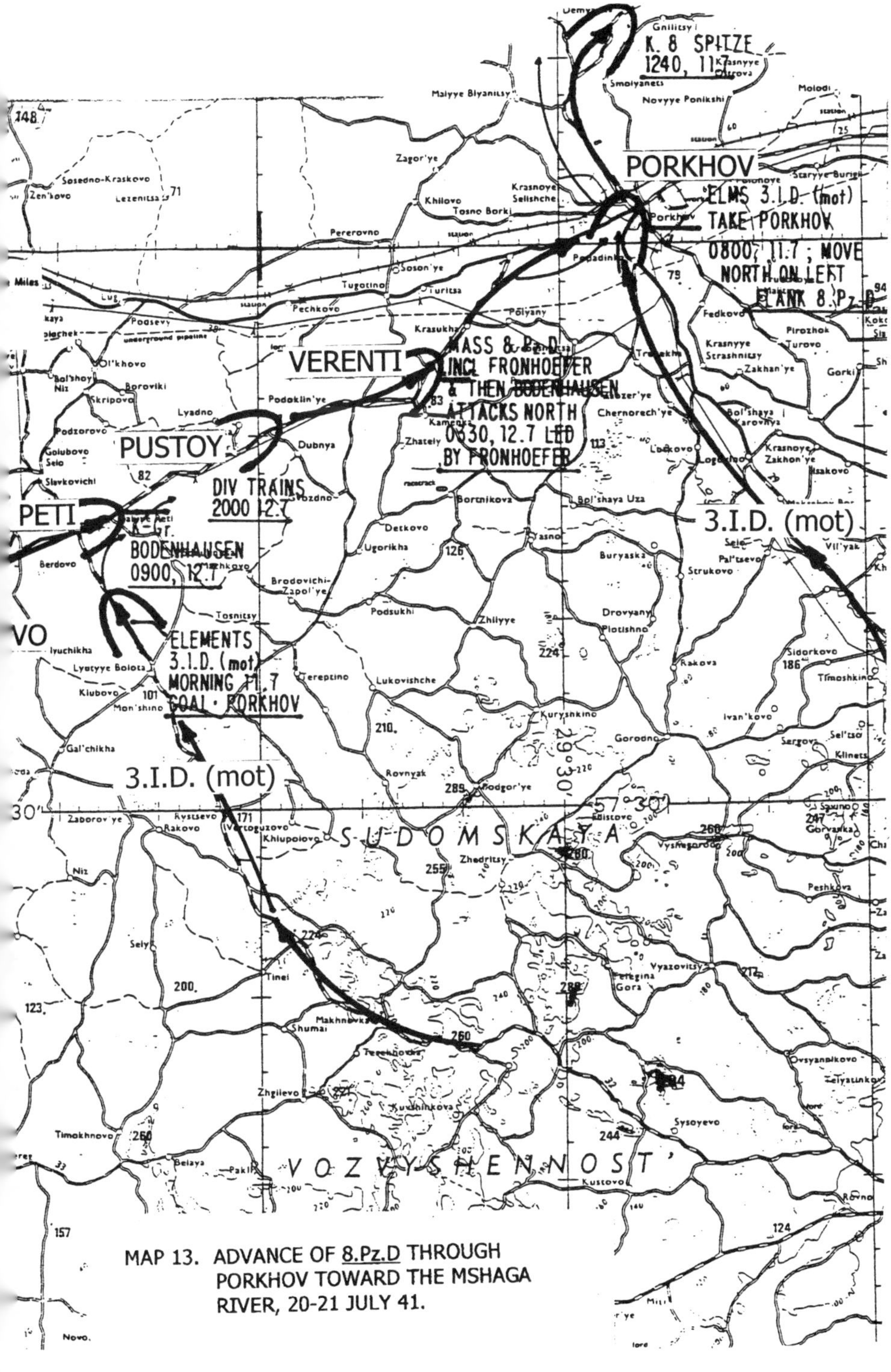

MAP 13. ADVANCE OF 8.Pz.D THROUGH PORKHOV TOWARD THE MSHAGA RIVER, 20-21 JULY 41.

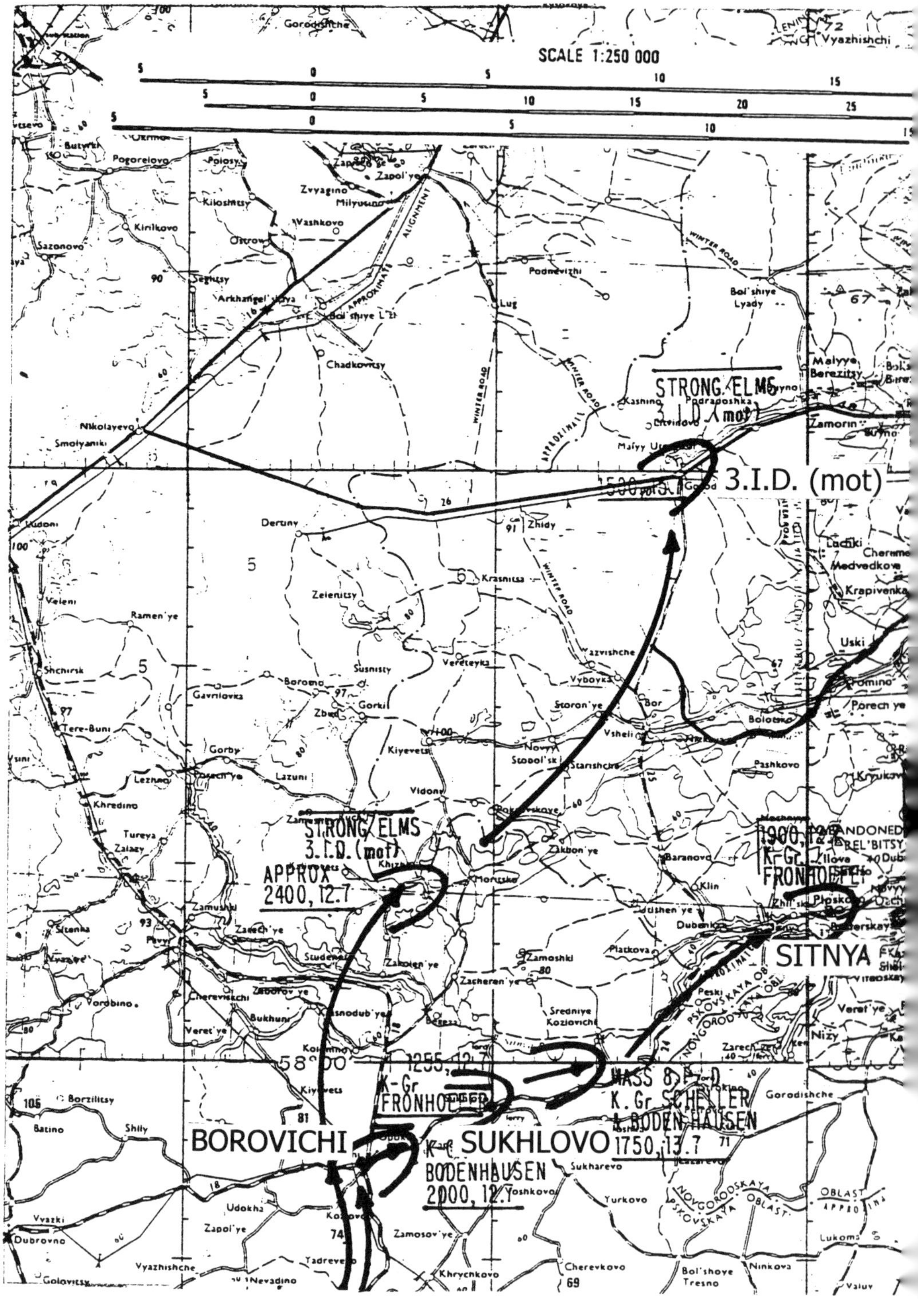
SCALE 1:250 000
STRONG ELMS
3.I.D. (mot)
3.I.D. (mot)
STRONG ELMS
3.I.D. (mot)
APPROX
2400, 12.7
1900, 12.7
K.Gr.
FRONHOEFER
SITNYA
1255, 12.7
K-Gr
FRONHOEFER
MASS 8. P. D.
K. Gr SCHELLER
& BODENHAUSEN
1750, 13.7
BOROVICHI
SUKHLOVO
K.Gr.
BODENHAUSEN
2000, 12.7
WINTER ROAD
NOVGORODSKAYA OBLAST
PSKOVSKAYA OBLAST
Nikolayevo
Deruny
Zelenitsy
Zhidy
Krasnitsa
Gorodishche
Vyazhishchi

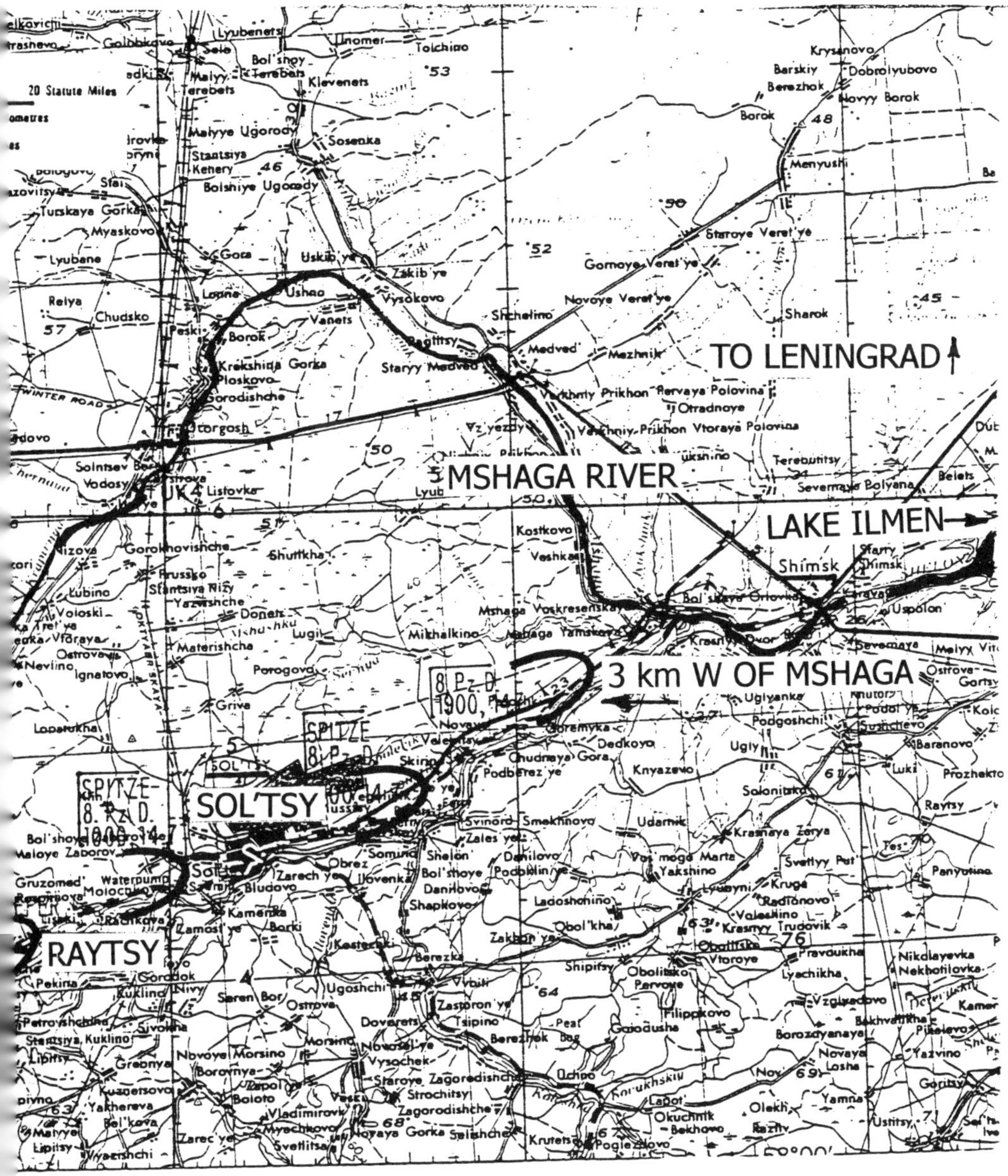

P 14. ADVANCE OF <u>8.Pz.D</u> TO THE MSHAGA RIVER ON THE ROAD TO LENINGRAD, 12-14 JULY 41.

20

Summarizing the Drive of the 8th Panzer Division and Analyzing Offensive Maneuver War from its Experience

In the period 0305, 22 June through1900, 14 July 41, *8.Pz.D.* advanced 742 km through Lithuania, Latvia, and European Russia. The division commander led his reinforced organization through three distinct periods of fighting. From 22 June - 0630, 26 June, Brandenberger pushed the division through a period best described as an ultra-blitz culminating in an operational coup de main at the Duenaburg bridges that gave German *H.Gr.Nord* the clear possibility of reaching Leningrad, its strategic target for the entire campaign, in a time frame of mid-July 41. From early 26 June - 1 July, the commander of *H.Gr.Nord* immobilized *8.Pz.D.* and the entire *LVI.A.K.(mot)* through his incapacity to seize the fleeting opportunity offered by the seizure of the Duenaburg bridges to push the mobile force through a disintegrating enemy to instant victory in the Baltic. During this period of operational immobility, *8.Pz.D.* "advanced" 27 km in a tactically inspired widening of the Duenaburg bridgehead. Finally unleashed by Leeb, from 2-14 July, Hoepner as commander of *Pz.Gr.4* directed *LVI.A.K.(mot)* and *8.Pz.D.* to the Mshaga River in an advance of 413 km while simultaneously moving *XXXXI.A.K.(mot)* approximately 455 km by road along a parallel route. Hoepner misdirected *8.Pz.D.* during this period into a difficult area for movement and through a tough but extraneous defender who simply could have been bypassed; the result was a period of advance best described as an interrupted blitz. The entire period can be summarized as follows:

8.Pz.D. Advance 22 June - 14 July 41

Time	**Characterization (km advance) (rate of advance)**
22-26 Jun	Ultra Blitz (299 km) (75 km/day)
27 Jun - 1 Jul	Operational Immobility (27 km) (5.4 km/day)
2-14 Jul	Interrupted Blitz (413 km) (32km/day)

Figure 9 presents the daily movement of *8.Pz.D.* and gives the reader a finer cut at what actually happened. Figure 10 summarizes the cities reached by *8.Pz.D.* daily and Figure 11 characterizes the daily advances verbally but in a useful systematic format. Figure 9 shows that during the ultra blitz the Germans were immobilized for approximately 26 hrs, giving them only three days during which they were actually in movement including of course the hours of almost full darkness at night. During the period of actual movement, Brandenberger pushed the division predominately along one main highway with the division strung out in columns of battle groups and supply service elements along approximately 70 km of road. Figure 2, for example, on 24 June 41, shows the advanced elements of the division in Battle Group Crisolli 192 km into enemy territory. The remainder of the division lay strung out behind it for approximately 70 km of road, the farthest forward 45 km of which had no contact with any German units on either side. The division moved 100 km farther forward into Lithuania on that day in an extremely narrow, elongated column. Brandenberger during the ultra blitz faced chaos in command and control, extreme uncertainty about the location, size, and intention of enemy forces, and meeting engagements

1941		Distance (km)	Comments
Jun	22	92	Crisolli.
	23	0	Halt of approx 26 hrs.**
	24	100	Crisolli.
	25	100	Crisolli.
	26	7	Crisolli over Duena bridges, 0635, 26 Jun.
	27	3	The division on line.
	28	3	The division on line.
	29	21	Scheller.
	30	0	The division on line.
Jul	1	0	The division on line.
	2	19	Scheller. Bodenhausen advanced 33 km.
	3	44	Scheller. Bodenhausen advanced 16 km.
	4	42	Scheller. Crisolli in similar distance advance.
	5	27	Crisolli now as Schwerpunkt.
	6	0	Road construction east of Goliseva.
	7	22	Scheller as division Schwerpunkt.
	8	28	Scheller as division Schwerpunkt.
	9	4	Scheller as division Schwerpunkt
	10	105	Fronhoefer becomes division Schwerpunkt.
	11	25	Fronhoefer, mass of.
	12	66	Fronhoefer, mass of.
	13	8	Fronhoefer, mass of.
	14	26	Fronhoefer and Bodenhausen.
Total distance:			742

*Names are those of battle groups that achieved maximum division advance.
**Halt from 1645, 22 - 1900, 23 June 41.

Figure 10. Daily Advances by 8.PZ.D. 0001-2400, Unless Otherwise Noted.

dominated by chance or imponderable circumstances in the initial contact. Brandenberger, his subordinate commanders, and general staff officers seemed to revel in this situation. In the chaos of war and the greater chaos of mobile war, they dominated the pervasive uncertainty, chance, and danger by a robust command and battle style that brought order out of chaos and translated finally into successful advance. Map 1 illustrates among other things the chaotic dispersion of *8.Pz.D.* on the first day of the campaign. The map also shows a counterbalancing "order' in the situation because the *Schwerpunkt* battle group has seized the day's operational target and the division has in fact remained focused on its mission of deep penetration towards Duenaburg. Late in the afternoon, the two largest battle groups, Crisolli and Scheller lay 46 km straight line distance apart but actually about 77 km apart over the roads that Scheller would be ordered forward. Battle Group Bodenhausen would be behind Scheller and the division trains even farther back still in East Prussia. Note also that the "Spitze, *8.Pz.D.*, 1220, 22.6" comprising *K.8* would remain 21 km south of Ariogala for the rest of the day adding a wide lateral dispersion to the division. For the entire advance

1941		**Location Advanced Elms 8.Pz.D. End of Day**
Jun	22	Vicinity Ariogala (13 km east)
	23	Vicinity Ariogala (12 km east)
	24	Vicinity Seta
	25	Zarasai
	26	Duenaburg (7 km north)
	27	Duenaburg (10 krn north)
	28	Duenaburg (13 km north)
	29	Duenaburg (34 km north)
	30	Duenaburg (34 km north)
Jul	1	Duenaburg (34 km north)
	2	Seksti (Scheller) (Bodenhausen actually near Rezekne)
	3	Rezekne (5 km north)
	4	Goliseva (I km east)
	5	Krasnoye
	6	Krasnoye
	7	Vel'ye
	8	Pushkinskyegory (5 km west)
	9	Pushkinskyegory (o.6 krn west)
	10	Shmoylovo (adjacent to)
	11	Vereteni
	12	Sitnya (4 km east)
	13	Raytsy
	14	Mshaga River (3 km west near Lake Ilmen)

Note: Each of these cities is shown on one or more maps in the map section and underlined or overlined.

Figure 11. End of Day Locations of 8th Panzer Division in Advance through Lithuania, Latvia, and into Russia, 22 June - 14 July '41.

1941			**Characterization***
Jun	22	Motion/High Tempo (92 km)	**Generally:** Motion/High Tempo. 292 km advance in 4 days, 34 hrs., 30 min. from 0305, 22 Jun thru 0635, 26 Jun 41, and 7 km deep bridgehead.
	23	Halt (0 km)	
	24	Motion/High Tempo (100 km)	
	25	Motion/High Tempo (100 km)	
	26	High Tempo Bridge Coup (7 km)	
	27	Halt (3km)	**Generally:** Halt. Cautious Army Group Cmdr and temporarily weak Pz.Gr. and Corps Cmdrs Freeze Div into 27 km "widening" of bridgehead
	28	Halt (3km)	
	29	Halt (21 km)	
	30	Halt (0km)	
Jul	1	Halt(0km)	
	2	Motion/High Tempo (19 km)	**Generally:** Interrupted Motion. Impressive advance of 413 km even though interrupted by the cautious misdirection of the Panzer Group Commander.
	3	Motion/High Tempo (44 km)	
	4	Motion/High Tempo (42 km)	
	5	Halt (27 km)	
	6	Halt (0 km)	
	7	Motion/Low Tempo (22 km)	
	8	Motion/Low Tempo (28 km)	
	9	Halt (4 km)	
	10	Motion/High Tempo (105 km)	
	11	Motion/High Tempo (25 km)	
	12	Motion/High Tempo (66 km)	
	13	Motion (8 km)	
	14	Motion/High Tempo (26 km)	

Characterization Terms:

Motion	=	Operationally Inspired Advance Toward Distant Operational Target.
Halt	=	Either No Advance or Tactically Inspired Advance Toward Proximate Tactical Target.
High Tempo	=	Extreme Sense of Time Urgent Operational Level Mission and Associated Fluid Action
Low Tempo	=	Little Sense of Time Urgent Operational Level Mission and Associated Interrupted Action.

Figure 12. General Characterization of the Advance of *8.Pz.D.* through Lithuania, Latvia and into Russia, 22 June - 14 July 41.

to Duenaburg, Brandenberger and his Ia, Berendsen, would move the division similarly. They would keep the *Schwerpunkt* moving toward Duenaburg as focus and order in the drive and force the other battle groups and supply services to maintain the pace. The German command style was geared to master uncertainty and chance. Linked with an equally robust battle or tactical fighting style, the resulting German war fighting style is the primary factor that explains the motion of *8.Pz.D.* The analyst interested in inserting rates of advance in war gaming equations can do little more than relate in some realistic and systematic fashion, the primary factors of command and battle fighting style with the more concrete but secondary factors of terrain, road net, weather, night time, attacker's casualties, defender's posture, duration of operation, and force ratios.

In the period 27 June - 1 July 41, *8.Pz.D.* gained so little ground that it can be considered to have been immobilized. The division advanced only 27 km during this period, a rate of advance of only 5.4 km/day, modest enough to qualify as immobilization during the blitz against Soviet Russia. The relative importance of the primary and secondary factors stands out particularly clearly during this period of operational non-movement. No secondary factor held up *8.Pz.D.* in the Duenaburg bridgehead; the commander and chief of staff of *H.Gr.Nord*, overwhelmed by the danger of a situation in which *Pz.Gr.4* would range far ahead of the foot marching infantry divisions, froze *8.Pz.D.* in position as a function of that conservative command style. Unlike the case in which Brandenberger advanced in a division column over roughly 70 km of bad road with enemy forces all around him, Leeb would not advance toward Leningrad with a *Schwerpunkt Pz.Gr.4* far in advance of the trailing infantry armies and accept the risks necessary to achieve the quick victory demanded in the Baltic. Leeb's faulty command style and the temporary lack of energy and courage on the part of Hoepner and Manstein to keep things moving by impressing their will on the army group commander combined to halt the leading elements of the *Schwerpunkt* force for five entire days. No other factor, primary or secondary was significant in imposing a halt. The Germans had the numbers, weapons, functioning supply services and command and battle style in the panzer group, corps, and divisions to continue forward movement at a blitz pace.

In the period 2-14 July, *8.Pz.D.* advanced again at an operational pace toward the operational target of the Mshaga River bridges near Lake Ilmen and Leningrad itself not far beyond. During this period Brandenberger faced a medley of factors that both accelerated and decelerated the advance of the division. In terms of rates of advance, the situation developed as follows. Given the green light to advance on Leningrad, Hoepner accelerated *LVI.A.K.(mot)* and *8.Pz.D.* toward the Mshaga River. Manstein, for example, assigned Brandenberger the first day's mission to advance 85 km to Karsava (See Maps 4 and 5). Leeb, however, had in the meantime given a shaken Soviet command five days in which to recover its psychological balance and throw newly arriving forces into defenses in front of Rezekne (See Map 4). Brandenberger and his division, as a result, ran into strong Soviet forces along the main road to Rezekne and Karsava. Instead of advancing to Karsava between 0400 and midnight on 2 July 41, *8.Pz.D.* fought a series of tough engagements that slowed its entry into that city until 0830, 4 July 41. Instead of achieving 85 km/day, the division averaged 37 km/day as a direct result of strong Soviet defenses and difficult roads and terrain for the advance of motorized forces.

The Germans during this time were slowed below the required rate of advance by at least three secondary factors that the primary factors of German command and battle fighting style were unable to master in the brief time of one day initially allotted by the corps commander for the advance. Then, as *8.Pz.D.* reached Karsava on 4 July 41, Hoepner misdirected it eastward out of that city in a cautious, time consuming detour (the Mshaga lay north northeast from Karsava) to secure the eastern flank of *Pz.Gr.4*. As *8.Pz.D.* headed east it ran into paralyzing secondary factors of bad roads and swampy terrain. These factors halted it operationally from 4-6 July 41, in the area between Karsava and Krasnoye where it advanced only 39 km in the approximately three days from 0830, 4 July to 0400, 7 July 41 (See Map 5). Although Brandenberger and Manstein suggested reversing the division out of the swamp around Goliseva and sending it directly north along the big road to Ostrov and the Mshaga, Hoepner persisted in his misdirection of *8.Pz.D.* eastward. Hoepner's staff college command style of safeguarding the east flank of *Pz.Gr.4.* combined with the secondary factors of Road Net and Terrain soon joined by tough Soviet resistance slowed *8.Pz.D.* in its drive east limiting its advance from 0830, 4 July (advance through Karsava) to 0600, 10 July 41 (advance eastward out of Pushkinskyegory) a period of about six full days to approximately 54 km by road. The rate of advance—9 km/day—represented operational disaster for division, corps, and panzer group.

Early on the morning of 10 July, Hoepner finally acknowledged the disaster and boldly ordered Manstein to reverse *8.Pz.D.* westward out of Pushkinskyegory and send it north through Ostrov and Porkhov. He ordered it to reach Porkhov, 143 km distant by midnight of the same day (!). The advanced elements of *8.Pz.D.* moved 111 km on 10 July 41, 6 km east out of Pushkinskyegory and then 105 km towards Porkhov. Manstein gave the division a rest day on 11 July 41 during which it pressed the advanced battle group 25 km farther north while allowing its eastern neighbor *3.I.D.(mot)* to pass across its front. In the face of poor roads, difficult terrain, strong Soviet delaying actions, and developing adverse force ratios, *8.Pz.D.* went on to gain an additional 125 km from 12-14 July 41 before being halted 3 km from the Mshaga River.

As concerns rates of advance in the unique case of *8.Pz.D.* in the Soviet Union in the Sumner of 1941, the author realized that he tended to fall into a biased analysis based on the outcome of a particular phase of the campaign. When considering a period of rapid advance he looked for factors explaining motion and neglected factors tending to immobilize the division but temporarily overcome during successful advance. This psychological phenomenon might be termed, "immediate outcome" bias, and worked just as strongly when analysis of immobilization of the division was underway. The author found himself, for example, as the division was unable to move a single wheeled vehicle through the stretch of 1,500 meters of terrible road east of Goliseva, elaborating on the immobilizing details of road net and terrain (See Map 5). The researcher tended to neglect to tell the reader that the division commander ordered every tracked vehicle he could lay his hands on into an unbalanced battle group to move through the impasse to seize Krasnoye 26 Km farther east and break up any Soviet attempt to establish a defense line along the Sinyaya River (See Map 5). The point: even as the division lay immobilized operationally by road net and terrain, the division commander's superior command style resulted in a brilliant tactical advance and coup at Krasnoye that set the stage for continuation of the operational drive.

The brief summary above of the adventures of *8.Pz.D.* can be distilled into generalizations for rates of advance in mobile warfare. Although derived from the unique situation of the division between 22 June – 14 July 41 in the Soviet Union, the following factors apply to war past, present, and future:

General Factors Which Affect the Advance of a Ground Force

Primary	**Intermediate**	**Secondary**	
Command Style	Technology	Terrain	Attacker Casualties
Battle Style	Principles of War	Road Net	Defender Posture
		Weather	Duration of Action
		Night Time	Force Ratios

More specifically the factors apply to the advance of 8.Pz.D. as follows:

Specific Factors Which Immediately Affected 8.Pz.D. Advance

Primary	**Intermediate**	**Secondary**
Command Style	Technology	Defender Posture
Leader Front *(8.Pz.D.)*	Moderately	Terrain
Action Oriented Staff *(8.Pz.D.)*	Superior German	Road Net
Mission Style	Principles of War:	
Direction *(8.Pz.D.)*	Germans Seize	
Excessive Caution in Face of	Initiative, Achieve	
Uncertainty & Chance	Surprise	
(H.Gr.N., Pz.Gr.4)		
Battle Style *(8.Pz.D.)*:		
24-hour Action		
Battle Groups		
Reconnaissance		

In the listing above the most important factors that affected the movement of the division were command and battle style. The factors are centered on man, largely qualitative, difficult to put in mathematical equations, and override in importance both the intermediate and secondary factors. In *8.Pz.D.,* the primary factors that explain the forward motion of the division were those of a command style in which the division commander led from the front, a streamlined action-oriented general staff, and mission style tasking and orders. Primary factors included additionally those of a battle style with which the Germans moved 24 hours/day, fought in mission-tailored battle groups, and placed exceptional emphasis on air and ground reconnaissance. The researcher also identified factors intermediate in importance between the primary and secondary factors and essentially different from them. The intermediate factors comprised weapons and material technology, a factor susceptible of quantification, and the very different factor of the applicable principles of war, one extremely difficult to quantify. The more conventional rate of advance factors like, terrain, road net, weather, etc., are necessary for consideration in any analysis of rates of advance but susceptible to being overridden by both the primary and intermediate factors and, hence, systematically designated as secondary.

For the entire period the factors that explain the advance and acceleration of *8.Pz.D.* can be summarized using the above format as follows:

Factors That Made 8.Pz.D. Go (22 June – 14 July 41)

Primary	**Intermediate**	**Secondary**
Command Style	Technology:	Weather: Dry, Sunny, Warm.
Leader Front.	Moderate German	
Action Staff.	Superiority.	Night: Exploited by Div.
Mission Orders.	Principles of War:	Force Ratios: Favorable.
Battle Style	Germans Exploit	Combat Power Ratios:
24 hrs/day.	Initial Surprise.	Superior German.
Battle Groups.		
Ultra Reconnaissance		

And, the contrasting factors that explain the operational halt or deceleration of 8.Pz.D. are the following:

Factors That Made 8.Pz.D. Stop (22 June – 14 July 41)

Primary	**Intermediate**	**Secondary**
Command Style:	Technology:	Terrain: Difficult.
Excessive Caution in	Good Soviet Arty	Road Net: Difficult.
Face of Uncertainty	& Heavy Tanks	Defender Posture:
and Chance		Always Tough, Often
(*H.Gr.N.* and *Pz.Gr.4*).	Principles of War:	Strong Enough to
	Germans Allow	Halt Div.
	Surprise to Dissipate.	

The 742 km drive of *8.Pz.D.* through Duenaburg to the Mshaga River was a unique historical experience. The human actors, time, place, and weapons will never combine again in any time or any place. Within such a framework, the division achieved rates of advance that similarly were unique to the human actors and other aspects of the historical experience and will never be repeated. Stated thus, the picture of *8.Pz.D.* during the drive through the Baltic would appear to be of limited value in generalizing about rates of advance and forecasting them for future ground warfare. The challenge is one of grand dimensions—how can one generalize and forecast from a unique past historical event?

Although unique, the experience of *8.Pz.D.* can nevertheless be characterized in terms of factors, namely the human actors, time, place, and weapons that have defined the essential aspects of war fighting in all times and all places. To understand, for example, rates of advance of ground forces, the analyst must address the qualities and skills of the men, the physical setting, the performance characteristics of the weapons, and issues of time that play on the subject of success and failure in an advance. Just as surely, therefore, as the experience of *8.Pz.D.* was unique and not repeatable, the experience can be defined in terms of factors common to all other war fighting that has taken place in the past and to every consideration of war fighting that may take place in the future.

The study contends, for example, that the primary factors of command and battle style override the intermediate and secondary factors particularly in cases of extreme acceleration or deceleration. This contention suggests that rates of advance like many statistics can sometimes find themselves divorced from empirical reality. The panzer division of this study advanced at a rate of 74 km/day in the four days from 22-26 June 41. Being presented with this rate, the reader attempting to understand the advance of *8.Pz.D.* cannot be faulted for looking for the necessities and possibilities in moving a panzer division 74 km/day. The division, however, halted for one continuous period of 26 hours during the four days and actually advanced almost exactly 100 km each day that it was in motion. The frustrating point here is that even if the scientific analyst had predicted correctly the *rate* of advance of *8.Pz.D.*, Brandenberger, the Ia and the battle group commanders would have been assisted precious little by that statistic in preparing for and mastering the reality of 26 hours of immobilization followed by a move of 100 km in a single day. There may be too much focus in scientific analysis on the straight lines or gentle curves of trends and averages and too little attention to the jagged realities of unforeseen collision with an armed enemy.

The experience of *8.Pz.D.* on this point of the variability of the data is also probably not the exception but actually the rule. In the advance of *7.Pz.D.* farther south with Army Group Center, that division moved in a dramatic coup between 0305, 22 June and 2300, 25 June 41 to cut the main highway between Minsk, the capital of White Russia, and Moscow, the capital of the Soviet Union. The advance similarly involved a halt for one continuous period of about 24 hours around Vilna and a total move of approximately 340 km by road. The similarity between the two advances is striking. Both involved wildly different motion on consecutive days. In the case of *7.Pz.D.*, after approximately 20 km of tactically conditioned "advance" southeast of Vilna on 24 June 41—in effect, an operational halt—the division advanced 185 km during approximately 19 hours of movement on 25 June 41. These data represent extreme variations in advance rates. They reinforce the case for advance rates being largely due to uncontrollable and unpredictable chance effects and characterized by irreducible variability. Since war is the province of chance, the scientific analyst cannot consistently or accurately predict rates of advance. The best he can do is to help to design forces and operations that are robust in the face of the fog, chaos, and uncertainty of war.

There is no key factor that can be put in any set of mathematical equations and give consistent, accurate outcomes for rates of advance. It can be stated, nevertheless, that the primary factors of command and battle style predominated among the factors put together to explain the advance of *8.Pz.D.* and have always dominated in war fighting. Command style and associated battle (or tactical fighting) style, for example, through the consistency with which they override other factors are the collective key to rates of advance. The "key" then is command style, exemplified by individual, or in the case of the German general staff, corporate military genius. The "key," however, is no key at all for the scientific analyst using mathematical equations for probabilities of advance, because he cannot insert command style as exemplified, for example, by genius in his equations. Even if the analyst could insert it in his equations, that factor would be challenged in turn by inherently uncontrollable and unpredictable chance. In no other sphere of human activity must such a margin be left for this intruder, because it is in such constant contact with man on every side in armed combat. Chance increases the uncertainty of every circumstance and deranges the course of events.[35]

What then can be done to make military operations robust against the jagged variations in rates of advance associated with chance? The advance of *8.Pz.D.* reveals several elements of command and battle style in 1941 in combat against the Soviets that contributed to mastering the chaos of war. The elements contributed to a German conduct of operations so robust that *8.Pz.D.* was able on 23 June 41, (1) to halt and concentrate the division "mass" in a defensive scheme intended to break up and then destroy an advancing Soviet force of 300-400 tanks supported by motorized infantry and artillery, and, when it became evident that the force was veering off to the northwest, (2) to move out of its defensive posture into an advance of 100 km on 24 June. At least six elements in the command and battle style of the Germans comprised the robustness. The elements enabled the division to ride with the intermediate and secondary factors favoring an advance and to override the unfavorable factors. The six elements are the ones in bold type below:

Key Elements in Robust German Conduct of Operations

1. **Front Leadership** by Division and Battle Group Commanders.
2. **Streamlined Staff** Dedicated to Maneuver Through . . .
3. **Mission-Styled (Brief) Orders and Tasks.**
4. **24-Hr./Day Movement.**
5. Combat in **Ad Hoc Battle Groups.**
6. **Ultra Reconnaissance.**

These elements raise the question of the validity of applying the command and battle style of a German panzer division fighting against the Soviets in the Baltic in 1941 to ground forces operations today. It can be said, however, that examples from history make things clear and in addition afford the most convincing proof in the empirical fields of knowledge. It must be evident that German operations were robust because of the elements of style elucidated above and equally evident that Americans can emulate parts of that style to improve U.S. ground forces operations today. The point is not to make 1941 Germans out of 21st century Americans but to improve American capabilities to cope with uncertainty and chance in war, as it were, to ride through the rugged and uneven landscape of war rather than attempt to level it.

Note for Part Three:

1 See the English translation in, H. R. Trevor-Roper, *Blitzkrieg to Defeat: Hitler's War Directives* (New York, 1965), 50-51.

2 Cannon with 3.7 cm bore diameter and moderately long barrel 40 calibers in length or 40 x 3.7 cm long.

3 See, *Ia. Anlagenband 2 zum KTB. Einsatz Russland, Anlage 5 zu Gen. Kdo. LVI.A.K.(mot). Ia Nr. 210/41 g.Kdos. den 12.6.41.* U. S. Archives, Records German Field Commands, 8. Pz .D., Copy T-315, Roll 471, Fr. 001531.

4 See *Ia, Kriegstagebuch. Feldzug im Osten. Band 1, 8.Pz .D.*, U. S. Archives, Records German Field Commands, Copy T-315, Roll 483, Fr. 000631.

5 German divisions in World War II had no chiefs of staff or assistant division commanders.

6 See *Ia. Kriegstagebuch. Feldzug im Osten. Band 1. 8.Pz.D.*, U. S. Archives, Records German Field Commands, Copy T-315, Roll 483, Fr. 000636.

7 *Ia. Kriegstagebuch. Feldzug im Osten Band 1. 8.Pz.D.*, U. S. Archives, German Records of Field Commands, Copy T-315, Roll 483, Fr. 000641.

8 Field-Marshal Erich von Manstein, *Lost Victories* (Chicago, 1958), 183.

9 The southern *Spitze* (spearhead) of Battle Group Crisolli also negotiated the mouth of the Dubysa River at Seredzius on the Neman during this time.

10 This statement is made even though the Germans used members of Regiment for Special Disposition 800 (Brandenburg) disguised as Soviets as part of the coup de main team to seize those bridges.

11 The word mechanistic suggests itself because the eight factors are largely quantifiable.

12 This force turned out to be two companies strong and put up the usual tough Soviet resistance. See *Ia. Kriegstagebuch, Feldzug im Osten, Band 1, 8.Pz.D.*, U.S. Archives, Records German Field Commands, Copy T-315, Roll 483, Frs. 000652, 53.

13 An expressive French expression often used by the Germans to express the supreme quality of iron coolness in the face of danger.

14 See in *Ia. Kriegstagebuch Feldzug im Osten. Band 1. 8.Pz.D.*, U.S. Archives, Records German Field Commands, Copy T-315, Roll 483. Fr. 000657.

15 See Map 2 for locations of Crisolli at 2110 and Scheller at 2300, 24 June.

16 See, in *Ia Kriegstagebuch Feldzug im Osten. Band 1. 8.Pz.D.*, U. S. Archives, Records German Field Commands, Copy T-315, Roll 483, Fr. 000659.

17 The author has a German sketch of the action in which the team is called Sondereinheit Knaak after the Brandenburg *Oberleutnant* Knaak. See *Ia. Kartenlagen zum KTB. Russland Feldzug, 8.Pz.D.*, U. S. Archives, Records German Field Commands, Copy T-315, Roll 484, Fr. 000206.

18 *8.Pz.D.* U. S. Archives, Records German Field Commands, Copy T-315, Roll 484, Fr. 000206

19 See R.H.S. Stolfi, *Hitler's Panzers East: World War II Reinterpreted* (Norman and London, 1992), especially Chapter 8.

20 Manstein, *Lost Victories*, p. 185.

21 For these details and the following, see Georg Meyer, *Generalfeldmarschall Wilhelm Ritter von Leeb, Tagebuchaufzeichnungen und Lagebeurteilungen aus zwei Weltkriegen* (Stuttgart, 1976), pp. 17-73.

22 See *Ia, Anlagen J zum Kriegstagebuch Nr. 1, 56.A.K.(mot)*, U.S. Archives, Records German Field Commands, Copy T-314, Roll 1389, Fr. 000296.

23 See *Ia, Kriegstagebuch, Feldzug im Osten, Band 1, 8.Pz.D.*, U.S. Archives, Records German Field Commands, Copy T-315, Roll 483, Fr. 000669.

24 The *Schwerpunkt* battle group would move out at 0400 and anticipated a long day in which it would reach its target by approximately 2300, 2 July 41. In the actual event, the division would not reach Karsava until the morning of 4 July 41, being held up predominately by the factor of Defender's Posture.

25 See, Ia, Kriegstagebuch, Feldzug im Osten, Band 1, 8.Pz.D., U.S. Archives, Records German Field Commands, Copy T-315, Roll 483, Fr. 000694.

26 See *Ia, Kriegstagebuch, Feldzug Osten, Band 1, 8.Pz.D.*, U.S. Archives, records German Field Commands, Copy T-315, Roll 483, Fr. 000698.

27 See, Ia, Kriegstagebuch, Feldzug Osten, Band 1, 8.Pz.D., U.S. Archives, Records German Field Commands, Copy T-315, Roll 483, Fr. 000719.

28 See the brief, three-page written order of the division in *Ia, Anlage 9 zum KTB, Russland Feldzug, 8.Pz.D.*, U.S. Archives Records German Field Commands, Copy T-315, Roll 474, Frs. 000370-72.

29 See, *Ia, Anlage 9 zum KTB, Russland Feldzug, 8.Pz.D.*, U.S. Archives, Records German Field Commands, Copy T-315, Roll 474, Fr. 000430. The city noted in the message is immediately adjacent to Shmoylovo on Map 5.

30 Brandenberger wanted to route Bodenhausen through Borovichi farther north and then turn him northeast to advance on the left flank of Fronhoefer. Corps rejected this suggestion

31 See I*b, Kriegstagebuch Nr. 1, Russland Feldzug, 8.Pz.D.*, U.S. Archives, Records German Field Commands, Copy T-315~ Roll 490, frs 000021-23.

32 The KV-2 tanks were destroyed by the single, operable 8.8 cm *Flak* cannon still held by Battle Group Fronhoefer at that moment.

33 See Ia, Kriegstagebuch, Feldzug im Osten, Band 1, 8.Pz.D. U.S Archives, Records German Field Commands, Copy T-315, Roll 384, Fr. 000736.

34 See, for example, the data in *Ia, Anlage 4 zum KTB Nr. 1, Russland Feldzug, 8.Pz.D.*, U.S. Archives, Records German Field Commands, Copy T-315, Roll 490, Frs. 000776, 77, 78, 85, 86.

35 See *The Clausewitz Casyndekan*, Conceptual Index, Clausewitz, On War, analyzed and Indexed by Computer (Colorado Springs, 1969), p.126, for these comments on chance.

Gallery

The following section presents four photographs extracted from inividual frames of German Second World War weekly motion picture newsreels. The newsreels are presently held in the UFA Collection, Motion Picture Newsreels, 1933-1945, Hoover Institution Archives, Stanford, California. The author gives his special thanks to Mr. Remy Squires, Multi-Media/Film Reproductions Specialist, who combined technical skill with the capability to immerse himself in the historical content of the films to produce these photographs.

The Hoover Institution does not own the copyright to its German Second World War film collection and therefore it could neither grant nor deny permission to the author to pulbish this material. The Institution has no information in its records regarding copyright claims if any to this material. Neither has the author been able to discover copyright claims. With this disclaimer, thus, the author points out to the reader that the *Hoover Institution Archives* are the *location* of the original material presented here, and each photo caption acknowledges such with the acronym *HIA*.

Behind the Gun Shield. Gun commander at left gingerly raising his binocular for a look down range. The gun layer has his head pressed to the sight with his helmet visible immediately to the right of the gun commander's hand. The loader at right is in the act of flipping up a 37 mm round from a sharp downward angle into the open breech. By keeping his eyes focused on the breech and receiving the round blindly from the ammunition handler, the loader could reload a firing gun a remarkable 30 times per minute. (HIA)

North Africa. Commander of a late production version of an 8-wheeled armored reconnaissance vehicle in mid-autumn 1941. Note the supplementary armor plate protecting the turret front and gun mantlet by this stage in the war. (HIA)

Behind the Gun Shield. Unusual scene with gun layer and loader stripped to waists in direct fire with 105 mm howitzer against probably Soviet armored vehicles directly to front. Army Group Center summer of 1941. (HIA)

North Africa. German ammunition handlers passing an 88 mm antitank round towards the open, fuming breech at right. Here we have serious combat with the cannon in the ground fire role. Summer 1941. (HIA)

Index